The Diasporic Condition

The Diasporic Condition

Ethnographic Explorations of the Lebanese in the World

GHASSAN HAGE

The University of Chicago Press
Chicago and London

The University of Chicago Press, Chicago 60637

The University of Chicago Press, Ltd., London

© 2021 by The University of Chicago

Published 2021

Printed in the United States of America

30 29 28 27 26 25 24 23 22 21   1 2 3 4 5

ISBN-13: 978-0-226-54690-2 (cloth)

ISBN-13: 978-0-226-54706-0 (paper)

ISBN-13: 978-0-226-54723-7 (e-book)

DOI: https://doi.org/10.7208/chicago/9780226547237.001.0001

Library of Congress Cataloging-in-Publication Data

Names: Hage, Ghassan, author.

Title: The diasporic condition : ethnographic explorations of the Lebanese
    in the world / Ghassan Hage.

Description: Chicago : University of Chicago Press, 2021. |
    Includes bibliographical references and index.

Identifiers: LCCN 2021007567 | ISBN 9780226546902 (cloth) |
    ISBN 9780226547060 (paperback) | ISBN 9780226547237 (ebook)

Subjects: LCSH: Lebanese—Foreign countries. | Lebanon—Emigration
    and immigration.

Classification: LCC DS80.6 .H344 2021 | DDC 909/.049275692—dc23

LC record available at https://lccn.loc.gov/2021007567

♾ This paper meets the requirements of ANSI/NISO Z39.48-1992
(Permanence of Paper).

To the memory of my mother,
May Debs Hage

CONTENTS

When we consider that Lebanon's population of resident citizens was around 4 million in the first decade of the twenty-first century, the importance of its emigrant population and its descendants is beyond a doubt. Between the 1850s and 1880s, migration from the area of Mount Lebanon, often referred to by locals at the time as simply the Mountain, slowly evolved from the movement of a few individuals to—relative to the size of the Mountain and its population—a significant structural phenomenon. By the 1890s and until World War I, around one-third of the Mountain's population of roughly half a million had migrated to North and South America, and in smaller numbers to Europe and Australia. Today, it is safe to say that two to three times more people of Lebanese descent live outside their mother country than within it.

The intensity of this migratory flow has fluctuated, shaped by both local developments and the many global factors that have influenced such flows everywhere, in ways familiar to researchers of migration in other parts of the world. This fluctuation continued throughout the twentieth century, after Lebanon was constituted as a nation-state, and it continues to this day. Also, and again like everywhere else, what began as a one-way migration from Lebanon to the rest of the world was quickly transformed into a transnational network of relations among the various national and international points of settlement to which and from which people continuously traveled.

Because they are part of the vast state-supported mythology celebrating migration as a major Lebanese achievement as well as the realization of a Lebanese character essentialized as always predisposed to travel and adventure, the estimated numbers of Lebanese immigrants worldwide are invariably inflated. Brazil clearly stands out, with more Lebanese there than in

Lebanon itself. Next in numerical importance are Argentina and the United States (around 1 million each), followed by the Caribbean, Mexico, Venezuela, Canada, Europe, and Australia (between three hundred thousand and five hundred thousand each). Substantial settlements of Lebanese can be found throughout the rest of Latin America, the African continent, and the Arab Gulf region. Although only about 10 percent of all these immigrants (again, the estimates vary considerably) have retained their Lebanese citizenship, a far more substantial number remain attached affectively, economically, and politically to their homeland in some way or another. Those continue to be an integral part of the Lebanese social formation. Overall, migration has been indispensable to the reproduction of the Lebanese nation-state. As Wendy Pearlman notes:

> According to the World Bank, Lebanon ranks first in the [Middle East and North Africa] region in terms of tertiary-educated emigration; 39.6 percent of the tertiary-educated population in Lebanon emigrated, compared to 12.5 percent in Tunisia. Egypt, registering less than half that amount, did not place among the region's top ten. Such emigration has contributed to lower rates of unemployment; according to figures from 2004–05, youth unemployment was 20.9 percent in Lebanon, compared to 30.7 percent in Tunisia and 34.1 percent in Egypt. Lebanon ranked first among the region's remittance receivers in absolute terms, remarkable given its small size. In 2010, Lebanon received 8.2 billion US dollars in remittances, compared to Egypt's 7.7 billion US dollars and Tunisia's two billion US dollars. Lebanon also ranked first among the region for remittances as a portion of GDP. In 2009, remittances accounted for 22.4 percent of GDP in Lebanon, compared to 5.3 percent in Tunisia and four percent in Egypt.[1]

Behind these remittances is a transnational socioeconomic reality comprising a variety of kinship, economic, social, affective, and cultural ties and affinities. This reality constitutes the wider terrain in which I have conducted my fieldwork and investigated what I call the diasporic condition. The term refers to how such a reality is experienced by those inhabiting it and how the experience, in turn, gives this sociocultural formation some of its distinctive characteristics.

Despite having taught and researched these questions for a good twenty-five years, I have come to the study of migration in a roundabout way, and it has been one of many research interests I've had over the years. I say these things because I think they leave a mark on my writing on the subject and help the reader understand some of my areas of focus. My doctoral dissertation was a study of Christian identification during the Lebanese Civil War, and though it examined the emergence of Lebanese capitalism as part of the history of modern sectarian identification, it barely touched on questions of migration as an analytical problematic. I was more attentive to the relation between Lebanese experiences of communal conflict, cultural pluralism, and class. When I finished my doctoral studies, the theoretical work underlying these issues became my main interest. This was easily transposable to the study of Australian multiculturalism, racism, and national and ethnic identification, in which I was increasingly becoming politically and academically involved. These preoccupations put me in contact with Lebanese ethnic organizations, as they are referred to in Australia, which in turn led me to become interested in Lebanese experiences of migration as such— first in Australia and then increasingly as a global phenomenon. Then, between 2000 and 2005, an Australian Research Council (ARC) Large Grant allowed me to conduct ethnographic research in the Lebanese villages of Mehj and Jalleh[2] and among their immigrant population worldwide.

I originally conceived the ARC project to compare migration from three different villages. Almost immediately, this scope narrowed to two as I quickly faced the impossibility of undertaking comparative work of such breadth on my own. But after three years of work in both villages and as my enmeshment in each grew, I had to settle on intensive work only with the people of Jalleh while maintaining enough contact with Mehj to permit some valuable comparative reflections.

When I started interacting with Lebanese ethnic organizations in Australia, I met several people originally from Jalleh. Situated in the North Lebanon Governorate, the village is about sixty-three miles from Beirut and north of Tripoli, the governate's chief city. It's also near my father's birthplace. In Lebanese parlance, this would make it near "my" birthplace— although I had been born and raised in Beirut, and I have visited it on only a few occasions. Nonetheless, because of this proximity, I have paternal relatives in Jalleh, some of whom I had met in the 1960s when I accompanied my parents on their visits to my father's ancestral land. These ties facilitated my contact with people from that village living in Australia and influenced my decision to choose it as a place to conduct my research. Let me stress, however, that while I have kinship relations with several individuals there, those aren't close relations. At the time of my study, I hadn't seen most of them for more than twenty years. I am emphasizing this so as not to create a false impression of a "native" ethnography: rural Lebanese village culture was foreign to me. I met more people from rural North Lebanon in my first year of involvement with the Australian Lebanese community than in twenty years of growing up in Beirut. And I can't say it was easy to establish intimate relations with people from Jalleh when I started my fieldwork. Yet now, after years of research there, I am indeed very close to my kin and to many of their neighbors. But it didn't start out that way.

I was in fact far more "at home" in Mehj, the second village I chose for my research. Mehj was much closer to Beirut, about nineteen miles north of the capital and north of the city of Jbeil (Byblos). So it was part of the geography of my youth. I had a friend there whose parents owned a traditional old stone house. Its basement had excellent acoustics, of which my friend and I availed ourselves for listening to music while smoking dope. I often returned to the house after I had become based in Australia until my friend himself left the country in the early eighties and I lost contact with him. Then in 1998, I was visiting Lebanon when a news item in *L'Orient–Le Jour*, the country's mainstream French daily, caught my attention. It reported on the French ambassador visiting Mehj to open a cultural center, at which time he declared how important migration from that village had been to Paris. I immediately wondered whether my friend had moved to Paris. I drove up to Mehj to inquire, only to find out that he had in fact ended up in New Bedford, Massachusetts. I also found out that the concentration of people from Mehj now living in New Bedford was even greater than in Paris. As all this coincided with my planning my ARC application, I immediately began contemplating the possibility of doing ethnographic work among the people of Mehj and its transnational population. I reconnected with my friend and through him with others still in the village, as well as some of those now living in France and in New Bedford.

To my mind at the time, a comparison of emigration from Mehj and Jalleh would be interesting, as the two villages are different in many ways. Jalleh is a very bland place from a touristic/aesthetic point of view. It's at the base of a small mountain, it has no river passing through it, it has no wilderness worth talking about, and its houses have no views of valleys or the sea. It's also in the more economically underdeveloped part of Lebanon. Despite its unambiguous modernity, life there feels like being part of a rural community, where houses are surrounded by orange and olive trees and where many nonmechanized agricultural practices remain, as we shall see. Like many Christian Lebanese villages, its mid- to late-nineteenth-century economic life was structured around the production of silk controlled by French manufacturers in Lyon. After the decimation of the silk industry following the rise of Chinese artificial silk, Jalleh's mulberry trees (where the silkworms were raised) were replaced by olive and orange groves. Most families in the village own their homes and at least some land containing

Table 1. Location of Jalleh's population

Lebanon-Jalleh	544
Lebanon-other	352
Australia	456
Venezuela	132
United States	130
Canada	38
Brazil	37
Arab Gulf	17
France	7
Nigeria	2
Sweden	1
Philippines	1

an orange or an olive grove or both. Everyone maintains their land's agricultural productivity through either their own labor or hired help, but no family survives solely on the output of that work. Jalleh has a locally owned private school and a small olive oil press, the "factory" (*el ma'mal*), as the locals call it. There is also a small bakery and a couple shops located outside the village limits on the main road, enhancing their economic viability. But the main sources of income in Jalleh are the villagers' employment in nearby towns as shopkeepers (20 percent of the village's working population), government employees (23 percent), and workers in a cement factory (31 percent)—along with, most important, migrant remittances to individual households as well as to public-works projects, including road maintenance and a village medical center with an ambulance. About one-third of the village's total population of 1,736 immigrated to Australia (as of December 2001, derived from the mayor's records). There is a small but significant presence in Venezuela and the United States as well (see table 1).

Mehj, on the other hand, is an extremely attractive mountain village, classically (in a Lebanese sense) embedded in a region both rocky and green. Unlike Jalleh, it had been relatively well integrated into the 1950s and 1960s circuit of Lebanese capitalism dominated by the nonproductive tertiary sector: tourism, banking, commerce, and services. Mehj became an early part of the national tourism circuit because of its location below a ski resort. Therefore, an important part of the village's winter economy initially developed to service the middle-class skiers passing through Mehj to get to the resort: shops for purchasing ski gear (or for renting it more cheaply than from shops up in the mountain), restaurants, and small hotels. When, as part of a worldwide trend, ski resorts began to diversify and transform themselves into summer resorts to ensure that their hotels attracted business all year round, this had a corresponding effect on Mehj's economic development. But such tourism is hardly important: about a quarter of the village population of around 4,000 (mayor's estimate) immigrated to New Bedford, Massachusetts, 432 to France, and 100 to Gatineau, Canada. What interested me about Mehj from a comparative sociological perspective was that its residents' dreams and fantasies of a "better life" were shaped in close contact with the Lebanese middle class they had come to know and deal with as customers. I suspected—and this was very quickly confirmed in the early part of my ethnography—that these hopes and desires were markedly different from those entertained by the people of Jalleh, given the latter's relative geographic isolation and socioeconomic position.

In the first half of 2000, I took leave from my University of Sydney job and secured a visiting position at the American University of Beirut. I spent a couple months each in Jalleh and Mehj, alternating between them every week or two. Sometimes, I commuted between the villages and Beirut for the day or for a couple of days. In Jalleh, my (re-kin-dled?) kin relations became my closest contacts, and they insisted I use a spare room in their household as my main accommodation in the village. In Mehj, the family of my old friend from school invited me to stay at their house. I acquainted myself with both villages through a familiarization with my hosts' respective circles of relatives and friends and was identified by other villagers as part of those circles. It was also through those groups that I began what I thought to myself as an ethnography of absence. Many people had left those villages for good, either for the city or for overseas destinations, but not all were considered absent. Some were simply forgotten—and, perhaps, had forgotten the village themselves—and were rarely mentioned. The truly absent, however, are those whose lack of presence is experienced by the village. Their absence is felt, and they're quite often talked about, because they maintain contact through combinations of visiting or maintaining property, various forms of communication, or sending remittances. They became the emigrants I considered, because they believed themselves and were judged by others to be part of the village's diasporic milieu that I was aiming to define. It was the global whereabouts of such people that I began to map and investigate.

By mid-2000, my research leave was coming to an end, and I had to return to Sydney to teach. Nevertheless, I managed to use the final five weeks to "return slowly" via some of the key locations where emigrants from each village were concentrated: Paris, New York, New Bedford, Vermont, and Gatineau in the case of Mehj, and Caracas and Cabudare, Venezuela, São Paulo, Boston, and Melbourne in the case of Jalleh. I spent only two to three days in each location, but having prepared my stay and established my contacts with the help of the villagers the month before, they were an exceptionally useful and socially intensive couple of days, enough to give me an initial concrete feel of the conditions to plan fieldwork in earnest in some of those places.

While I was staying in the villages, as further confirmed during my first worldwide trip to the main migratory locations, it became quite clear that some of the extended families that reached around the globe were a far more salient relational reality than the transnational village population as a whole. The intensity of the transnational circulation of money, affect, communication, and people within these extended families, which constituted each family as transnational, made the existing global relations between the villagers as a whole fade into insignificance. Indeed, relations between villagers were often enough nonexistent, even in the same settlement location. More village communal ties clearly occurred in places where there was a village association, but this wasn't always the case. Overall, however, I was struck by how individualizing migratory processes are, as well as by the fact that the transnational family is one of the few potent counter-individualizing diasporic forms of sociality.

Consequently, I wanted to center some of my research on the extended family as a transnational formation. I felt that if I could do my transnational ethnographic research by locating myself in the household of a specific extended family member living in each of the various global locations, this would give me a good vantage point from which to study the diasporic milieu as a whole; it would also provide the possibility for me to take the transnational family itself as an object of research. The attendant logistics involved proved to be one of the hardest parts of the research to plan but one of the more rewarding parts to engage in. Finding an extended family from each village with members settled in most of the village's key migratory settlement points was easy, but finding a family where the majority of those members could host me all around the globe involved a couple of failed attempts in each village. Somewhat miraculously, it happened. So between 2000 and 2003, I found myself making six trips around the world in which I was staying in the same households of the same extended family for each village.

The core ethnographic data in this book was obtained during the 2000–2005 period financed for this purpose by the ARC grant. It was the time when I could best afford touring the various diasporic locations around the world. But I continued to visit people from Jalleh and other places until 2015. I have also integrated research with migrants from Jalleh and its surroundings that I conducted in Australia during the 1990s. Hence, the book is more Jalleh centered. Some parts involve material acquired much later, between 2010 and 2015, when the key ideas behind the book were beginning to materialize. It can thus be said that the ethnographic material covers a period of more than twenty-five years. While my theoretical and empirical interests in the diasporic condition have, of course, changed many times over those years, I think the interest in the phenomenological and critical anthropological approach delineated above continued to grow until it came to dominate my analytical perspective. Thus, while some of the chapters contain previously published ethnographic material, overall the analysis of that material has changed, sometimes considerably.

I dedicate this book to the memory of my mother, a quintessential Lebanese diasporic subject. She was born in the 1920s in Santo Domingo, capital of the Dominican Republic and where my grandparents had migrated. My mother lived there until she was seven years old, when in the 1930s the family relocated to Bathurst, Australia. There she grew up. When she was thirty years old and had been living in Australia for twenty-three years, my mother went "back home" to Lebanon in the mid-1950s for a visit. She ended up meeting my father there, marrying him, and remaining until she was in her seventies. She finally returned to Australia in the early 2000s to be with my two sisters and me.

Introduction

"Migration is in our blood."

"We are cross-continental sailors and merchants from time immemorial."

"We follow in the footsteps of our Phoenician ancestors."

"Show me a Lebanese who is not fidgeting, wanting to go somewhere other than where he is. It is in the genes."

"Our ambition knows no borders."

"Show me a corner of the globe where there isn't a Lebanese."

"You know where you can find Lebanese people? Everywhere you hear Fairuz singing and see someone feeling emotional hearing her. And you know where you can hear Fairuz singing and see someone feeling emotional hearing her? Everywhere in the world."

"It's a shame your daughters don't speak Arabic. Allow me to say to you what I would say to my brother: you should never take the Lebanese existence in the world [*al woojood al lubnani bil 'aalam*] for granted. Many emigrants have crossed oceans and braved incredible circumstances to give the Lebanese this international presence. If your children are not learning to speak Arabic, how do you transmit this to them? How will you preserve your heritage? *Haraam* [shame]."

The above is a representative sample of statements and declarations Lebanese people have made to me while talking about the diaspora. While some remarks, such as the one referencing Fairuz, involve a distinctive creative flourish, most are commonly heard. Many are the object of derision by people with high educational capital, the "Phoenician ancestors" statement in particular. This claim of a Phoenician inheritance has a long history of being used by those trying to establish the Lebanese people's unique ancient, pre-Arab (read: anything-but-Arab) roots. It has an equally long history of being mocked by the Lebanese Left. But if we concentrate on establishing the falsity or absurdity of such beliefs, whether they're about bloodlines, genes, race, or transhistorically inherited national character, we miss the truth and the importance of the experiences that all this folk theorizing aims to convey. Chief among these is the experience of existing within a diasporic transnational, moral, and affective sociocultural milieu that, like all cultural milieus, is imagined to have a sui generis existence. That is, this milieu is experienced as inheritable and transmittable across generations. Second in importance among the experiences is that of believing in an intrinsic and quasi-natural link between this mode of transnational existence and being Lebanese.

To say that "migration is in our blood" might be an analytically inadequate essentializing formula, but it nonetheless conveys something important: the subject uttering such a statement finds it hard to think of a Lebanese mode of being that is not always already a transnational diasporic being.

This book is the product of years of research that has taken seriously the above experiences and the sociocultural realities they bring forth. I refer to both in a multiplicity of ways: diasporic modernity, diasporic being, diasporic condition, diasporic mode of existence, diasporic culture, diasporic lifeworld, diasporic space, diasporic reality. All, for me, aim to communicate slightly (but critically) different variations on the same key point that my ethnographic work repeatedly validates: diaspora is a way of being in the world and a way in which the world comes to be. Thus, *diasporic* signifies a variety of qualities and properties that pertain to both the subjects of these experiences and to the social relations/reality/world/milieu/culture/environment in which these subjects exist.

How to come to grips with the transnational realities created by migration is one of the foundational problematics of what constitutes migration, mobility, diasporic, transnational, and cosmopolitan studies today. Each of these disciplinary and transdisciplinary approaches tackles the subject slightly differently, highlighting some of its many dimensions. A subject such as diaspora favors and even necessitates such a diversity of approaches. And this book, even while aiming to be a distinct contribution to an anthropology of Lebanese diasporic culture, embraces—as will be clear from the various theories deployed within it—such a multidisciplinarity. At the same time, however, it should be noted that diasporic anthropology in general, like most disciplinary and multidisciplinary analyses of migration and diaspora, has been more sociological and explanatory in its intent. That is, it has been an anthropology that participates in the general sociological endeavor of describing, explaining, and understanding as best as possible the nature, scale, social causes, and dynamics of migratory phenomena and their consequences. Such an anthropology does not differ from sociology or any other sociologically oriented discipline in its general analytical intent. It diverges only in terms of methodology and the dimension of the phenomena it chooses to analyze and emphasize.

Breaks and Continuities in the Anthropology of Migration

My approach here differs from this, but not so much because of a lesser commitment to the sociological project. This sociological orientation has produced a vast literature on the Lebanese diaspora as diverse as the diaspora itself.[1] While I have learned a lot about the state of the Lebanese in the world from this literature, I want to wed my research to what I consider a more specifically critical anthropological problematic associated with the quest for alterity.[2] This can be summed up with one guiding question: In what way does the study of a particular sociocultural phenomenon expand our knowledge of the plurality of modes of existing in the world? Studying something as intimately part of our everyday life and as connected with capitalism and modernity as Lebanese diasporic cultures are today usually isn't the ground on which such a "classical" critical anthropological question is asked. Indeed, such a question is more often associated with "exotic" or "primitivist" anthropology, where alternative forms of existence to our modern capitalist present are usually more pronounced. So there is something akin to a disciplinary challenge behind engaging in such an approach while studying something as "pedestrianly" modern as diaspora. It involves what Eduardo Viveiros de Castro has called "strategic exoticization."

This challenge of exoticization is also the challenge of maintaining some forms of disciplinary continuity amid ongoing transformations. Migration has been a favored ground for before-and-after narratives in anthropology. These form a genre of introduction to the history of the discipline that I have often heard in O Week orientation lectures welcoming new or prospective students. This genre takes pride in describing a break between a before, when anthropology was interested in premodern tribal cultures, an interest implicitly or explicitly portrayed as colonial and bad, and a present, where anthropology is interested in "everything." Here *everything* means modern or postmodern contemporary phenomena that can also be located in the West. This always includes migration. An accompanying narrative has it that the discipline was late in taking migratory flows into account, contributing to a general sedentary analytical bias by naturalizing the relation between identity and territoriality.[3]

While an important element of truth exists in this claim, when taken with the above before-and-after narrative it ends up disallowing the recognition of many analytical moments in the discipline's history, indirectly contributing to the preponderance of the sociological problematic mentioned above. These moments can be built on to create a distinctively anthropological contribution to studying diaspora.

In fact, it could just as easily be said that the movement of people, the circulation of goods, and the spread of cultural forms have always been at the core of anthropology as a discipline. Something as basic as Malinowski's study of the Kula is but one example. Ira Bashkow noted some time ago that the anthropologists who take the notion of flow as an innovation on a static conception of culture fail to acknowledge how much this idea is already present in the fundamental and foundational notion of diffusion in Boasian anthropology.[4] But perhaps least recognized of all as an antecedent to migration studies is the work on kinship and the study of population movements it assumes. After all, is it possible to understand something like an exogamous patrilineal patrilocal system, for instance, without seeing in it a theory of population movement? We would have had a wealth of data on what such movement entailed and, I imagine, a wealth of data on other key problematics of migration studies like acculturation, alienation, homesickness, and nostalgia had the early anthropologists been more interested in interviewing—and more phenomenologically inclined and able to interview—women who moved from their tribe to another and become subjected to a paternal law other than that under which they had grown up. Those anthropologists didn't, and they can be criticized for not doing so; but there is no need to engage in a classic "throwing out the baby with the bathwater" maneuver. As will be seen, drawing from key anthropological theories such as theories of reciprocity, animism, and kinship to think about the diasporic condition can give us interesting analytical angles that the sociological tradition does not provide.

Diasporic Culture between the Specific and the Universal

This takes us to a different but equally important concern present throughout the book. It regards how the study of this particularly Lebanese diasporic mode of existence affects and speaks to all of us, migrant and non-migrant, today. The universalizing *us* here is deliberate. One of the key arguments of this book is that Lebanese diasporic culture is the culture of Lebanese capitalist modernity. Certainly, not all modernities emerge as diasporic, and not all diaspora are modern phenomena. Nor is diasporic modernity a uniquely

Lebanese phenomenon. The concept captures an important dimension of Greek, Italian, Sinhalese, Irish, and Chinese diasporas, among others. But as far as I can tell, no modernity is as coterminous with its diasporic culture as Lebanese modernity. Indeed, as I will argue, there is no such thing as a Lebanese modernity that is not diasporic. Nonetheless, a critical anthropological approach invites us to investigate dimensions of this modern diasporic condition not unique to the Lebanese or to others who share a modernity similar to theirs. This is especially so today: it would be difficult to find a cultural space free from an entanglement with the experience of migration and the cultures it has secreted. Thus, in what we can call a classical anthropological move, I am examining a cultural phenomenon that I call the diasporic condition in a specific sociocultural space—not because this phenomenon exists only in this specific sociocultural space, but because this space is one in which the phenomenon is most clearly visible, easier to delineate, and as such made analytically available. This is particularly true of what I will call "diasporic lenticularity," a mode of existing in multiple realities. The aim is not therefore to just say, "Look at the Lebanese diasporic condition—how different and interesting it is." To be sure, this is something I also hope to achieve. But of equal importance is how such an analysis will allow the reader, as it has allowed me as a researcher, to go back to any space we inhabit with fresh eyes and see where and how elements of this lenticular mode of existence are present within it.[5]

Clearly, an anthropological perspective should never essentialize the relation between a cultural phenomenon and the people and space where one is studying it. As I have argued elsewhere,[6] most classical Western anthropologists have studied what in a first step is shown to be an exotic cultural form, working hard to show how radically different it is from dominant Western cultural forms. Yet in a second step that only superficially appears as paradoxical, they move to show that the culture they are studying, despite its exoticness and radical difference, speaks to something that exists within their own societies. Likewise, then, my aim in studying Lebanese social spaces where the diasporic condition stands out clearly is not to make that condition a specifically Lebanese cultural phenomenon to the exclusion of others. There is a universal dimension to this experience, even if some Lebanese themselves apprehend forms of diasporic being in a nationalist essentialized manner.

This vacillation between the specific and the universal is in the very empirical nature of things. Such dialectical thinking used to be taken for granted but is no longer.[7] The idea that the empirical is on the side of specificity is self-defeating. It always leads to an absurd ad infinitum reduction to the singular. If I were to associate the empirical with the specific, even my claim to analyze a "Lebanese" cultural form is unjustifiable. Indeed, both villages where I did ethnographic work are Christian, and there certainly is a specificity to the Christian Lebanese experience. But this descent into specificity will not end there. Indeed, not only are the villages Christian, they are Maronite. Thus, since not all Lebanese Christians are Maronite, even "Lebanese Christian" is an unwarranted generalization. Then there are questions of specificity related to the main determinants behind a certain wave of migration, such as the difference between what is referred to as economic migration dominant in early twentieth century and war-related migration that followed the Lebanese Civil War (1975–90). And so on. My point, however, is that cultural specificity is never as specific as it claims, just as universality is never as universal as it claims. To be empirically faithful to one's data is not about taking specificity as an anchor. It is about knowing how to cater to the continuous vacillation between degrees of specificity and degrees of universality at the very heart of ethnographic knowledge. I am always seeking to understand the extent to which a more general Christian Lebanese diasporic culture exists within a Maronite experience, while also being aware, as noted earlier, that this Maronite experience is itself evidently differentiated sociologically according to class, gender, education, national location, and so on. Likewise, I am always exploring to what extent from this Christian Lebanese diasporic condition one can speak of a Lebanese diasporic mode of existence and, in much the same way, to what extent a more general diasporic condition—*the* diasporic condition of the book's title—emerges from this specific Lebanese diasporic condition. This isn't an either/or matter. Finally, we must remain aware that the degrees of specificity and universality that emerge from the text because of the writing process themselves fluctuate according to the reader's interests and social and cultural background.

The Book's Structure

For my part, I examine a variety of people, spaces, and situations. Lebanese villagers celebrating one of them obtaining an Australian visa. A Lebanese Venezuelan mourning the fact that his life has become too centered on money. A Lebanese American blaming his sexual problems on migration. Members of a transnational family situated in various parts of the world arguing about the responsibilities associated with looking after their mother in Lebanon. A group of young middle-class returnees celebrating Beirut's relative lawlessness.

While each of these situations treats a particular dimension of diasporic sociality, my aim is also to show how they offer us a window on a diasporic condition shared by the Lebanese. In particular, I highlight their enmeshment in what I call the "anisogamic" and the "lenticular" mode of existence that defines the diasporic condition: an entanglement of multiple realities that are continually present and that differ in the way they are inhabited, their affective quality, and their intensity. I detail how this condition challenges our dominant conceptions of social reality. And finally, I show how, despite the diasporic specificity of the cultural forms I end up highlighting, they nonetheless speak today to those who aren't thought of as "diasporic" subjects.

The book is implicitly divided into two parts. The first part—the first five chapters—details the historical rise of Lebanon's diasporic culture, the way Lebanese subjects are constituted into diasporic subjects, and the key features of the diasporic experience. All those lead to explaining the lenticular nature of diasporic reality. The second part—the final four chapters—comprises case studies that aim to highlight the analytical benefits and insights obtained by analyzing various diasporic situations with the anisogamic and lenticular lenses.

Chapter 1, "Lebanese Capitalism and the Emergence of a Transnational Mode of Existence," deals with the rise of Lebanese diasporic culture. It argues that diasporic culture is not the culture of migration but the culture of Lebanese modernity. It begins in Lebanon itself. Migratory subjects are central to this culture, but someone doesn't need to have migrated to be part of diasporic culture. The chapter examines the first constitutive experience of the diasporic condition, what is referred to as the internationalization of the space of viability, the ability to look at the whole world as a place where one can make a living.

Chapter 2, "On Being Propelled into the World: Existential Mobility and the Migratory *Illusio*," deploys Pierre Bourdieu's concept of *illusio* to highlight the nature of migration as a mode of investing oneself in a social path that one hopes will yield something for the diasporic subject. The chapter explores the notion of migration as a quest for existential mobility, a sense that one is going somewhere in life. In addition, the chapter develops the relation between physical and existential mobility. It also shows how this desire for moving into the world is haunted by its opposite: a desire to remain and valorize home.

Chapter 3, "Diasporic Anisogamy," begins by examining a spatial comparative logic at the heart of the diasporic condition: the inability of diasporic subjects to look at a place without comparing it to other places. The chapter explores Lévi-Strauss's notion of anisogamy as reciprocity between parties of unequal status. It then shows how the comparative logic that animates diasporic being is traversed by an anisogamic logic based on the diasporic subjects' feelings of inferiority toward the lands they migrate to. It's not a racialized sense of inferiority but rather one grounded in a sense of belonging to a land that has failed to keep them.

Chapter 4, "From Ambivalent to Fragmented Subjects," begins by arguing that while the notion of ambivalence can account for a diasporic subject with two opposite yearnings—such as migrating and staying at home, modernity and tradition, the primacy of economic pursuit versus the primacy of a poetically and emotionally driven life—it can't account for the many situations in which the diasporic subject inhabits both yearnings, managing to do so by becoming fragmented, inhabiting multiple realities rather than being torn between those realities. The next chapter develops this conception.

Chapter 5, "On Diasporic Lenticularity," begins by arguing that if inhabiting a multiplicity of realities requires us to conceive of a fragmented multiple subject, then it also requires us to conceive of a social space made from multiple realities. The chapter examines what it means to inhabit and exist in a particular spatial location. It offers a critique of the monorealism characterizing the dominant conception of being somewhere, which assumes that someone can exist in only one location and rely on memory to relate to other locations. The chapter shows how people often experience themselves as existing in multiple places. It is this experience of inhabiting an entangled and flickering multiplicity of realities that is referred to as the lenticular condition.

Chapter 6, "Lenticular Realities and Anisogamic Intensifications," is an ethnographic examination of a particular mode of relating to the Lebanese news among the Lebanese in Sydney. The chapter shows how the notion of anisogamy and lenticularity allows a richer reading of what "reading the Lebanese newspaper" means. It shows that the reading is a particular mode of inhabiting Lebanon. Moreover, it demonstrates how a whole series of anisogamically structured affects shape the intensity with which the Lebanese in Sydney fluctuate between inhabiting Australia and inhabiting Lebanon.

Chapter 7, "The Lebanese Transnational Diasporic Family," is an analysis of the Neefa family from Jalleh as a network of transnational relations and as a diasporic milieu. The chapter examines the circulation of phone calls, money, and visits that constitute the family as a relational milieu. The elements that unite and divide the family are explored, the way it functions as a corporate whole and the contradictions and tensions that divide it. The chapter also examines the cultural milieu the family members share and the strategies of cultural distinction they establish among themselves. Then it relates how a minor disagreement between two family members became a transnational conflict that laid bare the lenticular nature of the realities in which the family is constituted as such.

Chapter 8, "Diaspora and Sexuality," takes as a case study a Lebanese man who blames his sexual problems on migration. It explores the migratory trajectory of the person involved, examining the dominant forms of male sexuality in the village where he had grown up and the transformation of his experience as he moved from Lebanon to the United States. In particular, the chapter explores how the anisogamic undercurrents that undermined his marriage to the daughter of his richer and better-educated maternal uncle became articulated to the anisogamic dynamic that traverses the relation of Lebanese immigrants to the United States.

Chapter 9, "Diasporic *Jouissance* and Perverse Anisogamy: Negotiated Being in the Streets of Beirut," examines how the anisogamic and lenticular nature of diasporic reality is inhabited playfully by middle-class immigrants to Europe and the United States who visit Beirut and enjoy what they see as its relative lawlessness. The chapter explores how existing in a lenticular reality made from both the lawful spaces of Europe and the United States and the lawless spaces of Beirut is the condition of possibility of enjoying lawlessness. The chapter then shows how this gives room for another form of sociality to emerge, what I refer to as "negotiated being," where the relation to the other is not regulated by law.

A Critical Anthropological Approach to Diasporic Culture

As I've already noted and as the above suggests, the critical anthropological problematic of finding within diasporic culture an *other* sociality permeates the analytics of the text. Let me reemphasize, however, and it should become clear as the reader proceeds through the text, that I don't see this critical anthropological quest for cultural alterity as an alternative to the sociological project of understanding diaspora as a social phenomenon. But I do want the reader to keep in mind that notwithstanding the desire to elucidate certain dimensions of Lebanese diasporic life, this search for "an *other*" sociality that tests our accepted categories of thought is *also* an important driving intellectual quest behind this book. The willingness to "do" anthropology (in the philosophical sense of the word) with one's ethnographic material is a necessary corollary of rethinking the adequacy of our categories. This is akin to what Holbraad and Pedersen describe as the "willingness to stage the encounter with ethnography as an experiment in conceptual reflexivity."[8]

If approaches like those I am delineating here have been rare in the study of migration and diaspora, it's because the sources of funding for migration-related research, such as the United Nations, governmental and nongovernmental organizations, and private foundations, have encouraged a preponderance of sociologically oriented applied problematics in the field. And while this is not as pronounced in cultural anthropological writing as it is in sociological and social-anthropological writing, very few migrant-related researches don't see in migration a governmental problem or another that it aims to treat: a problem of transnational mobility or a problem of settlement and assimilation from the receiving country's perspective; a problem of brain drain from the sending country's perspective; or an economic problem involving gains and losses for all the governments concerned.[9]

To be clear, the above is not only true of government-funded research. The research guided by a social justice standpoint shares a similar problem-oriented analytic posture. Here, instead of migrants being a governmental problem for the state, it is the state or the dominant culture that is seen as a problem for the migrant in the forms of racism, discrimination, failed hospitality, and so on. In anthropology, this has paralleled what Joel Robbins has described as the discipline's articulation of the figure of the "suffering subject."[10] The corollary of this anthropology is that, as in other disciplines, the research field is often treated like a crime scene: somebody has committed a crime against, or at least done something very bad to, the migrant, requiring a meticulous analysis of the social forces and conditions leading to the criminal offense. So the research acquires a forensic ethos: Who committed the racism? Who committed the exploitation? And who committed the marginalization? Though at least, in the style of TV detective Columbo, we know the likely suspects from the start of our investigation: patriarchy, colonialism, racism. The aim of analysis, then, is to find out how these injustices occurred. While I myself have inevitably engaged in this kind of social science often, highlighting a critical anthropological approach in this book allows me to minimize, without totally absenting, questions such as racism from the analysis. Instead, I have endeavored to focus on phenomenological questions concerning the nature of the diasporic lifeworld, on situations where people define for themselves, and struggle to achieve, whatever they conceive of as a viable life.

It should be said that for someone who in previous works always prioritized questions of racism and knows how diffuse racism is in the Western/colonial social body, there is something refreshing—and I would even say postcolonial—in researching immigrants of non-Western background living in Western metropolises without centering the research on how white people interact with or think of them. I discovered this firsthand when I started presenting part of the book at conferences in Australia and elsewhere. Some Australians whose ancestry was other than white European approached me to openly express their disappointment that my work is "no longer as political." But white Australians as well, accustomed to my discussing racism, were often looking at me as if wanting to ask, "What about us? We don't care if you say that we are really bad racist people, but surely you can't go through a whole paper without noting that we exist or mentioning us at all!" That is, I discovered—not so much by design as indirectly—that something infused with a Fanonian postcolonial narcissistic desire arises when implicitly informing readers from the white established cultures, "Sorry, but immigrants aren't thinking about you every second of the day, you know. They have other preoccupations."

A perspective interested in questions of lifeworld and viability necessitates an analysis combining the sociological with a more cultural phenomenological approach. To be sociological means being analytically receptive to the work of social relations, to questions of power, and to the social specificity (class, gender, etc.) of social experiences. In this sense, an unsociological anthropology would be extremely poor indeed. A cultural phenomenological anthropology, meanwhile, emphasizes the cultural unity of such experiences, the milieu in which they all happen. To me at least, the two approaches are indispensable and point to what appear as coexisting, coproducing, and yet contradictory realities. It's an old, irresolvable contradiction, the kind we should aim to dwell in productively and exploit analytically for all it's worth, rather than have misplaced Hegelian fantasies of resolving and transcending: to claim that there is a reality not experienced in a sociologically specific way would be ludicrous, but at the same time there must be "something" that remains the same in order for "it" to be experienced in different ways. Otherwise, the very idea of different experiences of "something" would be absurd. This is similar to the contradiction faced when we claim that identity is fluid and changing: on one hand, a claim to the contrary is absurd, but on the other, without "something" that stays the same while being constantly fluid, all we have would be just a series of different identities, not a fluid identity. By its very nature, writing can oscillate only between the sociologically specific and the culturally general, between what changes and what is continuously the same. This book is not different from others in this regard. Nonetheless, to highlight the above-mentioned critical anthropological approach is to bend the stick, as Bourdieu would say, in the direction of a cultural anthropological study of diaspora as a general milieu. *Milieu* here is understood in Georges Canguilhem's sense of the word in his classic work, "The Living and Its Milieu." It's worth quoting him at length to fully grasp, albeit in an abstract manner at this stage, the ramifications of choosing such a research object.

> In Newton's day, the problem facing mechanics was that of the action of distinct physical bodies at a distance. It was a problem that had not existed for Descartes. For him, there was only one mode of physical action, impact, in only one possible physical situation, that of contact. This is why we can say that in Cartesian physics the notion of milieu has no place. But it was difficult to extend the Cartesian theory of impact and contact to the case of separate point particles, since in this case they could not act without being confounded by this action. As a result, we can see that Newton was led to pose the problem of the means of the action. Luminous ether was for him the fluid that served as the vehicle of action at a distance. This explains the passage from the notion of fluid as a vehicle to its designation as a medium [milieu]. The fluid is the intermediary between two bodies; it is their milieu; and to the extent that it penetrates these bodies, they are situated within it.[11]

To me, diasporic culture is this particular fluid/milieu/intermediary in which the Lebanese and their transnational networks, born out of migration, are situated and which at the same time penetrates them and helps constitute them. It is the environment or ecology in which these migratory networks emerge and flourish. Clearly, people don't live in one or another of such defined milieus but in a multiplicity of them that intermingle, mix, fuse, and shape one another. Nonetheless, and as long as this intermingling is recognized, we can take a particular milieu as our object of analysis, which is what I do here regarding Lebanese diasporic culture. This milieu is experienced differently by people as they interact with one another and as I am interacting with them while doing this research. But through my examination of the various specific ways in which it is lived, I aim to reflect on what can be said about it as a milieu: its specific features, the elements of its identity, and the kind of subjects that are part of its constitutive makeup.

Strange as this might sound, the study of diaspora as a transnational cultural milieu or lifeworld has not been a common perspective in any of the disciplinary and transdisciplinary fields that take it as an object of analysis—not even in anthropology, which, theoretically, is more disposed to delineate cultural formations of this type. This might sound like an arrogant and ill-informed thing to say, but it's not. If there is cultural analytical work associated with hitherto existing approaches to transnationalism, it is mainly concerned with globalization and with the global cultural conditions that facilitated the formation of transnational realities—such as the conceptually ubiquitous time-space compression—rather than with forms of transnationalism themselves as culture. In anthropology of migration and diaspora, cultural analysis has been more prevalent and productive in the analysis of migrant cultures or the cultures of migration, as in the early works of Gil Bottomley[12] and Marie de Lepervanche[13] in Australia, Roger Rouse[14] in the United States, or Pnina Werbner in the United Kingdom.[15] These works, however, are more often than not studies of cultures of settlement, examining either the transformations of traditional cultural forms that occur during migration and settlement or the classical problematics of assimilation, acculturation, culture maintenance, and the relation with the host national culture. Of equal foundational importance is the work of Arjun Appadurai on the processes of de-territorialization and re-territorialization of cultural forms.[16] Clearly, the above studies and those issued from them offer important windows on the actual makeup of diasporic cultures, especially the transformations and variations in their key constitutive elements, such as kinship, food, and religious beliefs, and the social relations articulated around them. Nonetheless, it remains the case that such investigations do not delineate a common transnational cultural milieu as an object of analysis. Indeed, their interest lies in the opposite direction, in the differentiating processes happening within that milieu.

Where there has been a clear interest in transnational formations, as in the foundational texts on the anthropology of transnational networks primarily associated with Nina Glick Schiller,[17] the dominant analytical attention, encapsulated in the very notion of network and its emphasis on relations and ties, has been sociological or social-anthropological rather than cultural. Appadurai's earlier concept of ethnoscapes certainly moves in a transnational cultural direction, which played an important role in directing us toward anthropological conceptions of transnational cultures.[18] However, I aim to delineate less of a "scape" and more of a transnational diasporic state of being, along with a transnational diasporic environment or milieu.

As I moved among the various locations of this milieu trying to define conceptually and practically the kind of ethnographic project I was initiating, I kept finding myself trying to answer two issues from the moment I began reflecting on my research. It's useful to clarify those questions right from the start. The first was methodological: if I'm claiming to research "a" shared diasporic culture but a culture that exists in many locations around the world, and as such involves moving between different locations around the world, am I doing a multisited ethnography? The second was whether my desire to research diaspora as a transnational milieu implies that my research object was a diasporic "community." Is there a necessary relation between shared milieu and community?

A Not-So-Multisited Ethnography

Is it the case that if one's research is spread in a multiplicity of geographic locations, then one is necessarily engaging in a multisited ethnography? The concept has often become a routinized buzzword in the study of transnational migration, in the sense that it has been vacated of the reflexive power present in the work of those who introduced it as a concept.[19] It seems enough to be doing research in a couple of international places for a work to be named multisited ethnography. The reader might think that in my case, having spent much of my time zooming among eight different locations around the globe, I can't but be totally in favor of multisited ethnography. The fact is that I did start my research thinking of myself as doing exactly that. Now I simply find the idea not so much conceptually as practically difficult. That is, it's not a question of being for or against it. It's more a question of whether one can do such a thing. If we take site and ethnography seriously, I simply don't think that such a thing as a multisited ethnography is possible.

For my first couple of trips around the world, moving from one geographic area to another and staying with the family members I was working with went fine. I could have felt that it was possible to engage in a multisited ethnography—except for a simple problem. I was constantly suffering from jet lag as well as health problems associated with too much flying and too much eating and drinking on the run. Conducting multisited ethnography was unhealthy, especially for (most) people who have teaching and families to go back to and therefore can't take all the time they might wish to take. They need to cover the various sites in a limited amount of time. The body of the anthropologist, even a postmodern one, simply can't cope with such fast and intensive traveling for long. I thought it amusing, as this fact dawned on me, that none of the people who have written about migration and multisited ethnography have mentioned something as mundane as the problem of jet lag. I still wonder how they practically managed this multisited ethnographic research themselves.

Perhaps someone younger than I could have coped physically with this, also someone with no family to rush home to and unequal child-rearing labor to negotiate with their partner and make up for. But even if these responsibilities weren't an issue, for me an even more serious problem simply made multisited ethnography an untenable proposition. In my first couple of trips around the world, I found it relatively easy to stop in France, meet some members of the family, leave for Cabudare, Venezuela, meet some other members of the family, leave for Boston, and so on. But after a while, the issue of landing and leaving became a far more difficult affair. It wasn't so easy to just land and leave, as if I were floating above the cultures I was researching: people's problems, my own relation to them, people's expectations of me, my expectations of them, the questions I was asking, the social relations I was becoming aware of—all these things changed and complexified the site. As they say, it was getting thicker. Increasingly, it was simply becoming impossible for me to do what I was doing at first: just hopping around. In many ways, thick ethnography is not a matter of choice but a function of one's degree of immersion. After a period of becoming more immersed in certain social relations, we are forced by them to be either a thick ethnographer or no ethnographer at all. It was not ethnography but the relation to the field itself that was getting thicker. Thicker and stickier, I might add: as I became more involved I became more subjected to the socio-gravitational forces that pull us into a social field and make it very hard for us to remove ourselves from it.[20] I am interviewing X, with Y and Z sitting around. X says something that I know Z feels strongly about. Z knows that I know she feels strongly about it. So the feelings generated by the interview and the analytical labor it requires slowly became much more complex and more demanding. Now, each landing in the field and each departure were major affairs, and the time between them was less and less touristy and more and more socially, psychologically, and analytically demanding and exhausting. I was facing a choice that, in fact, made the whole issue quite clear to me: one site, if it is to be engaged in thoroughly, was already an exhausting enterprise. How can someone study multiple sites in such an involved way? So I decided to completely forget about the possibility of working with a third village as I had originally planned in my research grant application. I simply couldn't be involved that intimately with more than two families at the most, I thought. As it turned out, I only managed to work with the two families until 2003. After a while, even two families was becoming too much, as I mentioned in the preface. I had to stop working transnationally with the Mehj family and become more centered on the Jalleh family alone.

But regardless of the number of families I could work with, it was also clear that if I was committed to study a transnational family or a village as a global phenomenon, then I couldn't treat all the locations where each one of their members existed as separate sites. I had to treat all these locations, dispersed as they were, as just one place. However, if I am treating the whole family with its various locations around the globe as one site, is this really a multisited ethnography? Perhaps it is, but this would be at the expense of making light of the meaning of an anthropological site. If we are to maintain a concept of the site as something with which a person must spend an inordinate amount of time and labor to become familiar with it, then I wasn't studying a multisited reality. I was studying diasporic culture from one site: the site occupied by the transnational family. It was a globally spread, geographically noncontiguous site, but it was nevertheless one site. It was still physically demanding to study such a global site, but at least this was a more realistic way of defining my research object. Most important, I felt that this way of conceiving of my project was more in line with my desire to highlight diaspora as a milieu in which transnational Lebanese relations are located rather than as a specific culture of settlement that would necessitate more of an emphasis on migrant-host community relations than I am allowing for. This leads us to the other question I noted above concerning the link between culture and community.

And a Not-So-Imagined Community

If a village, or even a national, diasporic population shares the same culture or the same milieu, does this immediately make for a village or a national diasporic *community*? Transnational community was and remains a flourishing concept in diasporic and migration studies, and every diaspora seemingly is such a community whether it likes it or not. The concept has been used in all kinds of contexts, including by a number of anthropologists in my own field of working on Lebanese villages spread around the world, in which case the concept becomes an extension of the idea of the global village.[21] As I have already noted, when I began to globally locate the migrants from each of the villages I was researching, there clearly was no *necessary* strong sense of transnational community among them. I thought hard about whether in claiming that people share the same milieu or the same culture one is also claiming that such people form a community. My answer was always no. I could think of many cases where people share the same culture without their forming a community in any of the senses of the word available to us. Still, in a kind of uncritical inheritance, I found myself unreflexively using the concept of transnational village community to refer to the village and its emigrants. Indeed, I had to work on myself, and I continue to, so as not to lapse involuntarily into the language of community.

In contrast, villagers certainly had a sense of belonging to a village whose members are globally spread around the world. But to say that they formed a global community and that they had a communal sense of belonging to a transnational community of villagers was stretching it in many cases. When I returned to the studies that discuss transnational communities to look for the evidence produced to indicate that the members of a village diaspora constituted a community, there was very little of it. Stephen Castles's and Ralph Grillo's warnings against the facile usage of this concept rang particularly true.[22] It seems that for too many people, the fact that some people originate from the same village or nation and are spread around the globe was enough to make them a transnational community. What's more, the lack of empirical evidence of connectedness didn't appear to bother some of the researchers concerned. This was particularly striking when I raised the issue with some of those who used the concept at various conferences. There seemed to be no need to show that any specific enduring social relations between the villagers existed for them to constitute a community. Why? Because apparently, these villagers constituted an imagined community—and here is another concept that has been wildly circulating for some time now.

It's truly striking how much of a passe-partout the notion of imagined community has become in the field of diasporic studies. This is not to take anything away from Benedict Anderson's originality when he himself deployed the concept.[23] It just seems that for a long time now, it has become an excuse for not doing any empirical work that tries to establish that a group of people form a community. When an individual presenting a paper on a diasporic community is asked for any evidence to show that the diasporic group that person is studying is a community, that person reacts with a superior look and informs the questioner that "it doesn't work this way," because the community being studied is an "imagined community." Here "imagined community" seems clearly to have very little community in it and a lot of imagination by the researchers concerned. The issue becomes about whose imagination we are talking about here.

This influenced my attempt to locate my ethnography with the extended diasporic families where evidence of their members' experience as a transnational community was far more materially grounded—which, just to be clear, isn't a term I oppose to *imaginary community*. But I am nonetheless pleased to let the reader know that the extended transnational families I studied weren't "imagined" by me in any facile way, even if becoming conscious of them requires a definite imaginative act. They are nevertheless existing familial communities, with a definite analyzable ensemble of social relations that constitutes them. In fact, these families weren't "imagined" at all in Anderson's proper sense either. Usually, each member *did* have an empirical sense of exactly who each person was that belonged to the family and where they were located, even if they had never met them. As an aside, I must stress that during that period of my research, I enjoyed and I really recommend the study of such not-so-imagined communities when analyzing diasporic relations. They are both analytically and psychologically good for you as a researcher—much better, and far more socially useful, than the study of imagined but non-existing communities.

ONE

Lebanese Capitalism and the Emergence of a Transnational Mode of Existence

Jalleh, 16 August 2003

It's 3:30 p.m., and I am sitting on the veranda of Luis's house. We're having the ritu-alistic after-lunch ahweh, *and the men are starting to nod off on their seats, as it's the time of their afternoon siesta. But no one has gone to lie down in the bedrooms on the cooler side of the house on this hot summer afternoon. Everybody is waiting for Jameel to come back from Beirut. Five minutes of silent somnolence and Luis says, "That's it, I am going to bed. I don't see the point in waiting. He has been given assurances that nothing is going to go wrong." He stops for a fleeting second and says, "They're going to give it to him this time." This is the nth time he had proclaimed a variant of the last sentence since Jameel left in the morning. Trying to act like a diviner in close contact with cosmic uncontrollable forces but sounding every bit like the exact anxious opposite.*

But no one has to wait that much longer. Less than a minute later, Jameel's car reaches the top of the village's main street and is now visible from our veranda. Ev-eryone gets up. The car disappears behind houses for the time it takes to reach us. It reappears and slowly turns left off the main street and into the wide cement driveway that leads straight to us. Jameel's younger brother, who is driving him, slowly moves the car as far as it can go before it reaches a more elevated cement slab, about twenty meters from the balcony where we are. Jameel gets out. He turns to us and waves with a hand clutching a bunch of white papers. His body is erect, and he gives us a broad grin . . . There's no mistake . . . He's got it . . .

"I told you!" Luis shouts in a feeble attempt at making us see the scene unfolding before us as a confirmation of his divining powers. Everyone on the veranda wakes up from their slumber, descends the few steps separating the veranda from the driveway, and rushes toward Jameel to congratulate him. They are screaming and hugging him, and he is screaming and hugging everyone. Jameel had just obtained a visa to join his uncle in Australia.

This was his third attempt. For the first, I also happened to be around to see him come back from the two-hour drive between the Australian Embassy in Beirut and the village, a stoic smile on his face, but his body slumped and his spirits broken. And for the second attempt, I was waiting for him at the Australian Embassy, looking bemusedly at the people lined up next to a We Only Accept American Dollars sign as he came out looking defeated. But now he stands before us as if a completely rejuvenated man. It's both banal and extraordinary to note the difference between a despairing and a hopeful body: a body that believes in its future.

Jameel's hope is a contagious hope. Indeed, while everyone is congratulating him on his visa, clearly happy for him, most are as clearly happy for themselves. After all, in succeeding to get a visa Jameel has reaffirmed the village's collective belief that migration does not have to be something one endlessly desires and dreams about without it ever eventuating; it's a living fantasy, both an aspiration and a practical possibility—a sometimes difficult possibility given increasing visa restrictions around the world, but a possibility nonetheless.

Along with a number of other frequent daily occurrences such as discussions about private or public remittances; media reports about business success (e.g., Carlos Ghosn and Carlos Slim), social fame (e.g., Amal Alamuddin Clooney), or film fame (e.g., Salma Hayek); or the celebration of "happy" emigrant news from one part of the globe or another, Jameel's visa success works to represent migration as a viable endeavor. It reaffirms migration as something worth investing one's effort in, or at least keeping on one's horizon. In the month I was in Jalleh, around the time Jameel was preparing to leave for Australia, I was aware of four others from the village getting ready to migrate: one to Dubai to work in a financial institution; one to Ghana to work with his uncle as a supervisor on a construction site; and two to the United States to join other family members and, like Jameel, not knowing what their employment prospects would be. At the same time, I met two couples, one from Melbourne and the other from Montreal, who had returned after a long migration to resettle permanently in the village. There were as well many emigrants who were back for a short visit. I witnessed many people talking about what to do with public (and sometimes private) remittances they or others had received. I also attended meetings to discuss building a football (soccer) field with a donation to the village by a Saudi-based immigrant, who wanted the field named for his recently deceased father. All such events reaffirm the village's diasporic connection and the viability of its migratory aspirations.

To be sure, Jalleh also has an abundant history of diasporic suffering, failures, and pain. Moreover, there's an implicitly and explicitly expressed desire to stay at home that continues to manifest itself at every stage of the migratory process. As we shall see, this desire is an important feature of the diasporic condition, and it sometimes even gives shape to a kind of anti-migratory counterculture where everything linked to tradition and home is valorized, and everything linked to migration is derided and devalorized.

But despite all this, in the village, as in the rest of Lebanon, the positive images of migration continue to overshadow all others. To be sure, no one goes around actively repressing the negative images; they're simply not dwelled on too much. More important perhaps, the negative images are left for individuals (and writers and artists) to express, while the positive ones are institutionalized. Indeed, it can be said that migration and the belief in migration in Lebanon are akin to an institutionalized faith. As with every faith, the believers don't dwell on the thousand times their faith failed them. They dwell on the success stories. It can also be noted here that successful emigrants function like "saints of migration": they become a sublimated ideal of the true believer. They are possessors of that transhistorical Lebanese migratory spirit mentioned in the introduction, and their very presence works to further reinforce people's belief in migration as a viable path in the search for a better life.

When I was writing this passage, the well-known Brazilian-French businessman of Lebanese descent, Carlos Ghosn, had been jailed in Japan. Carlos is a quintessential patron saint of Lebanese migration. As with actual saints and as noted above, people name their children after him, hoping that through the naming some of Carlos's Lebanese migratory spirit will find its way into their child. Far from ruining his reputation as a Lebanese success story, his being put in jail is seen as part of the difficulties the Lebanese must go through on the road to diasporic success. What's a saint who hasn't been persecuted? Indeed, a big billboard appeared in Beirut at the time, proclaiming, We Are All Carlos Ghosn (fig. 1).[1]

Given this affinity, it's not surprising to see that elements of religious faith are continuously entangled with migratory faith. In Jalleh and Mehj, each village's Maronite saints along with the Virgin Mary and Saint Charbel, Lebanon's quintessential saint, are present at every moment of the migratory process, helping people obtain a visa, helping them travel safely, and helping them settle but also, in some cases, helping them remain and resist the lure of migration. Migratory faith, like and along with religious faith, is ubiquitous throughout the diasporic landscape.

When I began my research in the two villages, I would ask some people preparing to leave, "So when did you start contemplating migration?" They invariably looked at me as if my question was absurd, and their answer was

Figure 1. We Are All Carlos Ghosn. Photo by Jeremy Arbid.

inevitably a variation on "I've been thinking about migration ever since I was born." It didn't take me long to recognize the naïveté of my question. I was assuming a migratory subject who at some stage, after his or her formation as a social subject, suddenly begins thinking about and "deliberating" the possibility and viability of migration as if for the first time. It struck me that this was the kind of assumption implicit in some rational choice theory approaches to migration.[2] My Lebanese subjects were unambiguously communicating something different to me: they are always already born in a cultural space and a milieu where questions of migration impose themselves in a matter-of-fact and inevitable manner in their everyday lives. In Jalleh and Mehj, as in the rest of Lebanon, one would have to struggle to find someone whose life is being lived without questions of migration and diaspora being part of it. It's important to stress, however, that understanding that everyone's life is entangled with questions of migration does not mean that everyone is actively contemplating migration. Biao Xiang's critique of the governmental origins of the category of migrant and his introduction of the "would-be migrant," the person devoting his or her life to trying to migrate, are crucial and important steps in broadening our analytical horizon of what the diasporic entails.[3] But thinking about and being affected by migration can take many forms, including refusing to be seduced by and to yearn for migration. What all these references to migration denote, including the latter, is the existence of a diasporic culture as a common milieu that affects people in a variety of ways. A Beiruti physician captured this notion reasonably well when he described migration to me as "a bug that pervades the social environment. It affects people differently, but everyone catches it the moment they breathe the air." It is the emergence of this viral environment that I want to delineate here.

Indeed, diaspora is often thought of as anywhere outside "the homeland." Many articles speak of people moving between the diaspora and the homeland. The "and" signals the relation of these places but also their separate identities. And of course, in the classical conceptions of diaspora, the homeland figures as a place of origin, sometimes mythical, and as a "yearning." Thus, to begin thinking about diasporic culture by saying that it is impossible to think of a Lebanese life that is not always already diasporic takes us in a somewhat different direction. It entails the uncommon claim that diasporic culture is not only the culture of immigrants outside Lebanon but also the culture of the Lebanese in Lebanon from "the moment they breathe the air." Abdelmalek Sayad long ago argued the impossibility of understanding immigration and the culture of settlement without understanding the culture of emigration.[4] In a slight variation on this, a key argument I am developing here is that important features of the diasporic condition emerge in Lebanon before being part of the culture of the *mahjar* (the overseas space of migration). Or to put it differently, I am proposing that diasporic culture begins as a culture of emigration before also becoming a culture of immigration.

Furthermore, asserting that a diasporic subject is not necessarily a subject who has actually migrated will help us highlight that actual migration, as opposed to being entangled within a migratory culture, is merely one mode of being part of diasporic culture. It's not even a necessary one from an experiential point of view. Objections could be immediately raised that migration historically precedes the formation of "a diaspora" and that a transnational diasporic culture is practically and logically, not just historically, unthinkable without actual migration. This is all true. Yet neither of these objections prevents us from arguing that migration is merely one among many trajectories and endeavors that constitute the diasporic universe.

To make an analogy that helps clarify the coexistence of such apparently paradoxical propositions, we can say that migration is to diasporic culture what surfing is to some Australian, South African, and American beach cultures. Surfing is at the core of those beach cultures. At most beaches, beach cultures formed historically around surfing practices. And surfers, with their various modes of inhabiting the ocean and the beach, their habits and relationalities, their fashion, and so on, have constantly shaped these beach cultures. But a beach culture is the culture of a whole beach town. And despite the continued primacy of surfing in such beach cultures, surfing nonetheless becomes only one feature of the culture among many. This is true even if the beach culture remains experienced by many as unthinkable or, perhaps more correctly, unimaginable without surfing. It's in much the same way that we can say that migration, despite its historical and practical importance in bringing about diasporic culture and despite its imaginary dominance, is only one mode of the wider diasporic culture it has nonetheless historically brought about and of which it remains the most distinctive feature.

Of course, diasporic culture becomes what it is for us today, the milieu of the considerable transnational migratory network, thanks to various migratory practices that spread it and transform it. But, as I will argue, seeing this culture at its point of emergence, where certain diasporic dispositions among Lebanon's population come to the fore, gives us access to key features that might otherwise escape us if we are approaching diaspora from the angle of immigration and settlement rather than emigration and the homeland. This will be an integral part of arguing, as I have intimated I will, that diasporic culture is not an offshoot but the very culture of Lebanese modernity.

At first glance, this argument appears to raise questions that make it unworkable. If diasporic culture is located in Lebanon just as much as in the countries of settlement, and if it is not necessarily the culture of migrants or those who have migrated in the past, doesn't that mean that everything is diasporic? And if so, doesn't that leave us with no space left for a local Lebanese culture that's not diasporic? The questions are difficult only if we accept that the assumed answer here is, Surely there must be a space outside diasporic culture. In fact, I am indeed contending that there is no such thing as non-diasporic *modern* Lebanese culture. This is because, to reiterate, my aim is to show that diasporic culture is the very culture of Lebanese capitalist modernity. To the extent that a non-diasporic culture exists, it is in those "minor" places where capitalist modernity has not taken hold.

The Emergence of Lebanon's Diasporic Modernity

Most academic accounts of the history of Lebanese migration and the transnational networks it gave rise to are grounded in the history of the stunted development of Lebanese capitalism.[5] World-systems theory, dependency theory, and theories of underdevelopment are mobilized either separately or together to account for this history. The research shows how the Lebanese Mountain's migratory processes, which began in the mid-nineteenth century, were a feature of the limited, dependent, and ultimately stunted form of industrialization that followed the capitalist penetration of what was then a predominantly quasi-feudal region. The processes were triggered by French interest in the quality of Lebanese silk and the ensuing industrialization of silk production. This industrialization brought about changes commonly associated with European capitalist modernity, such as the straining of the relationship between peasant and feudal lord,[6] the severing of the peasant's connection to the land, the spread of the wage form of payment for labor and of a monetary economy, the rise of individuality at the expense of kinship solidarity, and the transformation of gender relations. Silk-based industrialization was, however, short-lived, ending with the global decline of the silk industry that began at the end of the nineteenth century. Yet its transformation of the Mountain was irreversible, particularly through the migratory movements that accompanied it.

Dreams of international migration took root and began spreading in the Lebanese Mountain at the same time and with the same intensity as the circulation of capitalist relations of production. They further intensified with the decline of the silk industry and because of the sectarian violence marking the transition from a Druze-dominated feudalism to a Christian-dominated capitalism. The 1860 massacre of Christians by Druze was particularly significant in this regard. But it's important to stress that international migration, and the kind of social dispositions and modes of thinking that it presupposes and that we'll soon examine, did not begin because of industrial decline or war. Indeed, this movement began at the very beginning of the industrialization process. It's at this point that we need to be cautious about how we formulate the relation between capitalism and migration.

It's very clear, even from the very short account of the period given above, that a structural understanding of the causes of emigration grounded in theories of uneven development (particularly Wallerstein's *World Systems Theory*), with their emphasis on "the penetration of capitalist economic relations into peripheral, noncapitalist societies creat[ing] a mobile population that is prone to migration abroad,"[7] has much purchase on explaining nineteenth-century Lebanese migration to the world. Nonetheless, and despite the explanatory power of the above, I think that the way causality is spoken of and imagined in these structural theories is not unlike the milieu-free Cartesian forms of causality critiqued by Georges Canguilhem, as quoted in the introduction. It is good to carefully think through what it means to say, as in how it's often formulated, that the introduction of capitalism "caused" the rise of migration. Such a notion of causality invites us to think of the two phenomena as external to each other and existing in a temporal sequence in which the cause precedes what has been caused, as in the general positivist formula φA causes φB: first we have capitalism, which triggers or is followed by migration.[8]

What's at stake in this critique of externality can be appreciated when we compare a statement such as "Capitalism causes migration" with another common claim about the Mountain at the time but also made about the history of capitalism in general: "Capitalism causes the spread of wage labor." It's clear that in this second statement, the notion of cause is used rather loosely in that there is not much difference between saying "Capitalism causes the spread of wage labor" and "Capitalism is partly defined by the spread of wage labor." This is so because wage labor is an intrinsic feature of capitalism, and the latter is unthinkable without the former. One is not external to and cannot precede the other. They are co-constitutive. The same kind of co-constitutive relation is not implied in the first statement, "Capitalism causes the spread of international migration." This is what I mean by migration being imagined as extrinsic to Lebanese capitalism when such causal claims are made. Yet my argument is that it is precisely *in* this co-constitutive manner that we need to think of migration in relation to Lebanese capitalism if we are to fully understand it. We need to see international migration as an intrinsic dimension of modern Lebanese capitalist culture, the existence of one unthinkable without the existence of the other. Likewise, we need to see international migration as being as constitutive of Lebanese capitalist modernity as wage labor. Therefore, diasporic culture needs to be understood as not so much the by-product of Lebanese capitalist modernity—something that comes after, in the way an effect comes after a cause—but the very form that Lebanese capitalist modernity takes.

The reason this has not been explicitly argued before is not because of an inability to conceive of an intrinsic relation between capitalism and migration. Histories of European capitalism often contain statements in the form of "Capitalism causes migration from the country to the city," where causality is loosely used to mean that country-to-city migration is an intrinsic part of the formation of capitalism. If there is a difficulty here, and a difference from how the relation between capitalism and wage labor is understood, it is because "capitalism" is thought of as delineating an "economic" reality, and neither "migration" nor "mobility" is seen as intrinsically "economic" in the way something like "wage labor" is. But this externality takes a different turn and becomes even more pronounced as soon as we start thinking about international migration. This takes us closer to the problem we are pointing to.

Even theories aiming to emphasize the international structural interconnectedness of the world economy, such as world-systems theory, seem unable to consider international migration as an integral component of a world capitalist system, the way country-to-city mobility is considered an integral part of the rise of capitalism from a national economic perspective. Instead, international migration is continuously presented as a "result" of capitalism. This is particularly disappointing regarding world-systems theory, for in this sense it proves unable to theorize culturally what it theorizes economically. It thus invites a Euro-normative national account of the culture of capitalist modernity at the very moment it tries to transcend it. Yet this naturalizing of international migration is precisely what's needed if we are to think of it from a global and total economico-cultural perspective.

These arguments have significant ramifications. For a start, to say that international migration is part of the very culture of Lebanese modernity is to think of non-Euro-normative modern forms or at least of variations on them. We move into the territory of "alternative modernities."[9] To be sure, it doesn't mean simply saying that Lebanese modernity is international "rather than" national. It's to be able to realize, with more complexity, how the form of internationalism represented in diasporic culture is the very form taken by Lebanon's modernity as experienced locally.

Diasporic Consciousness as the Internationalization of the Space of Viability

While the capitalist penetration of the Mountain did mean the spread of wage relations, historians of this period have demonstrated that men overall remained attached to their land, and the wage earners in the silk industry were mainly women. Men looked down on the idea of being in a wage relation, and their dreams of upward mobility continued to be marked by a quasi-feudal idealization of themselves as autonomous landowners. These desires were partly responsible for Lebanese migration dominated by an entrepreneurial imaginary that favored, at least as a normative aspiration, even the smallest mercantile venture over industrial wage labor. But the dominance of this imaginary doesn't mean that all Lebanese immigrants were able to become small entrepreneurs. Khater and Avery have effectively subjected the myth of the dominance of hawkers among the Lebanese in the United States to an empirical debunking.[10] Yet, useful as such debunking is, it's important to also direct our efforts toward understanding the myth's existence and persistence. For even if it's certainly the case that many Lebanese have ended up working as laborers, particularly in the United States and Australia, we still need to understand why, for instance, they often see such positions as transitional and still aspire to more autonomous working conditions. We also need to understand the difference, say, between Lebanese migration and Algeria's labor migration to France.[11] Although Lebanon was also somewhat colonized by the French, unlike the case of Algeria, Lebanese migration did not predominantly take the form of migration of wage labor to the French colonial metropolis. Myth though it might be, small in scale but still capitalist, entrepreneurial desire was the real force that made the Lebanese diaspora what it is.

We can say that Lebanon's modern diasporic culture is the national and international mode of existence of its underdeveloped capitalism in the same way that modern colonialism/imperialism is the national and international mode of existence of advanced capitalism. Both initiated and continue to involve forms of international mobility and resettlement. Both involve creating permanent transnational networks. Both are powered by the dynamic of capitalist accumulation. The biggest difference is that settler colonialists "migrate" with the support of their state and more often than not with a sense that they are transnational subjects capable of *occupying and appropriating* the spaces they go to in a way that diasporic subjects cannot. In this sense, taking Lebanon as an example, we can say that diasporic culture is the poor capitalist countries' colonialism. The colonizing subjects experience the world as organized by their own nation-state and their own national law as their turf. Transnational space becomes their national space as well as their national law writ large. Diasporic subjects such as the Lebanese, on the other hand, have always seen themselves as being subjected to or having to negotiate with, confront, submit to, or move in the shadows or between the cracks of an already Western-occupied world organized by laws not theirs. Still unlike labor migration, Lebanese migration involves subjects infused with an ethos resembling that of settler colonialists, only to settle for the crumbs, leftovers, and marginal spaces within already colonized nations. We can productively see this diasporic culture as a form of colonial gleaning. Its end result might be, at best, an ethnic neighborhood as opposed to a colonial settlement; but these neighborhoods came into being not as a result of people being transported against their will, or because of any state planning to import labor, or because there was a special relationship between where they originated and where they settled. These neighborhoods came into being because people experiencing new forms of needs and economic compulsions could (financially and conceptually) imagine that they could exist and make a living anywhere in the world. For a Lebanese villager, this was certainly a revolutionary transformation, and it takes us into the heart of the diasporic condition as it emerges in Lebanon.

Mireille is the only person in Jalleh with an arts degree (sociology), and she aspires to write a social history of the village herself (although since I met her in 2000, she has migrated to Australia). "Migration from Jalleh started a bit later than in the rest of Mount Lebanon," she tells me.

> This is partly because of the region's marginality within Mount Lebanon itself, but it's also in part because silk growing lasted longer in the village than else-where. There was still a *kerkhana* [spinning mill] operating here during World War I. It was providing the British army with silk for making parachutes. It was owned by my grandfather. When it stopped operating, my grandfather decided to move overseas. He already had a son in Australia, a son in Brazil, and a brother in Canada. His daughters, including my mother, all remained either in the village or in Beirut. He was still an energetic man, but he had never migrated before. He thought the time had come to go and invest the money he had, thanks to the *kerkhana*, somewhere overseas. My mum told me that he spent more than a year trying to work out where to go to make a living. She said, "He was like a kid looking at shelves of chocolate in the su-permarket, trying to work out what to buy." Every night over dinner, he would say, "That's it, I've decided I am going to . . . ," and every night it would be a different place. Finally, he went to Brazil.

While not everyone had the luxury of treating their migration "like a kid looking at shelves of chocolate," the more important dimension to note here is the capacity of Mireille's grandfather to see the entire world as a space where he could potentially make a living, which by the turn of the twentieth century had become a far more generalized social fact.

Speaking of the decline of the silk industry, Akram Khater notes, "Silk, then, had lifted hopes, only to dash them for most Lebanese peasants; it brought into view new possibilities for life, only to snatch them away."[12] While this is undoubtedly true when speaking of local Lebanese conditions, it's also important to say something that Khater more than amply demon-strates but does not explicitly spell out: silk, while dashing hopes locally, had also globalized the space of hope by linking the Mountain to the world-wide economy. It is hard to imagine the significance and immensity of this seemingly banal change in one's conception of oneself and one's relation to the world. The Lebanese Mountain dwellers, particularly the Maronites, have long had relations with Europe. But this wasn't any relation, nor was it simply the consciousness of the world "out there." It was a form of transnational being involving a radical expansion of the space where they felt they existed naturally, and where they felt entitled to go and struggle for a viable life: *"Blehd Alla Wehss'ah"* (God's country is wide), as the saying went.

More than colonial settlers dependent on routes traced for them by their state, those Lebanese imagined themselves as capable of going anywhere in "God's country," and they actually did depart their homeland and settle in astonishingly remote parts of the world, save for China and Japan. Captured and reconstituted into modern transnational subjects by the international capitalist economy, the Lebanese Mountain dwellers stopped mapping their aspirations and perceiving their livelihood within the geographic confines of the village and its surroundings. This internationalization of the imaginary space of social viability—how Mountain dwellers experienced locally the space of realizing their human viability as global—is what I want to emphasize as a cornerstone of the diasporic modernity as it emerges in Lebanon.

European modernity freed people from viewing their viability as lying only within the confines of feudally defined regions. But it was mainly a national consciousness of viability that replaced the narrow feudal regionalism. An international consciousness of viability came with colonialism and particularly settler colonialism, but as already noted, the path of such mobility was drawn by the European state, its interests, and its capacity to "explore" or invade other countries. In Lebanon, one moves almost immediately from a regional/feudal space of viability to an international one. Modernity endowed the Lebanese Mountain's peasants with a sense of being situated in the whole world, not just in Lebanon, in a way difficult to imagine in many places elsewhere—certainly not among the French or the English peasantry.

There is no doubt that Lebanon's national space, particularly its city space, did not offer the opportunities that urban areas offered in Europe during feudalism's dissolution. But it would be too simplistic to think that merely the absence of national/urban opportunities led to internationalizing the Lebanese outlook. For this absence of opportunity could just as easily have led to a shrinking of the imagination and a redeployment of the self within the confines of the village. What's more, an opportunity is far from being an objective opening in the social. It is a relation. Internationalizing the space of viability can't be merely the result of absent national opportunities, since by its very existence it is shaping what constitutes a viable national opportunity.

It is often said that while many migrations emerge from economic need, migrants can't be exceptionally poor, as they need some financial means to migrate. Consequently, one needs to regard migration not simply in terms of economic lack but also in terms of economic capacity. The expansion of Lebanese capitalism certainly included the distribution of a greater economic capacity to migrate. As Khater points out, "Unfettering the peasants from the land is but one part of the puzzle of this migration movement; another was money. It took money to leave the village, buy a ticket, bribe officials, pay off the sarrafs [money changers], stay at hotels along the way, and take care of oneself in the first few days—at least—of arrival in the new country."[13] And, as highlighted above, economic capacity was not the only necessary capacity. The ability to think of the world as a space where one can settle anywhere to invest one's money or one's labor was also of significant importance. Many other "capacities" facilitated either the possibility of migrating or the possibility of just thinking about migrating. Education, access to information about the world through the clergy if not school, connections to foreign merchants, industrialists, or politicians—all work as capacitating powers. Kinship networks are important enabling forces as well, but sometimes the opposite is true: freedom from kinship networks, particularly relative freedom from obligations and duties toward kin, can also be an enabling factor.

At this point, it should be stressed that a capacity to migrate is not a reason to migrate. Migratory discourse is structured by three themes: need, desire, and capacity. Needs convey elements of an experience of necessity, particularly but not exclusively economic. Such needs change and fluctuate socially and historically. As with all capitalist transformations, Lebanese capitalism entailed new forms of dissatisfaction and new needs. The changes in forms of consumption and taste that accompanied the capitalist transformation of Mount Lebanon have been well documented.[14] These changes continued well into the twentieth century. Fuad Khuri, one of the first local anthropologists of Lebanon, wrote a piece comparing Douma and Aramti, two villages unequally developed in terms of capitalist development. He shows how increased capitalist penetration created differences in the sense of satisfaction and security experienced by the village population. As he put it, "The annual income per capita in Douma is fourfold that of Aramti, and the family size is only half as large. Yet the people of Douma show less economic security than those of Aramti. Higher standards of living appear to induce less security, while the subsistence economy of Aramti produces more security."[15] We can imagine that a similar process began with the Mountain's capitalist transformation.

Desire conveys an affective dimension articulated in dreams and fantasies of leaving one's homeland to inhabit other lands and make more money. It, too, is shaped by macro-historical processes. Thus, as with needs, Lebanese migratory desires were affected by how international capitalism was accompanied by a greater diffusion of information about "lands of opportunity" throughout the world but particularly of idealized images of life in the West. As Samir Khalaf, for instance, points out in relation to migration to the United States, "The literature also abundantly references the importance of the Chicago Fair in 1893 and that of Saint Louis in 1906 for attracting and spreading immigrants all over the country."[16] Such images of the West were also relayed by emigrants, especially returnees, and by the growth of an international media. Further, they were propagated by the rise of Western schooling. French Jesuits and American Protestants engaged in a competitive drive to establish schools throughout the Lebanese Mountain, giving the region its best educational network.

Capacity then combines with needs and desires in various ways, according to people and to circumstances. Some might express a strong need to leave but say they are unable to do so (no capacity) and in fact do not wish to if they could help it (no desire). Some might express a strong desire to migrate without either having the capacity or experiencing migration as a need. All the possible combinations have come up in the field. A big difference exists between the settlement of those who migrate primarily driven by need and those driven primarily by desire (even if this is never an either/or situation). How much someone is driven by each alters during migration, certainly over the long term but sometimes day to day. What might have begun as a desired migration can end up very quickly being reduced to a matter of necessity. A number of times, people have said to me something along the lines of "Migration is not what I imagined it to be. If I didn't have to stay, I'd go back home immediately." Crucially, while each of these variables has its own history and an autonomous development process, they are also equally interdependent, and they variously affect one another. This continues to be the case today.

Jbeil (Byblos), 22 March 2007

Today I had a long chat with Tony and Raymond from Mehj who own a carpentry shop in Jbeil. Tony is very upset about the "economic situation." He goes through all the problems in detail: suppliers who provide poor materials, customers who do not pay, bribes that need to be paid at Beirut's port. He describes to me how he confronted a customer for giving him a bad check: as he threatened him with legal action the customer collapsed in tears, begging forgiveness as he started to tell Tony how his wife is going to leave him and how he is having difficulties keeping his children at their school. Tony becomes visibly upset and tells me, "It's just unbearable, unbearable. I'd leave [i.e., migrate] tomorrow if I could."

I note that Raymond, who co-owns the shop and is clearly supposed to be as affected by those problems, is way too calm, especially when compared with Tony, who produces one emotional outburst after another. As it's Raymond on his own who sees me out of the shop, I ask him why he seems so calm compared with Tony. He gives me an amused look and says, "Why? Because no matter how bad things are, every night I go home to sleep, I open my bedside table, I see my Canadian passport, and everything becomes fine. That's why."

We see here how for Raymond, the capacity to migrate decreases both the need and the desire to, while the opposite happens with Tony. Yet both operate with a consciousness of the whole world as a space of viability where they can enact their needs and desires according to their capacities. This embryonic transnational consciousness born out of Lebanese capitalist modernity, and as such an integral part of it, was bound to develop further as Lebanese migration sutured Lebanese villages to an extensive global network that increasingly transformed the village itself, making it more and more of a transnational hub.

A short visit to any Lebanese village today can quickly dispel the false stereotype of it as a space where a simple "mono" national culture lingers on, with the village serving as a point of departure to and arrival from complex transnational multicultural spaces. It's indeed striking how the available literature on migration leaves the reader with an implicit impression that international cultural complexity and hybridity are always on the side of the cultures of destination, whereas the villages that immigrants leave are simple and monocultural. Though this might be true of some places, it is certainly not true of Lebanon. The literature on vernacular cosmopolitanism aims to dethrone the urban, upper-class, Western bias of the conceptions of cosmopolitanism that preceded it,[17] yet international travel is still written about as a precondition for access to such cosmopolitanism. However, it doesn't take long for an observer who becomes conscious of this bias to note how misleading such an image can be. Indeed, the very opposite is true: what is astonishing is the extent to which any village in Lebanon is constituted by a multiplicity of transnational cultural forms, enhancing villagers' consciousness of the world as a space for investing themselves and making a living.

For an outsider to become conscious of the diasporic nature of this multiplicity requires a bit of work in Mehj, as he or she must disentangle the diasporic and the skiing-related transnational cultural forms. Still, it's not that difficult to note the diasporic specificity of the Vermont Basketball Court and Le Cine-Club Mehj-Paris amid the ski-rental shops and giant posters for Rossignol and K2 ski equipment. In Jalleh, however, diaspora-driven transnationalism is much clearer. When I initially stayed there, the mayor immediately took me on a tour of the village "real estate," where houses built or renovated with migrant remittances were referred to by the geographic location of the emigrants funding their construction: this is a Saudi Arabian villa; this is American, Brazilian, Australian, and so on. And just like the village's external public spaces, home interiors are also full of diasporic connections. Photos of emigrant family members are often displayed on living room walls or tables or on top of the television. Next to the photos are always little touristy souvenirs sent home by the emigrants or brought back by someone who has visited them. In the house where I lived in Jalleh, there's a canvas depicting a waterfall somewhere in Venezuela, a Native American dream catcher, and a wooden map of Australia that has a clock in the center and a miniature Tasmania dangling from the mainland on a golden chain.

But diasporic relations do not only mark the village's material culture. There is, of course, the intensification of technologically mediated interaction with emigrants, which has changed dramatically during my research as forms of global communication became cheaper, faster, and more interactive, particularly with the introduction of Skype and WhatsApp.[18] The latter became pervasive long after my main fieldwork period (2000–2005). Then there is the constant flow of returning emigrants, who in the way they walk, dress, cook, and eat become living diasporic monuments in themselves. In public gatherings, one can hear all kinds of international exclamations that can make for a truly multilingual cacophony, sometimes uttered by the same person: "*Por favor*, come here, *viens chez moi, ya habibi.*" Furthermore, throughout the region from Jalleh to Mehj today, the first names Felipe, Sol, Christo, Bob, Mario, Christina, and Carlos increasingly compete with the traditional and ubiquitous Maronite Charbel and Maroun, along with the equally traditional and ubiquitous Pierre, Georges, Antoinette, Raymond, Jean, and Jeannette, French names popular since the nineteenth century. There's even a diasporically driven revival of traditional names once seen as too archaic with the rise of modernity but now fashionable again thanks to someone's international rise to fame. Salma, for Salma Hayek, is a clear example. Finally, we must note, along with village-specific social and symbolic diasporic forms, a continuous flow of nationally produced discourses concerning migration that are learned in schools and are diffused in a variety of media—particularly Lebanese folk poetry and folk songs, a ubiquitous tradition extremely rich in diaspora-related themes: travel, separation, return, waiting, and yearning. All this works to intensify the internationalization of the space of viability at the core of Lebanon's diasporic culture today.

As I have aimed to show in this chapter, this internationalization implied a transnational mode of existence, a diasporic state of consciousness and orientation toward the world that the Lebanese acquire in Lebanon, before and even without migrating, even if the problematic of migration is central to this mode of existence. As I emphasized, I speak of this as a mode of existence because this consciousness was not merely a consciousness of the world but a consciousness of the world as an opportunity-rich place where one can invest in one's future and where the quality of one's own being was at stake. If European modernity primarily brings forth a nationally driven subject, diasporic modernity brings forth an internationally driven subject. It is to the specificity of this mode of investing oneself in the world and being transnationally driven that I now turn.

TWO

On Being Propelled into the World:
Existential Mobility and the Migratory *Illusio*

Amin Maalouf, in his biographical novel based on family archival material, tells among others the story of his great-grandfather's migration to the United States.

> My future grandparent stayed in Beirut for three years, a city he came to cherish, and where he will return to live on a number of occasions throughout his life. The city was then in full expansion; a development accelerated by the massacres of 1860. Many people who, until now, dozed lazily in their Mountain villages, thinking themselves protected from the ferocity of the world, experienced in those events a sudden awakening. The most audacious chose to go beyond the seas—it was the start of an immense migratory movement hardly interrupted since. First, in the direction of Egypt and Constantinople, then further and further afar, toward the United States, Brazil, and the totality of the American continent as well as Australia. The less adventurous—often those encumbered with a family—were content to "go down" from their village toward the harbor city, which bit by bit, began to have the allure of a metropolis.[1]

In a revealing passage, Maalouf portrays his grandfather, a man educated in an American-founded Protestant school, delivering a speech about the virtues of the English language. He proclaims it "the most necessary of all those that one can study." This was not only because "books in English contain, let there be no doubt, innumerable forms of knowledge, in all domains, which is not the case of other languages," but more important, he declares, because "the poor among us just as much as the rich will have to leave for the United States or toward Australia, if not immediately, at least in the near future, for reasons no one ignores." And so the grandfather ends up exclaiming,

Long live the English-speaking countries!
Long live English![2]

"I force myself not to smile hearing these pathetic and incongruous ex-clamations," writes Maalouf after relating this—with a hint of Francophone chauvinism. But, as he goes on to note, the speech reveals how much leav-ing had become a taken-for-granted fact in the Lebanese Mountain. As he put it, "to leave or not to leave" very quickly became, and has remained, the Mountain's "to be or not to be."[3]

The question of being is intimately linked to the concept of viability I in-troduced in the previous chapter by speaking of the internationalization of its space. To speak of a space of viability is to speak of a space where the wor-thiness of one's life is played out. Capitalist modernity in the Mountain and later across Lebanon took the form of a generalized circulation of diasporic aspirations that weren't merely some among others but aspirations integral to viability. The questions raised by becoming conscious of the world as one's space of viability—whether to migrate, where to, for how long—were all experienced as concerns that put the worthiness of one's existence on the line and continue to be to this day.

Mehj, 13 June 2002

Rose is talking with me as she chops the parsley for the tabouli salad. A proud and tough woman, she taught French at a primary school in the town of Jbeil for more than thirty years, and she retired last year. Her husband is sitting in the living room. He is seventy-six and moves with difficulty. Rose is ten years younger. As many in Mehj explained to me, she has always been known in the village as ikht il' rjehl (the sister of men). This is a common Lebanese term for strong-willed women. The term has no sexual connotations. It's more a gender-based behavioral definition.

Soon I discovered that Rose isn't liked by any of her brothers and sisters. Indeed, they are quite openly hostile to her. They have described her to me as selfish, scheming, and interfering, and worst of all, they hate how she deploys her being a French teacher to intimate a sense of status distinction. I initially tried to convince myself that all the family's prejudices were simply sexism toward a strong woman, so I showed Rose a lot of solidarity. She repaid my expressions of support by often inviting me for dinner and telling me endless stories about the village and its people. Although I never stopped showing her solidarity, soon, and partly because of how she spoke of other people, I also found myself sympathizing with how the rest of the family perceived her.

The dislike the family has for Rose never translated into complete ostracizing. She is always invited and is always present at family gatherings. But this dislike has indirectly led—and as far as I can see, without any premeditated scheming—to a rather severe punishment. The rug of family networks needed to migrate has been pulled out from under her feet, or more exactly from under her son's feet. Her son, Robert, is in jail for forging checks in a desperate attempt to save from bankruptcy the business he had inherited from his father. As Rose chops the parsley and explains to me what happened to her son, she waves her knife, looking particularly bitter and threatening. She is directly blaming her niece and nephew in Gatineaux. "We didn't want Robert to take over the business," she says. "We wanted to sell it. It was in the middle of the war and nothing was going well. It was migration or nothing. I begged them, but they simply provided excuses. I looked after them more than their mother did when they were kids, and they left my son here with nothing to look forward to. Are we not allowed to live as well? They are all des salauds [bastards]. They could have helped him, but they left him here to rot instead."

This linking of migration to life and non-migration to "nothing" and to "rotting," but only by those in the grip of an unfulfilled migratory desire, is one of the most enduring associations at the heart of diasporic culture. In both Jalleh and Mehj, I met people who weren't interested in migrating. What was interesting was how they invariably acted as if they were resisting migration. That is, while they didn't desire it, they couldn't be indifferent to it. One man kept declaring to me that he didn't want to migrate and that he was "contented" in Lebanon. He repeated the word so often that I became suspicious that maybe he really couldn't migrate and so was making a virtue out of necessity. But soon enough, when I got to know him and his family better, I realized that in fact, he could easily migrate if he chose to. He was genuinely content to stay. I had to work on my inherent cynicism vis-à-vis the concept of contentment and stop putting it in scare quotes every time I used it. It made me appreciate how radical the affect of being contented is in the face of the desire to improve and progress that is the dominant ethos of capitalist modernities. More important for our immediate ethnographic concerns here, I also realized that this man's need to repeat that he is contented was a form of incantation. It worked as a counter-spell aimed at protecting him from being lured by migration. Clearly, the latter was experienced even by the nonbelievers as a dominant ensnaring force permeating their village.

Despite this dominance, the idea of migration as an artificial and superficial lure that takes someone from the authenticity of traditional life is not exactly rare. It's present in everyday folk antimigratory discourse and a common theme in the literature concerned with migration produced by Lebanese writers living both inside and outside their homeland.[4] We will see in more detail in the next chapter that the subject of diasporic modernity, like the subject of European modernity, is exposed to various centripetal and centrifugal forces. Accordingly, that individual experiences both the need to move and the yearning to stay "home," the desire to be free from tradition and the urge to "return" to it. There's no doubt, though, that the dominant modernist ethos in both cases is that of the need to move and to move on; the nostalgic yearning for home often plays a mere enthusiasm-inhibiting role. In this chapter, I will begin by examining the nature of the propelling force animating the desire for migration, then return to the counter-migratory desire for home and tradition and the interplay between the two.

The Migratory Gamble

"It's in the genes," Alissar says. She's been talking with me about how her grandfather, her father, and her brother were all what she calls gambling addicts. "They gambled everything on anything," she claims. I remark that I have heard many Lebanese immigrants speak of their own family like this, that indeed I speak of my own Lebanese diasporic family in this way too, so it can't be her family genes. She responds, "No, it's the migration genes. The migration genes and the gambling genes are one and the same." It's certainly the case, and well documented, that gambling is an integral dimension of Lebanese diasporic culture. I have encountered many problem gamblers throughout my fieldwork, and I have read accounts of Lebanese gambling elsewhere in the world.[5] In Australia, it's not rare for it to be a broadcast news item.[6]

I have noted that this kind of gambling is more prevalent among immigrants with entrepreneurial aspirations than among working-class migrants. That's why it wasn't surprising to see that the association between gambling with money and the nature of migration itself as a form of gambling was far more pronounced within the Chinese diaspora. In Australia, some have argued that there's a continuity between the form of risk taking associated with the Chinese presence during the gold rush and the gambling culture characterizing subsequent migration.[7] In the case of the United States, Sheng-mei Ma puts it very nicely:

> When Asian diaspora plays, it oftentimes comes to Las Vegas or a casino or venue with gaming devices. Las Vegas and the like provide the culmination of Asian diaspora. which is, in essence, taking risks in casting oneself out of home and into the unfamiliar, a gamble in view of all the variables and pitfalls. The euphoria of possible winning is always haunted by the keen or repressed sense of loss over homeland, identity, or even youthful dream on

the other side of the Pacific Ocean. Metaphorically, every facet of diaspora resembles gambling, with the high stakes involved in speculation with one's money and life and the uncertainty of return, pun intended.[8]

This is certainly the case with regard to the Lebanese diaspora. Consequently, it's hardly surprising that such a practice of leaving the safety of the village for unknown lands with no certainty of success is accompanied by a vast deployment of religious charms, icons, and spells. These are thought to provide some godly *baraka* (blessing) aimed at making fate more clement toward the voyagers and giving the cosmos a nudge to make clear the path of success before them—reminiscent of Lévy-Bruhl's description of gambling as having dimensions of what he refers to as "primitive mentality."[9] As we shall see, the migrant's religious practices and props, such as icons and amulets, are always supported with nonreligious practices of divination, particularly the reading of coffee cups, where a fortune-teller informs those about to leave what fate has in store for them.

One thing in particular clearly shows that in the eyes of the migrants themselves, diasporic success is more a question of baraka than of rational planning and know-how. That is the fact that in their village, a successful migrant is considered more of a saint than simply a lucky person or a great practical planner. Certainly, he or she is thought to be all of those. But like a saint, the migrant's being regarded as both possessed and a possessor and dispenser of this diasporic baraka is what always comes to the forefront. We have already noted the We Are All Carlos Ghosn billboard erected in Beirut. No Lebanese would dispute Ghosn's business acumen. Indeed, some might try to claim it as a particularly Lebanese acumen. Yet most crucial for the Lebanese, who aspire to see their children become as successful as Ghosn, is his being possessed by a saintly baraka. And as with any saintly person, a secure way to channel a saint's baraka into a child is to name that child after him or her.

Given how the stories of migratory failure and misery abound and indeed sometimes predominate, and how very few Lebanese immigrants encounter the kind of success they dreamed about at the start of their journey, it would make sense to think of migration as a variety of the "cruel optimism" described by Lauren Berlant which makes people attached to the very things that are bound to hurt them.[10] But this would fail to see the "gambling" nature of the migratory process. The gambler (in the sense of the person consumed by gambling) does not gamble on the basis of a statistical likelihood of success. He or she only needs to know that winning is possible, that it has happened once and is therefore looming somewhere on the horizon. That once is enough. In much the same way, the believer in a saint's miracle does not base that belief on a high incidence of that miracle. It's enough to believe that a miracle has happened once and can therefore happen again. The same goes for the immigrants. They need only to believe that a successful migration has occurred once for them to become diasporic believers ready to take on the world and see whether they can conjure enough baraka to make the world smile at them.

The Migratory *Illusio*: On Physical and Existential Mobility

By speaking of migration in the previous chapter as an opening into the world, as a capacity to see the world as a space where one can invest oneself, and by extending this viewpoint to argue in this chapter that it's a matter of being, of what makes one's life worthwhile, and then, crucially, a matter of gambling with oneself, we are dancing around a concept of clear pertinence to us. It is Pierre Bourdieu's concept of *illusio*.[11]

For Bourdieu, illusio is a key dimension of those worlds we inhabit and endeavors we embark on, marked by belief in their worthiness. In being perceived as worthwhile, they in turn make our lives viable and worthwhile, in our eyes and in the eyes of those who share our illusio. These are the pursuits that give us purpose, as they simultaneously delineate and ground themselves in the worlds that structure the meaningfulness of our lives. According to Bourdieu, the etymology of the word includes what we commonly refer to as illusion: the key illusion here is that once society provides us with something that gives our life meaning, we end up thinking that life is intrinsically meaningful, that what animates us is akin to a transhistorical/transsocial destiny. We transform what is a social construction and distribution of meaningfulness into an essential/existential pre-social feature of life, in the way life is conceived in religious discourse: "We are on this earth to do *x, y, z.*" This transformation is particularly pertinent in our case, as statements such as "We Lebanese have inherited the Phoenician spirit," while not religious, engage in a similar mode of transforming the disposition to migrate from a sociohistorical construction into an essence possessed by the Lebanese and, in that sense, a transhistorical destiny.

But illusio, as Bourdieu reminds us, is also etymologically connected to *lusiones*, which has associations with *ludos*—that is, with playing and gambling. Here it is about playing the game of life by gambling with oneself. It is taking the chance of investing oneself in a life pursuit in the belief (rather than the knowledge or the certainty, which is why it's a gamble) that one has a future in it, that it will yield something—that is, that it will be rewarding.

Again, the concept's pertinence is particularly striking for understanding how questions of migration are experienced within diasporic culture as questions of investment of the self in a path where the worthiness of one's life is on the line.

Yet to speak of a migratory illusio is also to stretch Bourdieu's concept, though I hope usefully so. This is because for Bourdieu, illusio is linked to a specific orientation, such as toward a particular career path (carpenter, academic, businessman, artist) or at least toward a general sphere of social life (art, finance, manual labor). These paths define trajectories along which a person is propelled based on the social, economic, and cultural capital that individual acquires, inherits, or both. In this sense, a migratory illusio is more of a *meta-illusio*, in that it's not a path toward doing *x* or *y* or *z*. Rather, it's a path that marks the *possibility* of doing any one or combination of *x*, *y*, or *z*. That is, the migratory illusio doesn't trace a specific trajectory in the manner of "you will own a grocery store," "you will yearn to be a manual laborer," "you will be a lawyer," or "you will own a clothing factory." Instead, it opens up a path where the subject can be located in a space offering the possibility of a trajectory, as opposed to a location (i.e., the homeland) perceived to offer no trajectories at all. It imagines a move from one space experienced as a closure, as unable to provide any particular life pursuit, to another space imagined to open up such a possibility, without necessarily knowing what such a possibility might be or whether such a possibility will actually eventuate.

Indeed, as described in the opening of chapter 1, when Jameel arrives in the village with his visa and his hope-infused body, he's ready to go to Melbourne but has no idea what kind of job he'll seek there. He's not even sure he'll be successful in getting a job. "I just hope there'll be something for me there," he said to me. So it's not the encounter with a well-defined "something" that fuels the hopeful migratory body. It's the more general sense of a possibility of encountering "something." The knowledge, or preferably the sense and the belief rather than the knowledge, that there is this meta-possibility diffuses itself into the body, energizing it and preparing it for the possible encounter with the future. Therefore, it's illuminating to speak of illusio here. The depressed body is weighed down by a present in the form of "what there is" and, where it registers no open possibilities, "nothing." It slumps and becomes heavy. The hopeful body inhabits the domain of potentiality, of the "what might be" or the "about to be," such as Ernst Bloch's famous "not yet" that works as a principle of hope.[12] Even at the moment the successful Jameel returns from the embassy, we can see a hint of a Jameel already not fully "present" to the here and now, already transported to where the visa promises to take him. His body is made lighter as it is propelled toward a possible future. It's *on the move*, even though he hasn't migrated yet.

Immigration-speak often articulates together the oppositions between here and there,[13] something and nothing, stasis and movement. Here, there's nothing and we aren't going anywhere. There, there's something and we can go somewhere. Illusio, as the principle through which life pursuits acquire a meaning, adds a propelling force to such pursuits. Immigration is often analyzed using terms such as *push factors* and *pull factors*. But it's important to highlight the differences between a pushing or a pulling force on one hand and a propelling force on the other. Pull factors and push factors depict forces imagined as external to the social bodies they are affecting. They work on such bodies from the outside in, from society to individual. Like someone giving a boat a push, the force behind that push remains ashore, and the effect of the push wanes after a while. A propelling force, on the other hand, acts continuously from within the subject it is affecting, like a motor's relation to the vehicle in which it is housed. Therefore, to be captured by an illusio is to be animated by a social force better perceived as a propelling force. You are "driven" from within to pursue certain things you have come to believe are worthwhile. The movement implied here is more symbolic, or—better still, and as I argue—existential: a general sense that your life is going somewhere. To be sure, the sense of being propelled and the feeling of being on the move are not specific to the migratory illusio. They denote a mode of human existence that has been exacerbated by capitalist modernity everywhere. What's specific to diasporic modernity is how it combines this yearning for existential mobility with the desire for physical mobility. Yet the latter remains subordinated to the former: one moves around the globe so as to be "on the move." The migratory illusio can't be understood without understanding this combination.

On Existential Mobility

I ask Elie, who lives in Boston and is a distant relative of the Jalleh family I am working with, the obligatory question of whether he ever wishes to go back to Lebanon. He's just taken me to see his new restaurant. He and his brothers own a chain of Lebanese food outlets in the city and are doing very well financially. He is driving us in his "toy," a monstrously oversize yet magnificent black, gadget-filled, four-wheel-drive utility truck. He says that emotionally, he'd love to go back to the village, but, he quickly adds, there is no point in returning, for "life in Lebanon had no taste" (bala ta'meh). He continues by asking rhetorically, "What do you want me to go back there for? In Lebanon, one runs and runs and stays exactly where one started from" (Whahad byerkud, byerkud, w' byib'a matrahu). *"Here," he continues, "you work, and you have a sense of going somewhere." As he says this, his ute burns the highway at more than seventy-five miles per hour, which gives a further intensity to his words "going somewhere."*

The Lebanese are often said to think with their stomach, so to say that life has "a taste" means that life has both a meaning and a purpose. *Hayeht bala ta'meh*, a tasteless life, means a meaningless and purposeless life. But, as Elie makes clear, one experiences this meaningfulness and purposefulness best when one has a sense of "going somewhere." In Lebanese, as in the English "how is it going?" and in many other languages, the word used to denote "functioning well" is the same used to mean "moving well." In colloquial Lebanese, to say "I am well," you say *"Mehcheh'l-haal,"* which literally means "The state of my being is walking." When the state of my being is not walking, when *"Mich mehcheh'l-haal,"* I experience the need to position myself somewhere else where I can get going again. There is, then, the close association between the viability of life and a sense of existential mobility. Indeed, in listening to people's evaluation of what makes them migrate, one senses an inverse relation between migration, this all-important physical mobility, and existential mobility. Migratory physical mobility is contemplated when people experience a crisis in their sense of existential mobility. Or, to put it differently, it's when people feel they are symbolically moving too slowly or going nowhere—that is, that they are somehow stuck on the "highway of life"—that they begin contemplating the necessity of physically going somewhere.

Clearly, there is nothing distinctly Lebanese in this association between the feeling of "going nowhere" and the desire to move physically, except perhaps the strength of the emphasis. The word the Lebanese use to signify remaining where one began, *matrahu*, means "a place." But it also means "a dump," where one is thrown as a reject. Moreover, there is an even more damning meaning, albeit only implicit in the Lebanese usage of the term. A *matrah* is a place where the fetus is discarded after a miscarriage. To remain where one began symbolizes a miscarried social life, an illusio-less life.

Puerto la Cruz, May 2004

I am in Puerto la Cruz. The tourist information booklet I have indicates that here the weather is warm all year long. This is supposed to be one of Venezuela's main tourist centers. It's the point from which Venezuelans take boats and ferries to Isla Margarita, a prime tourist destination—not because of the beauty of the island but because it's a duty-free zone. Still, it is the Caribbean, and it is a tourist zone, so I've been imagining the good life: my chance to fuse work with a nice holiday . . . I'm looking for Toni, a young Lebanese man who recently arrived here from Jalleh to live with his uncle. There is a relatively large Lebanese community here, according to my information, but I only managed to get in touch with Toni through his family in the village.

Unfortunately, the part of Puerto la Cruz where I landed isn't attractive in the touristy way I was expecting, nor in any other way, to be quite honest. In fact, for an outsider like me, the place is easily experienced as an irredeemably depressed and depressing place.

Like everywhere in Venezuela, the main roads to Puerto la Cruz are exceptionally well maintained. The oil companies need good roads. What's more, with bitumen being an oil by-product, the companies get to sell it to the government. But inside the town, where the oil companies' trucks do not pass, the roads aren't always as good, and the footpaths need maintenance.

I've been driving through the night, and when I arrive early in the morning, kids in their early teens are asleep here and there on those cracked footpaths. They all have some kind of plastic container next to them. They seem to have been sniffing gasoline.

The worst thing, however, was a smell, a very bad smell, which every now and then invades the place . . .

I keep trying to convince myself that this is a tourist town. There must be more to it for people coming here to have good clean fun in the sun. The shopping area doesn't help. Shops are dirty, all selling cheap plastic things in every shape, and the clothes are all made with this shiny synthetic material in which all Latin America is drowning. And every now and then, there is still that awful smell.

I cross the shopping area very quickly and head toward the beautiful beach studded with coconut trees. The sunlight is stunning, and the sea looks great. You get your first glimpse at the possibility that you've landed in a Caribbean paradise after all. But not for long.

As you head to the beach, you quickly notice a No Swimming sign. And if you can't read Spanish, the smell coming from the beach drives the point home very effectively. The secret behind the smell is suddenly revealed. All the town's raw sewage goes straight to the beach, and to make things worse, every couple of minutes or so the wind sends the smell up the streets and into the shopping center.

The first to be hit by the stench are the restaurants lined up on the road opposite the beach. Like everything else, the restaurants are grubby looking. And the food in them doesn't look and doesn't taste the best.

Plastic city, cracked roads, gasoline sniffing, sewage, and the smell of shit: in this environment, one is struck by the unusually high number of Lebanese restaurants operated by Lebanese immigrants. All the restaurants sell shawarma and Lebanese sweets. I counted six shawarma shops and three Lebanese sweet shops, usually *adjacent to a shawarma shop and owned by the same people, on a stretch of beach road no more than 300 meters long. My mind is thinking the obvious: why on earth would anyone migrate to live in a place like this?*

I enter the restaurant, whose name my informants in Caracas gave me. A young man is serving the shawarma. It's Toni.

"You like it here?" I asked after some introductions and a cup of Lebanese coffee.

"I don't like working for my uncle. It is hard working for a relative," he replies.

"But do you like it here in Venezuela, in Puerto la Cruz?" I insist.

"I like the girls. There's lots of nice girls here. Nicer than the girls in Tripoli . . . and more willing to have fun with you."

I smile. "Is there anything else you like here more than Tripoli?"

Toni thinks for a while. "I am not living with my parents, that's good. I can do what I like."

"Except at work, right," I say jovially, "because there is your uncle?"

He nods.

"You want my honest opinion? I am wondering how someone can leave Jalleh for a place like this. Your village is so much nicer. This place is the pits. Why would you leave your village, the fig trees, the olive trees, the orange fields, the birds in the sky, and all that and come to a place like this?"

Toni looks at me, a bit puzzled for a moment. "Yes, I agree," he finally says. "I really miss the village, but there's nothing there. What can we do? I need to make a living."

"But couldn't you make a living like this [cutting shawarma] in Tripoli?" I boldly suggest.

His reply is surprisingly quick, as if he's thought about it before. "Yes, but I would be staying in it for the rest of my life. Here it is only something my uncle has given me until I find a better job."

"So you think you'll find a better job?"

He looks at me. "I don't know."

Here again, the relationship between symbolic mobility and physical mobility in migration is made clear. "I would be staying in it for the rest of my life" is the fear of being stuck. The issue is not "to have or not to have a job." It is "to have or not to have a sense of the possibility of going somewhere in life." Note that the promise of a better future here is encapsulated in the "I don't know." Better the uncertainty, which also means the possibility of mobility, as with Jameel earlier, than the perceived certainty of immobility. Among the more traumatic moments in migration is starting to feel that "there is nothing" where one has migrated to, and one becomes stuck in an unfamiliar rather than a familiar "nothing."

However, this sense of movement that gives meaning and purpose to life is not directionless. The positive sense of going somewhere does not include a sense of going backward. Existential mobility is associated with both a forward movement in time and a sense of progress. Consequently, it can be easily but mistakenly reduced to the classical modern capitalist drive for upward social mobility. This is particularly the case here, since this modern capitalist ethos intersects with the migratory illusio as they merge to constitute a diasporic modernity. Nonetheless, the language of existential mobility is premodern. Some overlap can be noted between the notion of existential mobility and Spinoza's notion of joy.[14] For Spinoza, seeking joy is to constantly seek a higher and higher state of agency and social efficacy, what he refers to as a move toward a higher "perfection." Of importance for Spinoza is that joy is not a high capacity to act but rather the *movement* from one state of efficacy to a higher state. But regardless of whether a desire for existential mobility is universal or not, what is clear is that it's a precapitalist yearning for existential mobility that, with the rise of capitalist modernity, increasingly takes the form of an aspiration to upward social mobility. It further transforms within diasporic capitalist modernity into the desire we have examined here: to move, be on the move, and invest oneself transnationally.

This mode of being driven by and toward existential and physical mobility is the active component of an individual's consciousness of the internationalization of the space of viability analyzed in the previous chapter. It's what makes this consciousness a seeking consciousness, not just a passive-observational one. As noted earlier in this chapter, despite the dominance of this centrifugal drivenness and sense of being launched into and toward the world, it is nonetheless tempered by a centripetal tendency to be directed toward and valorizing staying at home. This tendency, as is well known, is crucial to the nostalgic cultural forms integral to all diasporic cultures. I will be examining dimensions of this tendency and its ramifications next. What is important to remember here is that these states of consciousness are integral parts of the culture of Lebanese capitalism. That is, both are dimensions of Lebanon's diasporic modernity as it emerges in Lebanon long before they become an integral part of the transnational network woven by Lebanese migratory practices.

THREE

Diasporic Anisogamy

San Francisco, March 2001

I'm visiting Vivianne, who left Mehj five years ago (in 1996) to major in museum studies at the University of California–Santa Barbara. There she met Jack from LA. They married three years ago, and they now live in San Francisco. I first met the couple in Mehj during the initial period of my ethnography work in the village. They were visiting, and I had a good time chatting with them both, particularly as they had a good awareness of the colonial questions surrounding ethnology museums. They invited me to visit when I would be working near San Francisco, so now we're having Sunday brunch at their place. Joining us are Diane and Steve, another Lebanese American couple whom they thought I'd like to meet.

We're talking about trips when the conversation takes an interesting turn. "Can you ever see anything and enjoy it for what it is?" Jack says half-jokingly to Vivianne. He's complaining, partly to her, partly to all of us sitting at the table, that when they went on a Grand Canyon trip recently and were enjoying the breathtaking views, Vivianne had said, "It reminds me of the Qadisha Valley."[1] "I mean, man, this is crazy, right?" he says to us, exaggerating his sense of outrage for comic effect. "I've been to the Qadisha Valley and I loved it. But it's just one damn valley. How can you go to the Grand Canyon and think of the Qadisha Valley? Come on! And it's always like this," he declares. "We go to see this, and it reminds her of that. Is there anywhere on earth that can be seen that doesn't remind you guys of something in Lebanon?"

"That's so true," Steve replies, laughing, "Diane does that. I mean, how many 'reminders' of the whole world can one fit into a couple of square meters?"

"It's 10,452 square kilometers, thanks," Diane answers.[2]

Diaspora's Comparative Being

Mock outrage aside, Jack and Steve are touching on a defining feature of the diasporic condition. It's actually almost impossible for the Lebanese immigrant to see a place and simply enjoy it for what it is. If you're being taken somewhere with Lebanese people, they usually make the comparison for you before you get to the destination: "You wait till you see this, it's exactly like *x*." When I first arrived in Sydney in 1976, I had been taken to Bulli Pass, about sixty-three miles south of the city. I was told that it provided a mountain-to-sea view "exactly" like the one from Our Lady of Lebanon in Harissa. During the drive, I spent a lot of time listening to people speak about their memories of Harissa. I remember very clearly my Australian-born uncle, who was driving us and who had never been to Lebanon, telling me something like "The more we take people to Bulli Pass, the more I know about Harissa."

This permanent state of comparative existence is experienced not only in the lands of migration, where every situation, every object, and every street angle are haunted by another situation and another experience of a similar object and a similar street angle, but in Lebanon as well. Someone who's been "breathing diaspora" since birth is one who has grown up in an environment where there is constant mention of and comparison to other places prominent in her village's transnational diasporic imaginary. The moment that diasporic modernity as a cultural form becomes the very medium in which, and with which, people start to view themselves, their relations, and the issues they confront, a permanent transnational comparative logic takes hold of the modern subject. It is an integral part of the internationalization of the space of viability examined in chapter 1. If someone is contemplating further studies, it becomes impossible for that person not to ask whether those studies should be pursued locally or overseas. Even if a Lebanese villager applies for a factory job, it becomes impossible for her not to wonder how different it would be to do the same job in Sydney or Detroit and so on. To be sure, comparative logic as such is not specific to the diasporic condition. The modern European experience is also impossible to consider without using a comparative logic that is both spatial (e.g., comparing the city and the country) and temporal (e.g., comparing before and after).[3] What distinguishes diasporic modernity is that it entails accentuating the spatial at the expense of the temporal. This is particularly true in the comparative logic inherent in diasporic nostalgia, as we shall see.

Lévi-Strauss also saw comparative thought as a defining feature of modernity, though his view is different. In *Structural Anthropology*, he argues that this comparativist impulse constitutes a mode of relativizing culture and a kind of primary vernacular anthropology. "When the Jesuits made Greek and Latin the basis of intellectual training, was that not a first form of ethnology?" he asks. "They recognized that no civilization can define itself if it does not have at its disposal some other civilizations for comparison."[4] This is how generations of schoolchildren have since learned to put their "own culture in perspective," he tells us, and this is how they have been "initiated into an intellectual method which is the same as ethnography, and which I would willingly call the technique of estrangement [dépaysement]."[5] Yet to the extent that Greek and Latin are imagined more as part of another time than another place (although this opposition is never absolute), it can be argued that it is with diasporic modalities of being that a more genuine vernacular anthropology takes place. For it is the diasporic mode of being that entails the primacy of comparative spatiality over comparative temporality (Johannes Fabian's critiques of anthropology's temporality notwithstanding).[6]

This is also true of the related idea of progress, an even more fundamentally modern notion. Western modernity firmly grounds that idea in time: the experience of progress involves projecting oneself into a future imagined to offer the gains toward which one sees oneself as "progressing." It also involves experiencing an attendant sense of loss whereby the old days embody a now-lost simplicity, purity, nearness to nature, and so on. The diasporic condition entails a far greater spatialization of this temporality. The future is experienced as another place (the place one can or should or shouldn't migrate to), and so is the yearned-for past, the home space that one has left and which still embodies what has been lost. While often noted, not enough has been made of the significance of this accentuated spatiality.

But there is an even more important diaspora-specific feature of this comparative logic, a logic Lévi-Strauss saw as a scholastic exercise: its very raison d'être is for individuals to relativize themselves in order to know themselves in a different light. Here, thinking with Bourdieu's critique of scholasticism is of particular importance. When people like Vivianne look at one thing and say, "It reminds me of . . . ," they're usually not making an intellectualized, socially and affectively neutral comparison. Implicit in this "it reminds me" is also at least a hint of an exchange of comparative national offerings. That is, in the case of Vivianne, "it reminds me" involves saying to Jack something like "Thanks for showing me some of what your nation has to offer [i.e., the Grand Canyon]. My nation also has something that is grand and beautiful to offer the visitor." Diasporic comparisons, then, involve an exchange of valorized attachments to people, places, food, and many other things. What I want to highlight in what follows is that this exchange has an anisogamic logic to it. This anisogamic logic, articulated to the state of permanent comparison, is as important a distinguishing feature of the diasporic mode of existence as the others we have examined so far: the internationalization of the space of viability and the drivenness of the migrant illusio.

Anisogamy

Anisogamy is the concept used by Lévi-Strauss to refer to marriages between people of unequal status. But in keeping with Lévi-Strauss's orientation, I use "anisogamic relation" to describe any relation requiring a reciprocal exchange between people of unequal status, not just marriage. I also use the notion of "anisogamic strategy" to speak of the symbolic labor, in the dialectical sense described above, that is involved in maintaining these relations. To be clear, I don't see, as Bourdieu does, this dimension of practice as something opposed to Lévi-Straussian structuralist analysis. Rather, I see it as exploring a different dimension.

A successful anisogamic marriage involves reciprocal strategies of valorization. Both the dominant/high-status and the dominated/low-status parties must participate in this, and both parties see themselves as having an interest in "pumping up" the prestige/dignity/honor/status of the other *up to a certain point*. I witnessed an interesting exchange in Jalleh when a man from Beirut was visiting a villager's house to buy an old tractor. Over coffee, the man discovered that the father of the villager's wife had grown up in the same part of Ayn-el-Rummaneh, a neighborhood of Beirut, as he had. So he innocently asked the woman where her father attended school. Her husband intervened quickly and elided the question by saying, "My father-in-law was an exceptionally enterprising man. He left Ayn-el-Rummaneh and opened a café in Tabarja at the age of sixteen." It was clear to everyone that his father-in-law never went to school and was therefore of low educational status, but it was more important that the husband was seen to be doing the right thing in upholding his wife's father's reputation.

In an anisogamic relation, the high-status spouse would clearly want the low-status spouse to show some recognition of, and a certain degree of gratitude for, the higher socioeconomic or cultural status he or she has offered the spouse though marriage. At the same time, the high-status spouse would not want this recognition to be given in an overly obvious, obsequious, and submissive manner that would end up demeaning all concerned. A "thank you for saving me from my lowly roots" would not go over well.

To put down one's own origins is a shameful thing to do, both to oneself and to one's spouse, and it's always important to show oneself capable of speaking highly of one's own family. However, anisogamic logic is such that if the person of low status starts valorizing his or her family *too much*, it can become a sign of disrespect and lack of gratitude toward the high-status spouse. That is, valorizing should not be done to the point where it becomes a form of excessive boasting that can make the spouse of high status feel the need to remind the low-status spouse of those lowly origins.

There is always a need for the person of low status to show some gratitude to the person of high status for having helped this spouse experience upward social mobility. But, as already noted, it must be done with style and restraint so as not to demean oneself and one's high-status spouse. For the latter usually also has an interest in highlighting what is exceptionally positive about the low-status person he or she has married. After all, the high-status spouse chose to marry that person.

A successful anisogamic marriage depends, then, on both partners knowing how to valorize themselves, but not too much; how to valorize each other, but not too much; how to show gratitude, but not too much; and how to show pride, but not too much. It's an artful process of knowing where the boundary between self-worth and excessive narcissism is and how not to cross it. Other boundaries are those between pride and boastfulness, a healthy sense of appreciation of what has been received and excessive gratitude, and respect and servitude. Because of their dependence on all this subtle, symbolic labor requiring both a constant awareness of where one is positioned and constant adjustment to changing circumstances, anisogamic marriages can quickly degenerate from a process of mutual co-valorization to the exact opposite: an infernal dialectic of put-downs and devalorization of the other, compensated by over-valorization of the self.

The above is important in understanding the Lebanese diasporic mode of existence because the Lebanese—from the very moment they are captured by diasporic modernity, the moment they launch themselves into the world, even when they claim the spirits of their Phoenician ancestors and portray themselves triumphantly as a world-conquering people—actually see themselves in one important regard as lesser people when interacting with those inhabiting the lands to which they are migrating or want to migrate. They are ashamed of this self-perception, the source of which is not an internalization of the racist developmentalist schema of Western colonialism, which sees the world in terms of "advanced" white people and "backward" Third World people. Although, to be clear, they do internalize this racist schema and position themselves ambivalently within it.[7] Yet this does not explain how such a conception of themselves as a "lesser people" is present—even when they migrate to Third World countries, where they wholeheartedly adopt a Western racist conception of the natives.

What is behind this perception, then, is not the assumed degree of modernity and capitalist development of the Lebanese migrant's new country but something much simpler. It is a self-conception of coming from a country that lets go of its children because it cannot care for them. Or, as a Venezuelan Lebanese poetically put it to me, "We are the people whose country could not keep them." It is this primal sense of injury that unleashes the anisogamic sentiments at the heart of the diasporic experience.

Imaginary Anisogamy and Protecting the Good Mother

One evening in Melbourne as I am having dinner with my informants' family, George is lamenting the fact that Australians still think of Lebanon as "a desert with camels." He starts boasting about how beautiful Lebanon is and complaining about how ignorant Australians are. George's son can't help himself: "Yes, Dad, but the fact still is that it is you who migrated to Australia; it is not the Australians who migrated to Lebanon." "So what?" his father replies, totally evading the point raised by his son. "Just because they are rich doesn't mean they are better than us."

Again and again during my fieldwork, the fact that it is the Lebanese who migrate came up in ways reminiscent of some injuries of class: a source of shame that needs to be hidden. The deep nature of this injury emerges most clearly in the many ways it's evaded or swept under the carpet within Lebanon's diasporic culture itself. Indeed, we can say that the whole mythology of the enterprising Lebanese is partly an attempt to elide and not fully come to terms with the source of this injury: Lebanon's relative poverty and its inability to offer its people an acceptable distribution of economic well-being and sources of existential mobility. Despite the propelling power of the migratory illusio, the Lebanese diasporic subject is always riven with ambivalent feelings set in motion by this primal injury: love for Lebanon as one's homeland and one's family; shame that Lebanon is unable to keep its people; shame for experiencing this shame; and desire to protect what is good about Lebanon despite this injury.

One common mode of handling this ambivalence is by splitting Lebanon into a bad and a good side, with the split itself aimed at "protecting" the good side. Sometimes the split is gendered: "Lebanon is a good, lovely, caring place [female]. It's sad that we don't have a state [male] capable of protecting and caring for this goodness and distributing it among the whole population"; "If it weren't for the Lebanese state and what it has done to us, who would want to leave Lebanon?"; and "This country is heaven. The politicians turn it into hell. But for me it remains heaven. That's how I feel; I feel I am forced to leave heaven." Sometimes the split is between Lebanon as nature (good) and Lebanon as people and society (bad), as with this well-known joke: "When God created the natural world, the countries surrounding Lebanon got very jealous and said, 'That's not fair. Why did you make Lebanon so much more beautiful?' God agreed, so he proceeded to create the Lebanese to even things up."

This trope of the good mother unable to care for her children "because of x" is, then, the common way that the Lebanese migrant structures the ambivalent mixture of aggression and love, shame and pride, and valorization and devalorization felt toward Lebanon. It's also the basis for that migrant's anisogamic need to valorize and protect the reputation of "the good mother" in the face of those whose mother can keep them, a need that permeates diasporic discourse and the imaginary reciprocal relation entailed by migration. It's imaginary because it operates primarily at the level of the imaginary rather than explicit discourse. But it's also imaginary because there's not much indication that the host state is conscious of itself as entering into such a reciprocal arrangement.

Let us further clarify the meaning of *imaginary* here. It's not an argument that the Lebanese imagine a reciprocal relation that does not exist. Migration is, among many other things, a reciprocal relation. That is, reciprocity is one of its dimensions. That a host state or culture is oblivious to this dimension of the relation does not mean it doesn't exist. If the Lebanese immigrant or would-be immigrant is more aware of this dimension, it's because this individual has an interest in highlighting it. It stages the immigrant in a more viable moral light: being perceived as entering a relation of reciprocity is better than being perceived as, for example, a parasite or a beggar who is needy but has nothing to offer in return. Therefore, while the host state's and host people's failing to be aware of the reciprocal dimension of the relation doesn't mean it does not exist, it does mean that it makes for a very frustrating and paradoxical situation where the immigrant plays a game of reciprocity without a reciprocating party. This situation leads to the abundant strategies of over-valorization.

Perhaps more than as an imaginary marriage, the diasporic anisogamic relation takes the form of an imaginary adoption. The people whose mother could not keep them (though it's not her fault) are adopted by another mother who offers them the gift of a new social life. But given that this new mother is more often than not unaware of the reciprocal nature of the process, the immigrants find themselves in situations where their status as the people whose mother could not keep them is thrown back in their face rather than adroitly managed and kept hidden. This action is done implicitly by the receiving state and explicitly by racists, who if nothing else are experts in the art of finding ways to hurt—at least symbolically—those whom they racialize. When a Lebanese aims at highlighting the goodness and beauty of Lebanon, the racists reply with a mocking "So why did you leave if your country is so great?"

Overt racists are indeed good at rubbing salt into wounds in this way, but as noted, they only make explicit what is already implicitly happening. So the migratory subjects find themselves constantly engaging in a compensatory over-valorization of the homeland that seeps through the comparative logic examined at the beginning of this chapter. Nowhere is this anisogamic overcompensation clearer than in the antimigratory/anti-Western modernity literature produced by the Lebanese who have migrated and felt that the whole experience failed them.

Some of the work of Mikha'il N'aymeh (1889–1988), an important figure in the history of Arab literature, exemplifies this anisogamic diasporic literature. N'aymeh was a member of the Mahjar school, writers of mainly Lebanese background based in the Boston-New York area, that formed particularly around Gibran Khalil Gibran and N'aymeh himself. For all practical purposes, N'aymeh was someone who had received from his adopted mother, the United States, the gift of a life that would not have been possible in Lebanon. He studied arts and law at the University of Washington and was able to pursue his literary interests. He also can be viewed as having reciprocated this gift of a new life: he was drafted into the US Army during World War I and fought in France. But one gets a sense that N'aymeh increasingly felt disillusioned by the lack of recognition he was experiencing in the United States. He ended up returning to Lebanon after more than twenty years as an immigrant.

"Sa'at al-Kukku" (The Cuckoo Clock), a classic short story by N'aymeh, is taken as a simple but classic tale juxtaposing the culture of migration and the West to the culture of home, the latter emerging as the moral victor. Reading it for anisogamy yields further insight. The story is about an immigrant who arrives in Lebanon from the United States and bedazzles his new village with a cuckoo clock that comes to symbolize American modernity. One of those seduced by the clock (and by the immigrant) is Zumurrud, a woman hitherto happily in love with Khattar, her quintessentially Lebanese neighbor and fiancé. On her wedding night, Zumurrud must choose between marriage and life in the village or the promise of immigration and modernity embodied in the cuckoo clock. Deciding in favor of the clock, she elopes and leaves for the United States. The incident leaves Khattar, the simple Lebanese villager, brokenhearted, but it also transforms his attachment to his village. His yearning for Zumurrud becomes a yearning for the very Western modernity she preferred to the life he had to offer. His views about his own life are transformed: where he once saw beauty, he now sees ugliness. Khattar becomes ashamed of what he was initially proud, so he decides to migrate to the United States. After going through a difficult settlement period, he becomes financially successful, though he remains an unhappy man. The story then takes Khattar through a series of (mis)adventures, including encountering Zumurrud, now abandoned by her lover and doing menial labor to survive, leaving her a mess. In the end, Khattar returns to the village and to the pleasures of a simpler life.

Stories such as "Sa'at al-Kukku" have a quasi-universal structure based on a simple opposition between East and West, tradition and modernity, simplicity and complexity, love and money, home and away. Yet despite their simplicity, these "classic" oppositions still speak to many experiences I encountered in the field, even if the oppositions are rarely as sharp and caricatured. We shall look at some further manifestations of these oppositions throughout the book. What this chapter points to, however, is that loss is always imagined to be a loss of tradition, the simple life, and genuine human relations, and that it is experienced even by those totally captured by the propelling power of the migratory illusio. The experience's intensity differs enormously according to many variables, such as the cocktail of need, desire, and capacity to migrate referred to in the previous chapter, the ability to return, the stage of migration, and so on.

Whereas loss and yearning for tradition have been amply examined in the analytic literature on migration,[8] what I have aimed to highlight here and throughout the chapter are two things often missing from the analysis. First, this loss is articulated to an experience of a primal diasporic injury: having a sense that one belongs to a people whose country cannot keep them, generating an ambivalent feeling of being let down by one's country yet wanting to valorize it. Second, this feeling is itself articulated to an even more structuring dimension of the diasporic imaginary, what I have called diasporic anisogamy: a sense that migration involves entering a relation of reciprocity with a superior people, superior precisely because, unlike the immigrant, they have been cared for and kept in the fold by their country. Both processes highlight that the sense of loss is not merely a passive feeling that takes over the immigrant or would-be immigrant but also a strategic deployment in the struggle to construct one's viability in the face of devalorization.

I am finishing writing this chapter while in Lebanon during its October 2019 uprising. I notice with interest how much migration figures as a lament ("Look what you are making us do"), a problem ("Our youth are all leaving"), and a sign of governmental dysfunction ("We shouldn't have to leave") in the discourse of this revolt. "You've wasted the [people with] talents and given them to the foreigners," said a prominent banner in downtown Beirut on the very first day of the uprising. In familiar ways, it made the Lebanese government responsible for the "brain drain" caused by ongoing migration. It declared migration a problem that could be avoided if it weren't for the mismanagement of the economy by the political and economic governing elite. The mother's good, the father's bad.

As noted earlier, the discourse about migration being something bad that happens to someone has always been present in Lebanon, but it often took a backseat to an opposite, state-instituted celebratory discourse. Therefore, it's no surprise that when the state is suffering from a legitimacy crisis, the discourse that treats migration as signifying the adventurous and ambitious character of the Lebanese declines. Thus, the uprising brings to the forefront a discourse of migration as a social pathology. It can be heard everywhere: We are demonstrating because "we're sick and tired of having to migrate"; "I just got my degree. Why should I be looking for a job outside Lebanon?"; and then there's this guy holding a placard stating the names of all his friends who have migrated and telling them that he's demonstrating "because we want you back." "I don't want to be in a situation where my relatives ring me and say, 'Your father's not doing so well,' and I am too far to be able to do anything," says a man to a journalist interviewing him. Nonetheless, the participants in the uprising are in some instances people who have been living outside Lebanon and returned simply to join the revolt. A number of times since the uprising began, I've sat at street meetings where the conversation had to be held in English, because it was the only language that the participants shared as their Lebanese wasn't good enough. Such people had experienced the gains of migration, but they nonetheless also wanted a better state that didn't "cause" migration in the first place. Perhaps it was the woman holding a sign stating that she is demonstrating "for every drop of tears that has fallen at the airport" that spoke to their concerns. For this sign pointed not so much to a social problem as to a primal injury—the injury behind the anisogamic sentiments we have analyzed in this chapter.

FOUR

From Ambivalent to Fragmented Subjects

Jalleh, 14 September 2003

There's at least fifty people having dinner at Jameel's parent's house tonight. Tomorrow, he leaves for Australia. Ever since he had come home with his visa, he's been on a high, preparing for his departure. It's late in the evening, and we've already had a fair bit of arak (an anise-flavored distilled alcoholic beverage) to drink. Jameel gestures for me to come and sit next to him. He keeps gazing at the people around him and shaking his head as if in a state of disbelief.

"What's the weather like in Melbourne at the moment? Uncle Joe said it's still cold. But is it as cold as winter here?"

"Probably the same. Melbourne is colder than Sydney," I reply, but already Jameel isn't paying attention. He's again looking at the people around him and shaking his head.

"I can't believe I am leaving all this," he says. And then, the man who all week has been excitedly preparing for his departure, the man who for the last three years has been feverishly seeking a visa to go to Australia, turns to me and says, "Do you think I am doing the right thing?"

Jameel is gazing at the same space where, for the last three years, he has so often said to me, "There's nothing here." It's as if he's suddenly realizing that "something" is there after all, something he feels he's about to stop accessing in the way he's been accessing it before. For the person eagerly awaiting and failing to obtain a visa, a key reason that home is felt to be unhomely is because it has become experienced as a claustrophobic, suffocating enclosure. Researchers of home and homeliness emphasize security, community, and familiarity in the making of homely feelings, but they fail to highlight the importance of the feeling of openness to the world and to the future, without which homes can never be homely.[1] Thus, it's not surprising that after years of seeking a visa unsuccessfully and experiencing home as an unhomely enclosure, the moment one gets this opening to the world and to the future in the form of a visa, home reasonably quickly becomes homely again. As with Hegel's figure of that which comes into being by being left behind, the village stops being nothing the very moment that one can leave it. Literally overnight, the people and places that had been viewed disdainfully because they were thought of as being in the way, actively stopping one from leaving, or because they were seen as a simple reminder of one's state of "stuckedness" are now looked at nostalgically—with the added guilt of having unfairly directed at them all one's past aggression. Just as Jameel comes very close to leaving and is intensely focused on what is ahead for him, orienting himself toward Australia and, in a way, already inhabiting it, he wavers: his gaze on the space he is about to leave becomes nostalgic, and he is torn between leaving and staying.

This wavering is a classic trope of lay and analytical diasporic discourse, in which concepts such as being torn and being in between abound. Analytically, it has been studied predominantly as a form of ambivalence.[2] In this chapter, I show how the modes of analyzing phenomena such as this with the help of ambivalence, while undoubtedly pertinent, have worked against coming to terms with another mode of living these two contradictory orientations. Here, rather than occupying a position in between two spaces and being ambivalent and torn between them, one manages to inhabit both. The latter is what I am defining as "multiple inhabitance."

The Limits of Ambivalence

For a long time during my research, I deployed the concept of ambivalence to account for wavering. The concept was useful to denote a subjective state dominated by a sentiment of uncertainty and of mixed feelings concerning a decision one is about to make or a path one is about to take.[3] As implicit in the previous chapter's account of immigrants' feelings toward their country as the mother who could not keep them, ambivalence was also attractive because of its psychoanalytic lineage and its ability to account for desire's contradictory nature.[4] In addition, the concept gave me a word to describe situations where the migratory illusio's power to propel people into the world could coexist with a homely illusio that involves a counter-investment in staying at home and being subjected to its centripetal pulling forces. Moreover, I found myself deploying similar concepts, such as Spinoza's concept of vacillation,[5] to account for situations involving being subjected to multiple but contrary pulling and pushing and propelling forces, such as the uncertainty associated with staying or returning home after migration, and more generally, situations of being "in between" two cultures or of being torn between two countries.

Perhaps nothing captures ambivalence better than the lyrics of a Kabyle folk song quoted by Abdelmalek Sayad in his book *The Suffering of the Immigrant*. Here is a taste of it:

> And yet my heart wonders
> Whether it should stay or go,
> Whether it should go or stay;
>
> . . . .
>
> My heart asked me for advice, I told it to stay
> Whereas it wanted to go;
> So I told it to go,
> Whereas it wanted to stay.
>
> . . . .
>
> One day it went, but in its thoughts
> It came back before it had gone
>
> . . . .
>
> If I go, it wants to stay
> If I stay, it wants to go.[6]

There is little doubt about the prevalence of the ambivalence depicted in this poem within all kinds of diasporic cultures, nor is there any doubt about the pertinence of this sentiment in capturing what is going on in the folk song and the field. Yet the longer I was in the field, the more I was facing situations where I found the concept insufficient to account for my ethnographic data. Ambivalence could account for an experience that presupposes a unified subject suffering from a form of uncertainty regarding the choices, attachments, and investments he or she must make. In questions such as Should I do this or should I do that?, Should I go there or should I stay here?, the "I" is imagined to always remain intact as one: an "I" that is "torn between" but not a torn "I." It is clearly not imagined to be able to split and have some of it do this and some of it do that or, similarly, to have some of it go there and some of it stay here. That is, ambivalence was less suitable to describe a state, not of uncertainty by a unified subject but of fragmentation of the self into multiple subjects; a state where the subject is not so much uncertain about the space to occupy or the path to take as able to occupy two or more spaces at the same time. Ambivalence and in-between-ness were more on the side of either/or or in-between rather than on the side of both. And while the diasporic subjects I spoke with often experienced such ambivalence, they also experienced dwelling in this "both," in what I increasingly referred to as a state of multiple inhabitance. But it wasn't easy to rid myself of the tendency to collapse everything into the concepts of ambivalence and vacillation.

"You Are . . . the Two Roads"

It's the first year of my research in Mehj. Sitting on the second-floor veranda of Georges's house, Lilianne is "reading" Jo's cup of coffee, intensely scrutinizing the grounds left at the bottom of the cup.

"Ahead of you are two roads," she says to Jo.

Mona and Georges, Jo's sister and brother, start laughing. "You're sure it's not three this time?" Georges says in a mocking tone. "Shu . . . ush," says Fareedeh, their mum.

Lilianne is unperturbed. She's heard Georges and others mocking her fortune-telling before. And she's heard people specifically mock her when she says, "Ahead of you are two roads." Yet she still does it. "The cup always shows two roads," she once explained to me matter-of-factly.

For her part, Jo is used to the sarcasm. Every year around August, she leaves Vermont to stay in the village for a month. Every year, Lilianne must read her cup of coffee once. And every year, Georges, also visiting from Vermont (Mona, the youngest sister, is based in Gatineau), must mock the whole proceedings. "To demonstrate how modern he is," Jo quips sarcastically when talking with me about this later that day.

"Don't worry about him, keep going," she tells Lilianne. Lilianne keeps going. And as if to show how unaffected she is by Georges's sarcasm, she repeats her opening sentence: "Ahead of you are two roads." She continues. "Both roads seem to end pointing to the same place, but the choice is difficult." She stops and looks at Jo: "You are facing a particularly difficult situation here, for you don't even seem to have a choice." She takes a drag on her cigarette. "One road seems long and full of turns but with very few obstacles. The other is shorter . . . yes . . . [scrutinizes the bottom of the cup again]. . . but it seems very risky and dangerous."

Fareedeh couldn't help interfering this time: "Must be the road to Beirut."

Georges smiles, but Lilianne is looking at Jo very seriously: "You have to be very careful. For the danger is not just on the road. The danger is in you. When I look here, I see you. But you are not on either of these two roads. They are in you. You are, in yourself, the two roads" [Enteh binafsik el' tari'eyn], she says, finishing on this unusual and mysterious note what began as a classic routinized fortune-telling discourse. It's like telling Georges indirectly, "You want something different? Well, here's something different."

Lilianne puts the cup of coffee back on the tray in front of her, as if angry about what she just said. This is a very "cosmic" ending, and very un-Lebanese to my cultural ear. So I'm the one who has to refrain from laughing, while Georges is just looking at Jo and Lilianne, his eyebrows raised, appearing a bit more perplexed than usual. I wouldn't have made much more of this had Jo not replied, "All my life I've been two roads" [Tool 'imreh tari'eyn].

I think it interesting that what is to my mind an ostensibly rather nonsensical sentence makes immediate sense to her. "Do you mean you are always uncertain whether you made the right choice and whether you are going in the right direction?" I ask her later that day over lunch.

"Yes, I guess, sometimes," Jo replies. However, she quickly adds with more force: "But it also feels like part of me takes one direction and the other part takes another. I am going this way and that way at the same time, all the time. When I left Lebanon for the US, I always felt that part of me never left. And now I am here having a holiday with my mum, but I am also in Vermont. Not just thinking about Vermont but busy doing things long distance in Vermont. Like today, I spent three hours organizing [her daughter] Freddy's excursion to Banff."

I still vividly remember how, upon hearing Jo's reply, I felt that with a very simple explanation, she quickly made "you are the two roads" no longer sound like something written by Carlos Castaneda, as it had when I first heard Lilianne say it. This is how the sense of being in two—and on some rare occasions I have encountered, three—places at the same time slowly began shaping into an analytical problematic different from the question of ambivalence.

From Ambivalence to Multiple Inhabitance

As I noted earlier, at this early point in my research I was content with the work that the notion of ambivalence was doing for me. The sense of being torn between two countries, two cultures, two decisions, and so on did a good job accounting for states of being such as Jameel's "do you think I am doing the right thing?" or Sayad's Kabyle poem. Even the evening after the fortune-telling episode, I was still thinking about "you are the two roads" in terms of what it tells us about the torn and ambivalent state of the diasporic subject.

Just before going to Mehj that week, I was in Beirut preparing to head to the villages. My colleague Samir Khalaf at the American University of Beirut always generously let me share his office, and it was an opportunity to have many chats about his work and mine. I was explaining to him my idea concerning the migratory illusio and its propelling force. He quipped, "You're just going back to Lerner." He was referring to Daniel Lerner's *The Passing of Traditional Society*, a classic of American modernization theory as developed in Middle East media studies.[7] I was shocked at the suggestion. I remembered the book from my undergraduate years, and I remembered the lecturer literally mocking it. Its arguments and categories have been critiqued academically for more than half a century now, but given that they were an elevation of some commonsense ideas about US-centric conceptions of modernization in the first place, those ideas continue to circulate, regardless of the intellectual critique.

Thus, Lerner's was one book I was reading when I headed to Mehj. And no sooner had I started reading it than I indeed could see why my colleague would challenge me the way he had. Lerner's notorious opposition between two figures that lived in the Turkish village he was researching—"the chief," who was traditional, contented, and immobile, and "the grocer," who was modern, restless, and ready to go anywhere—might well be and probably is simplistic, as many have argued. Even so, his description of the modern grocer had definite resonance with the person propelled by the migratory illusio I was theorizing at the time. I admit that I was sheepishly worried that in my work, I, a committed postcolonialist, would end up recycling Lerner. This made me unconsciously cling even more to the concept of ambivalence, as I felt that without it my Bourdieu-inspired conception of the diasporic illusio would indeed turn out to be an uncritical fit with American modernization theory.

Moreover, this explains why, I now think, when I returned to my room the evening after the fortune-telling event and saw Lerner's book on my bedside table, I immediately thought that Lilianne and Jo's "two roads" highlighted a situation of ambivalence that critiques Lerner's fable-like exposition. Indeed, I experienced one of those moments when ethnography provided a more nuanced theory than the one being read in the field. I recorded my thoughts in my notebook that evening.

Isn't Lerner presenting us with the American modernist's version of the fortune-teller's "ahead of you are two roads"? Except his two roads, unlike Jo's, are an either/or matter. Either you take the road of the chief and remain a prisoner of tradition and locality, feel contentment, dislike economic calculative thinking, and desire to remain where you are, or you take the road of the grocer and embrace change, become exposed to media, and become able to project yourself outside the narrow confines of your physical surroundings. Feeling dissatisfied with where you are socially and geographically, you start to want more, to begin to live in a "world, populated more actively with imaginings and fantasies," and you start considering moving elsewhere.[8]

Lerner has no sense of ambivalence. Thus, it isn't so much that the two tendencies he describes aren't part of the structuring of the modernity/tradition dichotomy. It's more that they are presented as embodied in two different people and two different paths.

This text functions like myth. Myth can entangle what is separate and can separate what is entangled. In this case, Lerner's text does the latter, working to separate and project into two people what in fact always coexists entangled in the same person—namely, wanting tradition and wanting change, wanting to think economically and feeling shame at thinking economically, wanting to go and wanting to stay. Even if someone takes the road of the grocer, Lerner is unable to capture the sense of loss that this involves.

As can be seen, then, in those notes, although my own language was pulling me unconsciously toward a conception of multiple subjects, I was still thinking that Lilianne and Jo's "two roads" primarily implied a form of subjective ambivalence—even though when I questioned Jo over lunch as to how come "you are two roads" made so much sense to her, her reply didn't highlight subjective ambivalence. It was I who was unconsciously hoping to reduce what had been said to this state. "Do you mean you are always uncertain whether you made the right choice and whether you are going in the right direction?" I asked. And clearly even after Jo answered this with a "yes, but," I was still clinging to reducing the problematic of the two roads to a problematic of the torn-between-this-and-that diasporic subject. Yet this is clearly not what Jo's explanation entailed. She agreed that it could sometimes mean ambivalence. Nonetheless, what she insisted on was that she felt she was occupying two spaces at the same time. This situation involves more than a unitary subject being torn between two roads, between leaving and staying, between home and away, or between Lerner's modernity and tradition. To begin with, it entails the subject's fragmentation so that different parts of it inhabit those different spaces. This fragmentation is not the "result" of migration, though it develops differently in migrating. Instead, it's a structural feature of the constitution of the diasporic subject as traversed by the two opposite forces that make of that individual both a globally propelled and a homely subject. Sometimes this fragmentation is managed unproblematically, whereby the various fragments coexist and even complement each other, as in Jo's case. But sometimes it's experienced as a violent tearing apart, where two contradictory parts of the self are expected to cohabit the self. In what follows, I want to explore two cases involving very different ways in which it ends up being managed. While dissimilar, each case will help us understand some key dimensions of this fragmentation.

Leaving Gibran Behind

I am talking with Waheed in one of the very first of many conversations we had concerning his migration to Cabudare, Venezuela. We are, however, in Florida, where he stays for short periods to be with his son, whom he shares with Ana Maria, a Cuban American woman. While Waheed and Ana Maria's relationship was very brief and did not involve marriage, Waheed bought an apartment in Florida where she and their child can live. When he goes there, they all act, outwardly at least, as if they are a standard patriarchal nuclear family. Ana Maria has made us Lebanese coffee, and we're chatting about whether he made friends when he migrated to Cabudare. He replies in Arabic: *"Ya Habibeh, Leik, fee shee baddak tefhamo, Ashaab hoan ma fee."* The comment does not stand out to me. But later, when I translate it to English, I gaze at it, bemused. This is the exact translation: "Look here, my dear friend, there's something you need to understand, there are no friends here."

"O my friends, there are no friends" is a statement attributed to Aristotle. It was later analyzed by Montaigne, then much later taken up and dissected by Derrida in his *Politics of Friendship*.[9] Waheed has definitely read no Derrida, no Montaigne, and no Aristotle. But if, for someone who has read one or all of those philosophers, his statement stands out by its similarity to Aristotle's, what also stands out is the "here" that makes it different.

Unlike Derrida or Aristotle, Waheed is not making a philosophical/universal statement about friendship. His pronouncement is at the same time comparative, in the way diasporic comparative logic always is, and spatially specific. For him, there were no friends "here," which refers to a vaguely defined space that spans the United States and Venezuela. He made it clear during that conversation that he strongly believed that there were friends "there," in Lebanon. Indeed, this was the thrust of his conversation. In Lebanon, not only were there many friends but "friends were really friends." Here, in the US-Venezuelan space, "no one has time for anything. And everyone is for themselves."

I initially was amused by the similarity between Waheed's claim and the philosopher's but only mildly interested in it ethnographically, as I already had accumulated many similar comments made by Lebanese immigrants around the world. After transcribing and translating the chat we had on that day, I put the No Friends Here section in the folder I had titled "Diasporic

Nostalgia." I interpreted this conversation primarily as a variety of diasporic nostalgia in which everything is always imagined as better "back home," just as everything is lacking "here." In the Nostalgia folder I had bits of conversation about fruits and vegetables being better back home, about the sky and the sea being nicer, about family life being closer, and about coffee tasting better. And now I've got another bit about friends, I thought. It was all variations on the anisogamic nostalgia of Mikha'il N'aymeh analyzed in the previous chapter, though at the time I hadn't yet considered the analytical potential of anisogamy for the material.

It wasn't until a year later that Waheed's comment acquired further significance via a revelation, such as one has sometimes in the course of fieldwork, that made me remove the conversation from the Nostalgia folder and position it in a new one I titled "Diasporic Fragmentation." As will become clear, it wasn't really I who had the analytic insight—it was Waheed's maternal uncle, Georges, who had migrated to Venezuela long before Waheed and who virtually handed me the richer analytical space on a plate when friendship came up in a discussion.

In the mid-1950s when he was twenty-two years old, Georges arrived in Cabudare and eventually became a successful rice farmer. His farm was located near Barquisimetto, a city about four hours west of Caracas. In addition to his agricultural prominence, Georges was quite a powerful figure in the city, involved with another nephew in urban development projects. Although he was getting very old, he insisted on driving around and doing a lot of things by himself. I've gone with him on trips where he handed cash to soldiers at two army checkpoints in the city. Economically successful Lebanese migrants in rural Venezuela liked to keep the soldiers on their side. At the time I was doing my fieldwork, they were often worried that Chavez would mobilize the underclass mob to attack them and so felt it important to befriend the soldiers in case they needed protection.

While Chavez's mob never harmed them, it was after a less "revolutionary" violent assault on Georges that I had the conversation with him in which the subject of friendship came up. I am visiting him in the hospital. The week before, he had been shot by people who tried to rob him. It happened outside the bank shortly after he had come out with a suitcase full of cash, the monthly payments for his farm's manual laborers. This was the third time somebody had tried to steal money from Georges at gunpoint. Apparently, it always happened under similar circumstances—that is, after he left the bank carrying his employees' wages. Georges is now certain that the thieves have a collaborator who works in the bank, because he engaged in strategies to avoid predictable movements, and yet the robbery happened again. The first time, four years ago, he tells me, he gave the thieves the money and they didn't hurt him. The second time, he resisted them by knocking the gunman with the suitcase. So this third time, emboldened by his previous encounter, he resisted again and tried to take the gun away from one of the thieves. But then he got shot in both the leg and the stomach, and the thieves got away with his money.

But Georges doesn't want to talk about any of this. His wounds, particularly the stomach wound, which bled so much that he had to be put in intensive care for two days, have put him in a contemplative mood. It's now his third day out of intensive care, and he wants to talk to me about life. When I ask him how he is, he shakes his head. "Not good, not good. I am upset with myself, and Helena [his Venezuelan wife] is upset with me. I risked my life and nearly died to protect my money." He shakes his head again and repeats, "For money. That's what I did for money." And then he adds, "I did not start life oriented toward business and money, you know. I hated all this."

These last remarks surprise me, because I always thought of Georges as totally consumed by his businesses and happy with all the wealth and power they generate. "I was more like you," he continues.

> I was interested in ideas, poetry, and philosophy. Do you know that I was the first person in the village to actually read all of Gibran? Everybody talks about Gibran here and in Lebanon, but no one reads him. I read him. I read everything: *The Prophet, The Broken Wings*, all of them. People made fun of me. Even my father, I remember him saying sarcastically, "I wonder what Gibran's parents thought when he migrated all the way to America and sent them poems instead of money." Here he was thinking he was making fun of me, and I was actually thinking: I wish I could go away and write poetry.[10]

"So why didn't you?" I ask. Shaking his head again, he responds:

> I tried. My uncle was here [in Venezuela], he was childless, and he needed help. He enlisted my brother's help first, but that wasn't enough, and he asked for me. I didn't want to go. But my parents, especially my mother, kept insisting. My father was ambivalent, but my mother was relentless. My brother was sending quite a bit of money, and she wanted more. She put a lot of pressure on me, and I was still refusing to go. I hated the idea of leaving, and I particularly hated the idea of going to work in a shop. Mum was very upset with me. But in the end, I couldn't. My father had a stroke, and his medical bill became a burden, and Mum was using this against me for all it's worth. I decided to acquiesce to her demand, partly because, given Dad's health, I didn't want to

upset him, and partly to help financially. A man from the village was leaving to come here [Venezuela], and he told my father that he can take me with him.

You wouldn't know how miserable I was when I arrived. I sit in the shop and I start daydreaming and my uncle would say, "We were making more money when you weren't around. Maybe you shouldn't have come at all." And then my dad died shortly after I arrived, would you believe! I felt even worse. I gradually forgot about Lebanon, and I started making money and more money. Slowly, it became all about money. I left poetry and Gibran and everything that I love behind me in the village. I left them, just like I left the village itself and just like I left my friends.

You know, I was so upset with my mother for directly and indirectly forcing me to leave that I never spoke to her properly after that. She died, and I had hardly spoken with her since I left. She would say, "Come back for a visit; I miss you." But I think I wanted to punish her for making me leave. It was like I was telling her, "Well, you chose to make me leave and make money instead of having me around, so here, I am sending you money, lots of it, enjoy yourself." I never went back. I think I didn't want to be reminded of how painful it was for me to leave. Also . . . something happened to me. It wasn't easy. Anyway, I was the one who didn't want to leave Lebanon, and here I am now, the only one who hasn't gone and doesn't want to go back ever again.

Georges pauses for a second and then, like his nephew before him, he does a Derrida number on me: "I had no wife then and I missed my friends, but I didn't want to go. Now I have a wife. If it wasn't for my wife and family, there would be no one for me here. One thing for sure, my friend, there are no friends here."

I instantly recall his nephew Waheed telling me "there are no friends here" during our conversation in Florida, so hearing it again from his uncle is a bit droll. I do what I often do upon hearing what I consider to be routinized bits of conversation: I add an equally routinized comment to see how much of the same story as a total structuring device people end up adhering to.[11] So I say, "Yes, everyone is for themselves here," which was what Waheed and many others told me in the past. But Georges surprises me by not continuing the conversation in the same vein. "Everyone is for themselves here?" he exclaims questioningly. "That's very true, but who are the ones who put themselves before anyone and anything else first? Is it not we the Lebanese who emigrate? Who thinks it is more important to leave their family and friends for the sake of pursuing money? Is it not us the Lebanese? We happily settle somewhere and accuse the people where we settle for putting money before friendship, but is it not us the Lebanese who have done that to begin with? *Allah yel'an-na"* (May God curse us).

Clearly, Georges is still nursing the injury inflicted on him by his forced emigration. While his discourse begins as if it were a continuation of the classical anisogamic valorization of homely traditions against instrumental modernity, it contains a lot more.

One of the basic driving ideas behind Marx's concept of alienation in his early writings is the loss of work as a space of fulfillment and agency, an activity in which humans realize their humanity (their species-being, as Marx puts it). Capitalism brings about or generalizes the unfulfilling work, in which the workers become separated from their humanity. Work becomes a means toward a pleasurable end, not a pleasurable end in itself. Although not emphasized in existing reflections on Marx's writings, there is already a spatial "migratory" dimension in this well-known text of his: it involves the separation between the space of work and exploitation and the space of domestic pleasure and enjoyment, and the need to travel between them. Each day, the worker physically "migrates" between the two. While Marx's description captures an important reality, it is unlikely that this separation was specific to exploited workers only. His critique is clearly grounded in a romanticization of those whose work is their vocation. That being the case, it applies to all those whose work is a means to an end rather than an end in itself. Georges's experience shows us that migration can involve a similar kind of separation between a space of work that one doesn't really want to inhabit but must—a space where one is either being instrumentalized by others or instrumentalizing oneself—and the space of home, affect, poetry, and true friendship, where one really wants to be.

But although Marx's worker regularly moves between the space of work and the space of home, transnational migrants are unable to do so given the distances and difficulties involved. The immigrant learns to occupy the space of home differently: at a distance, imaginatively, and, increasingly today, communicatively. Otherwise, the immigrant can risk becoming totally imprisoned in the land of work and instrumentalization. From dwelling in what was supposed to be a means to an end, one gradually realizes that the means to an end becomes the end: an ongoing state of deferral. This is why migration intensifies the difference between the space of instrumentalization and the space of home, which becomes more starkly a subjective split, a separation between two selves inhabiting two different realities: an instrumentalized self, inhabiting the land of migration, and a homely self, inhabiting Lebanon.

In Georges's case, this split takes a dramatic and revealing turn. This is because his injury is more than just about being forced to migrate. It's as if, because it's his mother that forced his departure, Georges can't perform the classical anisogamic strategy of saving Lebanon the mother from the bad father of the governing elite, as we examined in the previous chapter. This failure compounds the injury of migration and leaves him with a basic distrust of a homely Lebanese anchoring, which he sees as poisoned to the core—so much so that he wants it to be cursed by God. There is another dimension to this injury, marked by the importance of the "loss of friendship" lament. Both Waheed and his uncle migrated to live with their kin. But they also migrated in their late teens/early twenties, a time when friends (the people who, unlike kin, we choose to associate with) are particularly important as a mark of autonomy and agency, hence a mark of distinction from kin and of growing up. Thus migration, which often involves a high dependency on kin in the early years of settlement, is experienced as a reversal of this trajectory. It is experienced as a process of infantilization and loss of autonomy.

Georges's migratory injuries were therefore quite extensive. But paradoxically, these work as a source of lucidity about some important dimensions of the diasporic condition. Unlike Mikha'il N'aymeh's romantic conception of the Lebanese as a victim of Western modernity yearning to go home, Georges's Lebanese are complicit in his valorizing the domain of self-instrumentalization in the pursuit of money at the expense of valorizing homely feelings, such as family and friendship. In the struggle between the money-seeking, instrumentalized subject and the home-seeking subject, the Lebanese who migrate willingly let the first dominate the second. Georges himself is clearly saying that he is not an ordinary Lebanese. He wants to valorize the second over the first. But "the Lebanese," here in the form of his mother, force him to do what "the Lebanese" usually do: prioritize money over home, poetry, and friendship. Interestingly, because "the Lebanese" (i.e., his mother) made him do this, Georges tore himself away from his home-yearning self and oriented himself to the land to which he immigrated, though he remains conscious of the scale of the loss. Unlike many whose desire for migration allows them to have multiple selves with multiple attachments, he can't cope with the multiplicity. As I am later to discover, this is even more dramatic than I first imagined.

I was back in Sydney when I typed my notes from this encounter. I stopped at a point where Georges says, "Something happened to me. It wasn't easy." I wondered what happened to him, and I wanted to ask him. Unfortunately, it was another two years before I returned to Venezuela, and by then he had died of a heart attack. When I visit Helena, his wife, I ask if she knows what he meant by "something happened to me." She does. She tells me that a year or so after arriving in Venezuela, Georges had a nervous breakdown and went to "live in the jungle." I try to learn more from her, but she says to ask his niece Reema, because "she knows. Her father [Georges's brother, who died long ago] told her everything." Here is an edited and condensed version of what Reema told me in a taped interview:

> According to my father, Georges became increasingly erratic after arriving from Lebanon. Uncle Toufic [Georges's paternal uncle] had a shop that sold all kinds of things, from furniture to antiques to suitcases, watches, and toys, and it was big and very busy. My father was the first to come from Lebanon to help him, but they were very busy and needed more help with the shop. They also suspected that some employees were robbing them and needed more family to act as supervisors. So they asked for Uncle Georges to come. He came, but he apparently couldn't cope with the intensity of the shop. After six months or so, he started behaving erratically. Dad said that Uncle Georges would have a kind of nervous breakdown and start swearing at everyone in Lebanese and acting very strange. He would have, like, an attack [*nawbeh*] and start smashing things. Apparently, even though they were very busy and they needed him, Uncle Toufic would say to him, "Take a break; go for a drive." One day, he went for a drive and didn't come back . . .
>
> Everyone was worried about him, and they called the police. But he came back two days later. He said he stayed in the forest, which everyone thinks is where the Monumento Natural Loma De Leon is now. But after he came back, he stopped shaving or taking showers, and he was behaving even more weirdly. Then he started disappearing for longer and longer, but he always showed up every week or so. Sometimes he would come to the house and take things. Like, he took a rifle and ammunition, which he said he was using to hunt.
>
> Apparently, this lasted for almost six months where he would appear every couple of weeks and refuse to answer if people asked him what he was doing. Then, my father said, something very strange happened. One day, Georges came back, cut his hair, shaved, and showered and put on his working clothes and went to the shop and acted as if the last few months had never happened. And he never again behaved strangely after that, ever.

This story exemplifies managing multiplicity through a borderline case in which this management becomes impossible. Because, as we have seen above, Georges is driven to migrate by his mother, leaving him without an emotional anchoring in Lebanon, his migration process ends with a traumatic severing of the homely part of the migratory self, performed dramatically in the form of an escape into the jungle. I want to finish this chapter with another ethnographic case that exposes the rich variety in how managing this multiplicity happens. This case takes us into the heart of the relation between diaspora and patriarchy.

Patriarchy as a Mode of Loss Avoidance

I first met Hind in Melbourne. She had just finished high school and was working at her parent's restaurant. She hadn't done well in her VCE (Victorian Certificate of Education) and didn't think she could get into university, but she expressed the desire to do further studies. We had a long chat about what she needed to do.

Five years later, I am visiting her parents, and they tell me that she has gone to live in Auckland. I mention to them that I'm going to Auckland for a conference, so they ask me whether I can take a package for her. I say yes, and that's how I got to meet her there. I ask her whether she still wants to go to university. She says she did, "but first I had to get away from Melbourne and from my family." I'm surprised, as I thought her family environment was nice and her parents loving. So I ask her why. Her reply is interesting. She says that she found herself increasingly sucked into working at the restaurant and that working for her father was intolerable.

"You know, he doesn't do anything other than act like the lord of the manor. He is great when he's welcoming people to our house or to the restaurant, you know, the way he welcomes you. But, as you know, his English is not so good, and he doesn't try to improve it . . . and he makes Mum do all the work. She cooks, she cleans, she even carries boxes, and whenever someone comes from the council or the government for whatever issue, he also gets Mum to deal with it. He doesn't even like to handle money, except receiving it and spending it. But, at least, he likes spending it on us. At the same time, when Mum is dealing with men, the very men he doesn't want to deal with, especially if they are Australian [she means Anglo-Australian] and young, he gets really jealous. And he has a bad temper. He has never physically touched any of us, but he can throw some unbelievable tantrums. He becomes really detestable. Then, late in the evening, after we finished cleaning the restaurant, especially if he'd thrown a tantrum during the day, he would come to Mum, sometimes he even starts crying, and he says, 'I don't know how you can cope with me, yaa habibti enteh [my darling], wallah enteh Maryam l'Adrah [God is my witness, you are the Virgin Mary].'

"I've seen it happen again and again. I tried to get Mum to challenge him, but she wouldn't do anything. She would tell me, 'Enteh ma btefhameh shee' [You don't understand anything]. It's as if being told that she was Maryam l'Adrah is enough for her. I found myself having to cope with this constantly. I also found

myself, like Mum, increasingly doing all the restaurant work [sometimes just to relieve her]. I was increasingly saying to myself that I had to get away from all this.

"One day, Dad asked me to get a box of Coke from the back shed to stack in the fridge, and when I went to the back, an Australian male friend of mine called in to see me and we started chatting in the backyard. Suddenly, Dad barged in on us, furious and acting as if he was waiting for the box of Coke. He started shouting at me and telling me things in Arabic and suddenly decided to speak English, just to tell me, 'You good for nothing . . . nothing!' right in front of my friend. I was embarrassed and started crying. That night, I was watching TV, and Dad came in. I was still very upset, and I didn't talk to him. He started crying and he said to me, 'Yah habibteh, I am sorry, walla enteh Maryam l'Adrah.' I knew straightaway that I had to leave the place as quickly as possible.

"A month later, I got invited to spend a week visiting some high school friends in Auckland. I went. After a few days with them, I just decided that I was not going back. I had enough of working in the restaurant and being Maryam l'Adrah. And I haven't gone back since. Mum and Dad weren't happy, of course, and they tried everything, but in the end, they've coped with it well."

I had often observed the patterned relation "man acting like 'lord of the manor'/woman doing all the labor" among Lebanese families who owned small businesses around the world. Hind's story dramatized it and made it much clearer to me. More important, as I thought about it, it started to dawn on me that in fact this relation is the very structure of how *iqta'* (feudal) patriarchy intersected with diasporic modernity in the nineteenth century.

As with all capitalist modernities, the silk industry's industrialization in Mount Lebanon unleashed a valorization of the modernization and freedom from tradition that capitalism brought, and reactively, it unleashed an opposite valorization of that very tradition that capitalism was undermining. These intersected with the opposition between the yearning to leave and the yearning to remain at home we have been examining so far. While all the people of Mount Lebanon had to find their way between these contradictory yearnings, historians of the period have clearly shown that most men were far more entrenched on the side of tradition. They looked down on the idea of working for a wage and valorized themselves as autonomous landowners, whatever the size of the land that they owned. As a number of historians have pointed out, patriarchal notions of honor remained articulated to landownership.[12]

In the eyes of Lebanese men, capitalism brought economic well-being but also a petty calculative logic which they, very feudally, looked down on. They "let" women do factory work, valorizing the additional money

brought into the household yet devalorizing the women morally for engaging in that same waged labor. In much the same way, the men saw the silk
factories as symbols of Westernization/modernization, and they increasingly used the fact that they've let "their" women work in such factories as a
symbol of their own Westernization. They, particularly Christian men, used
it as a mode of distinction and as a way of marking themselves as superior to the "backward" traditionally patriarchal nonmodern Arab Muslims
surrounding them. Yet at the same time, they feared the social and economic freedom the women were acquiring by engaging in capitalist labor.
The point is that from the perspective of patriarchy, women's insertion into
the capitalist economy meant a certain autonomy and freedom of circulation, which in the men's patriarchal feudal gaze (worried about honor) was
foremost worrying about sexual freedom and promiscuity. The silk factories
were known by their Turkish name as *kerkhanas*. Ambivalently, men started
referring to the *kerkhana* as a place where women were sexually/morally lax.
Slowly and well into the twentieth century, *kerkhana* became the name given
to brothels.

With the help of Annette Weiner, we can argue that this is a peculiar
mode of "keeping while giving" that marks Lebanese diasporic patriarchy.[13] Lebanese men faced the capitalist market by offering, indeed even
sacrificing, their women on its altar, keeping to themselves the feudal/tra-
ditional ethos they continued to morally valorize. This is the logic that was
made international through migration. Indeed, as Akram Khater points out,
many men thought of migration as a means to maintain their feudal sense
of self: a means to keep control of their land and not slip into the ranks
of the landless laborers.[14] Philip Hitti argues that Syrian (as the Lebanese
were then known) men migrated initially alone, but "before long, however,
the economic value of the woman was discovered. The nature of the work
in which the early Syrians engaged—peddling notions, laces, and under-
garments—lent itself more easily to women workers who had freer access
to homes. No sooner had the Syrian discovered that in the United States
woman was an asset rather than a liability than he began to bring over his
women folks."[15] But, as I am pointing to here and has been shown in detail
by Khater, this "discovery" of the economic value of women was made in
Lebanon before migration even began.

More important for me here, though, I am also arguing that this exploitation of the economic value of women was articulated to a diasporic patriarchal moral economy, through which men avoided splitting themselves
between a modern "capitalist" self, articulated to an instrumental, calculative economy, and a traditional "feudal" self, articulated to honorability and

the home. They did so by splitting the patriarchal family unit as a substitute for the splitting of the self as a unit. Faced with a division that pitted the morally valorized but economically valueless against the morally devalorized but economically valuable, men used their patriarchal power to keep to themselves what they morally valued yet still benefit from the economically valorized. They made the women that they continued to dominate the repositories of this morally devalorized but economically valuable subject position.

In this chapter, I began by arguing that while the notion of ambivalence can account for the person subjected to contradictory diasporic yearnings—such as migrating and staying at home, modernity and tradition, the primacy of economic logic and the primacy of poetry and emotions—it can't account for the many situations in which the diasporic subject inhabits both yearnings and manages to do so by becoming fragmented: "torn into pieces," with each piece occupying a space, rather than torn between spaces. I have shown that this tearing can be sometimes traumatic and sometimes undesirable, and it can lead the diasporic subject to avoid fragmentation or avoid its consequences. Nonetheless, this multiplicity in which the subject occupies more than one space remains an integral dimension of the diasporic condition. But if the inhabitance of a multiplicity of spaces requires us to conceive of a multiple subject, it also requires us to conceive of the possibility of inhabiting multiple realities. It is this conception that I aim to develop in the next chapter.

FIVE

On Diasporic Lenticularity

In the previous chapter, in examining Jo's reaction to being told that she is "the two roads," I noted how she normalized being a person not only in two parts but also in two places at the same time. "When I left Lebanon for the US, I always felt that part of me never left. And now I am here [in Mehj] having a holiday with my mum, but I am also in Vermont," she said. Jo's remarks not only invited me to take seriously the idea of the split subject but also made me face something I already had suspected well before that conversation: when people, in speaking about their or another's migratory experience, make statements such as "I am here, but part of me never left"; "No matter how long I will live here, I will always be there"; "I've tried to tell her that she now lives in Melbourne, but she acts as if she is still in Lebanon," they aren't being as metaphoric as they sound. Nor are they saying that they or the person they're discussing is in one place and thinking about or remembering another. Jo herself explicitly emphasized that she didn't mean something as routine as these circumstances. Immediately after saying that she was both in Lebanon and in Vermont, she stressed, "Not just thinking about Vermont but busy doing things long distance in Vermont." She was clearly highlighting the fact that she remained involved and, in one way or another, present and situated in both places.

Despite many accounts describing circumstances such as these, the dominant idea remains that someone can be situated in only one place at a time while remembering and invoking the other. This idea was also taken for granted when we examined comparative spatiality as a diasporic condition in chapter 3. For instance, it was the matter-of-fact assumption in Jack's account when talking about his wife, Vivianne, comparing the Grand Canyon to Qadisha Valley: Vivianne was situated in the Grand Canyon at that time, and she was remembering Qadisha Valley. Indeed, in his account Vivianne herself used the language of memory, saying, "This reminds me of Qadisha Valley." Thus, while most people would have no problem agreeing that comparative spatiality involves depicting a form of spatial haunting, where the ghost of one place is constantly lurking in another place, there is less agreement as to the ontological status of the ghost.

Undoubtedly, most see in the ghost the product of an invocation of the memory of another place, hence an ideational and affective entity that ends up floating around the place one is actually occupying. "Actually" here clearly refers to some idea of physical relationality and proximity. This chapter argues that the diasporic condition offers us a certain subversion of the matter-of-factness of this actually occupied place/remembered place—that is, an objective/subjective–like opposition—and thus a subversion of the assumed association of situatedness with physical proximity. It invites us to consider the possibility of the invoked and remembered ghostly space being as actually occupied as the place it is haunting, thereby offering us a way to think about multiple inhabitance. Certainly, this is not about the now accepted idea of multilocality associated with the fact that the time-space compression of late modernity has meant that immigrants can keep residences in and move between a multiplicity of places.[1] Multiple inhabitance as I am conceiving it here involves the capacity to experience occupying two places at the same time and being situated in them simultaneously without having to move between them. To understand this experience academically, we need to deepen our understanding of what it means to occupy and be situated in a space or reality. We equally need to see how remembering can itself be a practice and a different mode of occupying space, rather than the opposite of actual practical occupation. By its very nature, it invites us to regard situations such as the above not as the interaction between actually and not actually occupied places but as an entangled multiplicity of differently occupied spaces. Let us first begin by examining what it means to actually occupy a space.

On Being Somewhere

What is a person actually doing—or perhaps, to be more precise, where *are they* actually—when they say something like "I am in place *x*"? Anthropology as a discipline has perhaps more reason than other disciplines to reflect on this question, for its knowledge claims are often place-specific claims of "being there." Yet when introducing a series of articles on the problematic of space in a 1988 issue of *Cultural Anthropology*, Arjun Appadurai had to point out that "more than with any of the other human sciences, anthropology is based on circumstantial evidence. . . . But it is worth noting that the spatial dimension of this circumstantiality has not been thought about very much." He argues that the articles in that issue focus on "one aspect of the problem of space in anthropology, and that is the problem of place, that is, the problem of the culturally defined locations to which ethnographies refer. Such named locations, which often come to be identified with the groups that inhabit them, constitute the landscape of anthropology, in which the privileged locus is the often unnamed location of the ethnographer."[2] But five years later, in the early 1990s, Margaret Rodman was still pointing out that "place is a problem in contemporary anthropological theory. . . . Yet anthropologists who take pains to lead students through the minefields of conceptualizing culture often assume that place is unproblematic. It is simply location. It is where people do things."[3]

One of the issues of interest to us here is that the anthropologist who says "I have done fieldwork in a slum in Jakarta" and the person who says "I am living in São Paulo" are making claims that have a shared problematic. Neither the person who is "in São Paulo" nor the anthropologist doing fieldwork "in a slum in Jakarta" is situated in every single square meter of the space where they say they are. For the anthropologist, this becomes a question of reflecting on the limits of situated knowledge: when I say that I have done fieldwork in space x among people A, how many of people A have I really met, and how much of space x have I really covered?

Wendy's grandmother, Nahiyyeh, is from Mehj. Wendy's mum and Wendy herself were born in Montreal. They all live in that city's Saint-Laurent suburb, which has a substantial Lebanese presence. I meet Wendy in Mehj, and she's telling me that her grandmother doesn't go shopping except to Lebanese grocers, and she buys only Lebanese products. She cooks only Lebanese food and has no desire to speak French, much less English. Everything Nahiyyeh says, Wendy tells me, is mixed with either a reminiscence about or a comparison with things that are happening or have happened in the village in Lebanon. While describing this to me, Wendy says of her grandmother that "she lives in Montreal, but she acts as if she is still in Lebanon." The common way of understanding the distinction that Wendy is trying to convey, and that her own choice of words encourages, is to assume that living in Montreal involves relations of physical proximity, which entail that her grandmother is "really" living in Montreal, while living in Lebanon is a mental illusion, an "as if," brought about by a vivid imagination and a continuous remembrance of Lebanon. But is the difference so clear-cut?

To begin with, let us reiterate the critical question formulated above. Wendy is confident that her grandmother actually lives in Montreal. But how many parts of Montreal does one need to be in a relation of "physical proximity" to, to claim that one "is in Montreal"? Clearly, when one makes such a claim, one is in a relation of physical proximity to some parts of, or particular points in, Montreal, and one is either remembering or assuming the existence of the other parts that one is not in physical contact with. Already, we can see no clear-cut division between places experienced through physical proximity and places experienced through memory. Any actual inhabitance of, any experience of "being in" a place involves a selective physical relationality with some places based on proximity, some form of remembering based on experience (such as previous relations of physical proximity), and some acquired knowledge, which makes one confident of one's situatedness. Crucially, one must experience the parts one is connected to through physical proximity as part of a totality, the totality one ends up claiming to be inhabiting. That is, one must be confident of the metonymic nature of those parts.

But if we turn to Nahiyyeh above, is it really the case that her relation to Lebanon is an illusory inhabitance as opposed to her inhabitance of Montreal? After all, she is having a relation of physical proximity with certain Lebanese things: Lebanese grocer, Lebanese grocery, Lebanese cooking practices. She is also inhabiting the Lebanese language by insisting on speaking it rather than French or English. And sure enough, she is also remembering Lebanon. Yet Wendy doesn't feel as confident taking this combination of physical proximity to Lebanese things and invocation of memories of Lebanon to say that her grandmother is living in Lebanon. She feels compelled to add "as if" for a variety of obvious reasons: chiefly the fact that in her eyes, as it would be in the eyes of most of us, her grandmother has her feet, moves around, relates to people, deals with institutions and institutions deal with her, in Montreal, and Lebanon is thousands of miles away. The function of this "as if" is crucial, as it asserts that those bits of Lebaneseness that her grandmother is having a relation of physical proximity to are in her eyes metaphors rather than metonymies. Metonymies are extensions of the whole of which they are reminders. Metaphors are not: they remind people of a reality without being a part of the reality they are reminding people of. But does Nahiyyeh share Wendy's sense of the metaphoric nature of these Lebanese objects she is relating to? Is it not possible that she might be experiencing them as metonymies, as extensions of Lebanon in Canada, rather than as substitutes/reminders of the real thing? After all, the metaphoric and metonymic functions of things are a highly contentious issue. In the above-mentioned volume of *Cultural Anthropology* introduced by Appadurai, James Fernandez touches on this question.

When we consider the constraints of place upon our work, we should include in that consideration the problem of metonymic misrepresentation,
that is, the way that one place, which is simply a part of a much larger place—
whether a province, a region, or a nation—comes to stand for a whole place,
its particular problems coming to be perceived as the problems of the whole
place. And this is true even though, approaching the problem from another
more conscious perspective, we often cannot agree on a place that will stand
for the whole place. . . . In subsequent discussion it was recognized that given
Spanish provincial diversity it would be difficult to find any place in Spain
that could be admitted to stand for the whole place.[4]

Fernandez helps us see that the metonymic and metaphoric functions are
not straightforward things. But it's not the function of either metaphors or
metonymies to "stand for the whole place." It's enough that they relate and
allude to the place, either ontologically in the case of metonymies or epistemologically in the case of metaphors.

In what follows, I want to investigate the possibility that those groceries
Nahiyyeh is relating to can indeed be metonymic and that in relating to
them she's not acting as if she is in Lebanon but actually inhabiting Lebanon at the same time she is actually inhabiting Montreal. To be clear, let
me reiterate that the point is not to devalue the importance of physical
proximity. Even in the age of WhatsApp and Skype, when an immigrant can
be in continuous communicative contact with his/her family and friends
elsewhere, the yearning for the uniqueness, intimacy, and possibilities of
physical proximity remains an important dimension of the diasporic experience. Nor am I trying to argue that Nahiyyeh is situated in Lebanon
in the same way she is situated in Montreal, where she has been living for
a good forty years, or that the way she is occupying Lebanon is satisfying.
This would be a ridiculous claim. Nonetheless, I hope I do open the reader
to the possibility that she *is* inhabiting Lebanon *at the same time* as she is
inhabiting Montreal, even if not in the same way. My primary aim, then, is
to demonstrate that more than a neat binary opposition between inhabitance and remembrance, the diasporic condition is characterized by multiple
different modes of inhabitance.

In fact, the foregrounding of memory in diasporic studies has worked
in ways similar to the foregrounding of ambivalence described in the previous chapter.[5] Ambivalence allows us to see some things both common and
important, but in doing so, it disallows us from seeing the formation of
"split subjects," something less commonly accepted but of equal importance. In much the same way, the analytics of memory helps us account for

many important diasporic experiences. Yet a temporal bias, a conception of memory as primarily concerned with the past, works to hinder the possibility of considering memory as part of, rather than an alternative to, spatial inhabitance. Nowhere does this temporal imaginary show its limitations as much as in the study of diasporic nostalgia.

Diasporic Nostalgia and the Eurocentric Remembrance of the Past

The yearning for "back home" is considered an integral part of diasporic culture by both folk and academic discourse on migration. In the case of Lebanon, an abundance of mediatic, literary, and poetic production expresses or reflects on how the nation as a whole—or the village, the land one imagines to have left behind, back home—is often steadily yearned for and perceived to be what is lacking in the migratory present. This "back home" is quickly idealized and remembered ideationally as a place of plenitude and well-being, in opposition to the harsh land of migration, where a kind of reality principle prevails. In this sense, at least one dimension of diasporic nostalgia is certainly a variant of what Michael Herzfeld has called "structural nostalgia," a "collective representation of an Edenic order—a time before time—in which the balanced perfection of social relations has not yet suffered the decay that affects everything human."[6] Nostalgia here is the sentiment that some form of change, whether to personal circumstances or to society in general, has led to an experience of loss, whereby what is lost is imagined as more or less "perfect," a situation where particularly intense feelings of homeliness and oneness with the social and physical environment were supposed to prevail.

There is a certain touch of a universalizing claim in this conception of nostalgia. Psychoanalytic theory offers a similarly structured theory of personal development. Here the imagined past state of perfection is the fantasized state of being "fused" with the mother in the womb or on the breast. To come into being as a separate subject involves separating from the mother but also from this state of fusion itself. As such, the psychoanalytic subject is conceived as fundamentally nostalgic, always feeling a sense of loss (lack) and always yearning for that time of child-mother fusion before individualization occurred. But even when we think that claims of psychoanalysis are hardly universal and are far more specific to a certain modern Viennese bourgeois Jewish imaginary, we must deal with the fact that this same imaginary can be found in the monotheistic religious imaginary that predates modernity. Herzfeld's usage of the term *Edenic* perfectly captures this. Indeed, the myth of Eden as it presents itself in the Bible offers us a quintessential and paradigmatic nostalgic narrative involving three moments: imagined state of perfection (Eden), loss (the Fall), desire to recover at least inklings of the lost state (life on earth as the struggle for intimations of Eden) or, better still, to end up in heaven (a sublimated version of Eden).

This universalizing conception of nostalgia as an idealization of a past that never really existed is especially useful to describe diasporic nostalgia when it is grounded in an ongoing experience of disempowerment, in the sense of an experience of an *inability* to do certain things: inability to speak properly, inability to direct oneself, inability to socialize, and so on. This is made clear in the introduction to Hamid Naficy's well-known work, *The Making of Exile Cultures*, where he associates his nostalgic memories of separation from the homeland with "the separation from the native language and the control one has in using it—a control that is gradually diminishing."[7] It is useful to interpret this state of homesickness, from a Bourdieusian perspective, as a state emanating from a dysfunctional habitus—that is, a habitus that finds itself unable to strategize and improvise in the face of a radical newness. Nostalgia here denotes a disability, a sickness, which is indeed referred to as homesickness. It emerges from the unbridgeable fissure opened between the self and the environment when one finds oneself unable to strategize in a Bourdieusian sense. One takes refuge in the idealized memories of the past from the potentially traumatizing encounter with the present. Thus, it is certainly the case that this conception of nostalgic memory has a purchase on an important dimension of the diasporic experience. Yet for all the work it can do, it suffers from some important limitations.

Let us begin by examining a classic case of everyday nostalgic feelings emerging from a position of powerlessness, as recounted by Toufic, a man from Jalleh living in Sydney. He's telling me about an incident that occurred in his early days in Australia.

I had been here for around six months and I was driving back home to Punch-bowl from Liverpool, where I had gone to see the owner of a petrol station who had advertised about a job. I can't remember exactly where now, but it was pretty deserted. And I got this flat tire and I had no spare. I couldn't speak English, not that there were many people driving by. I started walking. Then it got dark, and as I was walking I started to think of myself heading to the village. Sometimes when I returned late to the village from Tripoli, I used to have to take a bus that stopped a fair distance out of the way. So I had to walk the rest of the way home. But invariably, I meet someone I know driving up and they give me a ride. And that's how I began to think of home. I started thinking, "Soon someone I know is going to turn up." I started remembering all the people with whom I took rides. I could even remember the details of their car, the sound of the horn, what they said to me. I got so engrossed by my thoughts that I really thought I was home. And when I heard a car coming, I turned around, hoping it would be . . . for some reason I just thought it was my brother. But it wasn't . . . [*He has a tear in his eye. The story he was telling happened ten years earlier.*] I had to walk all the way home. I arrived home around three o'clock. I couldn't speak with anyone the next morning. [*Sighs*] *Su'bi el'hijra* [Migration is a difficult thing]. I rang my brother and talked with him for an hour afterward, even though using the phone at the time was very expensive. I kept telling him, "I need to go back. I can't stand it here," and he was telling me, "No, you don't need to come back at all. I need to go to Australia."[8]

On one hand, the moment of nostalgia in this narrative presents itself as being like any other nostalgic discourse. Yet there is something about the nature of its remembrance that is both banal and obvious and yet exceptionally important in its difference: it's primarily a memory of another place, not the memory of another time. Even if, as already noted above, there are situations where diasporic nostalgia involves a remembrance primarily about another time, it's nonetheless the case that it is this remembrance of another place that makes for its specificity.[9]

Now, to be clear, most academics working on nostalgia take it for granted that notions of time are closely entangled with notions of space. The past we remember is always a past that happened "somewhere." And it is well known that when immigrants remember the place they come from, they often remember it frozen in the past, where they left it. Indeed, the story of the migrant returning home to realize that things are no longer what they were in the past has mythical dimensions in diasporic culture. Yet there is a certain Eurocentrism in our understanding of nostalgia when this entanglement of time and place is used to iron out the difference between a remembrance primarily centered on another time and one primarily centered on another place. This is because the concept of nostalgia most commonly circulating in Euro-American social theory is heavily shaped by a Western romantic tradition marked by the idea that nostalgia is a remembrance of a past that can never be accessed again. As with Lamartine's famed lament in "Le Lac" as he mourns the passing of his love,

> Why can we not keep some trace at the least?
> Gone wholly? Lost forever in the black?

Will Time that gave them, Time that now elides them
Never once bring them back?

It is because of the irrevocable passing of time that the past can no longer be accessed, and it is this that makes for the pain of the nostalgic moment. As Pickering and Keightley define it, nostalgia in this tradition is the "longing for what is lacking in a changed present . . . a yearning for what is now unattainable, simply because of the irreversibility of time."[10] Herzfeld's perception of nostalgia as referring to a "time before time" continues this temporally leaning conception.

It is precisely in that question of "irreversibility" of time that an important difference between a temporally and a spatially inclined remembrance comes to the fore. For surely, we can't speak of irreversibility in the same way when speaking of remembering another place. This is what the above account by Toufic makes clear. The object of his nostalgia might well be laced with a memory of another time, but because it is primarily that of another place, it is available for access: he accesses it by phoning his brother (today, migrants can also access where they come from through various social media visually, almost continuously, and very cheaply), and he can realistically contemplate visiting it (even if it's constantly changing in time). Indeed, for all we know, he is constantly accessing it at least affectively. But most important for us here, he is also accessing it through the process of remembrance. Memory is an important component of the process of, rather than being a substitute for, inhabitance of place. Lamartine himself in "Le Lac," when confronted with the irreversibility of time, asks the landscape to carry the traces of what is passing so it can remain accessible.

O Lake, caves, silent cliffs and darkling wood,
Whom Time has spared or can restore to light,
Beautiful Nature, let there live at least
The memory of that night

This idea of making the surrounding environment "carry" one's memory brings us to a particularly important dimension of nostalgia. Remembering, even when it is remembering the past, is not a passive state of mind but a variant of Lefebvre's famous "production of space,"[11] a production marked by what is being remembered. That is, when we argued in the case of Nahiyyeh that the inhabitance of particular spaces commences with direct relations based on proximity to some metonymic elements of the landscape, the metonymic function of these elements is not something that can be treated as given. It is itself produced experientially while remembering: space is produced in producing the elements we directly relate to as metonymic.

In his wonderful *The Weight of the Past*, Michael Lambek describes how in Madagascar "the ancestral past permeates present-day Mahajanga and its environs." As he puts it, "Behind gates and fences, in groves on the outskirts and in the distant countryside, at night, in cupboards, in tombs and under wraps, in embodied practices and in moral imagination, lies the past—all the more powerful for remaining discreetly concealed and protected; set apart but immanent."[12] This landscape marked by memory does not just come about simply with the passing of time. It is also an accumulation of a long history of remembering practices that mark themselves on and shape the landscape into what it is. In much the same way, the surrounding landscape becomes marked and shaped through the practices of remembering another place. It is through these productive practices that the landscape becomes a diasporic landscape. In a way, I am arguing that rephrasing Lambek and replacing "the past"/another time with "another place" will give us a pretty good idea of the nature of the diasporic world: Another place permeates the present-day spaces of the diasporic world. "Behind gates and fences, in groves on the outskirts and in the distant countryside, at night, in cupboards, in tombs and under wraps, in embodied practices and in moral imagination," lies another place—"all the more powerful for remaining discreetly concealed and protected; set apart but immanent."

Nostalgia and Producing Diasporic Space

As with all diasporic cultures, nostalgia for the food "from home" has a prominent place within the Lebanese immigrants' daily life. I once asked a young person from Jalleh living in Venezuela if I could see a random selection of email exchanges she's had with her cousins in Australia and the United States. I was curious to see what sort of things they chat about. The emails were in English, and in looking at what she showed me I came across this sentence: "I have to go: the eaters have come back." When I inquired what "the eaters" referred to, I was told it was a nickname for her parents. This apparently began when one of her cousins complained that when she goes to her Venezuelan boyfriend's house, people eat and dance; but when her parents have people visiting, "all they do is eat." And it is indeed the case that the direct relations based on proximity to food (the processes of acquiring ingredients, cooking, and eating) are central to the metonymic construction of inhabited space.

Part of the history of early Lebanese migration is one of deprivation of familiar fruits, vegetables, and other ingredients. One interesting element of this deprivation is the emergence of creative practices of substitution. A man from Jalleh who has lived in Bathurst (a rural town in southeast Australia) since the 1940s tells this story:

> Although some tahini arrived by boat every now and then, we used to go through long periods without it. Sometimes, we used to really crave tahini dishes. Finally, we improvised: either Mum or Dad, I can't remember, probably inspired by the similarity between the texture of peanut butter and that of tahini, decided to grind some of it with garlic and oil, and we used it as a substitute for tahini sauce with a grilled fish. Long after, when tahini became widely available, I used to sometimes crave the peanut sauce!

In this climate, the very encounter with yearned-for fruits and vegetables triggers strong intimations of home. Home food not only evokes security in that it represents a culturally determined basic need for nutrition, it also provides a clear intimation of familiarity in that one knows what to do with it, how to cook it, how to present it, and how to eat it, thus promoting a multitude of homely practices (unlike facing the unknowable: e.g., Salman Rushdie's description of the Indian migrant facing the English kipper in *The Satanic Verses*). Furthermore, food provides a clear focus for practices of communality, especially in terms of collective eating, whether in private or in public spaces. In the following interview, a Lebanese woman from Sydney tells an exceptionally graphic story of the homely intimations triggered by an encounter with Lebanese cucumbers—of which the Australian Lebanese, except for some who managed to successfully grow them in their garden, were deprived until the late seventies.

NAYLA: It was incredible. I was visiting my sister, who lived on the other side of the station. On the way back, I stopped to get some beans for dinner, and here they were . . . I touched them . . . I held them in my hands. They were firm. It was like touching my mother [her mother lived in Lebanon]. Shawki, the shopkeeper, saw me, smiled, and nodded: "Yes, Lebanese farmers are growing them down near Liverpool. No more mushy stuff." That's how we refer to the Australian cucumbers. I bought two kilos, although we were poor then, and they were very expensive. I ate one on the spot in the shop. Adel [her husband] used to say, almost every day, how much he missed the taste of Lebanese cucumbers. When Adel came back from work that day, I made a tomato and cucumber salad with garlic and lemon, because that's what I really felt like, and brought it to the table and said to him, "close your eyes," and I put the plate in front of him. When he opened his eyes, he looked at the plate and it took him a little while to realize what I was making such a fuss about. And then [*laughter*] . . .

ADEL [her husband, *interrupts, laughing*]: No, don't tell him . . . it's very embarrassing.

NAYLA: Yes . . .

INTERVIEWER: Come on, you must tell me, what did he do?

NAYLA [*laughing*]: He got up, he kissed me, and he started dancing and singing something like, *Ya 'ayni 'al khyar* [rough translation: Oh, I love you, cucumbers]!! [*Everyone laughing*] It all sounds so silly now. But the cucumbers really made us happy. It was like reuniting with a close relative.

In the homely scene generated by the cucumbers, we see both the nostalgic sentiments they trigger and how the practices of constructing metonymies of Lebanon—represented above in the making of the salad, which makes the cucumbers yield their potential metonymic homeliness—are at the same time practices of producing Lebanese homely space in Australia. We should note the emphasis on how the cucumbers are imagined to not so much "remind" people of their kin as "reunite" them with these loved ones.

Just as food provides the basis for homely practices within the private sphere, it also provides the basis of practices of Lebanese home-building in the public sphere—fostering intimations of Lebanese homely communality. An article in the *Sydney Morning Herald*, whose coverage of the food scene in Sydney dates to the immediate postwar era, describes the process:[13] "As each wave of immigrants to Australia settled in, little knots of eateries, evocative of the old world, served as meeting places where lonely groups of migrants chatted in their native tongue and recreated the tastes of home."[14] An article in the same newspaper some twenty years earlier describes a more specific process involving the "Ceylonese Tea Centre" in the early seventies: "It isn't surrounded by the neat green slopes of tea bushes—only the roar of Castlereagh Street traffic—but it's the nearest thing to home for the 5,000 or so Ceylonese who live in Sydney. . . . At night, if there is a special occasion, the Ceylonese gather to eat food characteristic of their spice-rich island. . . . The Tea Centre invites Ceylonese wives to cook their favourite dishes for the celebration held at the restaurant."[15]

Although the tradition of public eateries has never been dominant among Lebanese migrants, longtime village clubs continue to provide an alternative. On weekends and on specific occasions, someone's house or a hall is transformed into a "village party." Men and women sit around large bar-becues of grilled meats, chicken, and garlic. Often, the party ends with a *dabkeh* danced to the sound of traditional mountain shepherds' music.[16] Nonetheless, this production of Lebanese homeliness is always entangled with the many things that also give a clear sense of being situated in else-where, from the beer to the "backyard" to the color of the sky.

New Bedford, Massachusetts, 14 August 2005

Today I visited Najeebeh, who migrated with her two children from Mehj to the United States in 1983. Her husband died of a heart attack in Lebanon during the civil war. Her children have moved away from home, and she now lives by herself.

As soon as I enter her apartment through its front door, I face a set of stairs that takes one from left to right up to the second floor. I am immediately struck by two very cozy-looking lounge chairs directly under the stairs. There is a coffee table between them and a picture of Saint Charbel above them on the wall. This space stands out even more when I get into the living room and realize that the furniture there is no-where near as comfortable looking and looked after as the furniture under the stairs.

I can't help asking Najeebeh about that space. "You seem to have looked after that space especially well."

She smiles and she says, "Yes, it brings back my favorite memory of the war in Lebanon. . . . We lived in Ayn el-Remmehneh, and during the bombing the whole family used to sit together under the stairs. Although it was scary at the time, when I remember this, my heart yearns for that moment when we were all cuddled in together. Especially now that my husband is dead, and my children are far from me. When I sit under those stairs, it makes me feel like everyone is still with me. And that I am still in Lebanon."

"You miss Lebanon during the war?!!" I said, astonished.

"I know it sounds funny. I have often thought about that too. But it no longer reminds me of the war. It just reminds me of Lebanon as the land where my family were together . . . as soon as I sit under those stairs, that's where I am taken."

Clearly, Najeebeh is not yearning for the war. She yearns for a sentiment of familial togetherness that she has effectively managed to cut off from the cir-cumstances that produced it. It is that sentiment that she uses to produce her nostalgic space. At one level, the production here of diasporic space through nostalgic remembrance is a variant of what Appadurai called "de-territorialization" and "re-territorialization";[17] but what is re-territorialized is not a culture or an event but a sentiment of homeliness, which is after all what is yearned for in most nostalgic feelings. However, this is not where it all ends.

For the re-territorialization of a Lebanese sentiment in New Bedford is used by Najeebeh to territorialize herself in Lebanon as well. We end up with a re-territorialization that is really a strategy of territorialization. That is, we end up with a space that is not a transformation of, and a substitute for, Lebanese space but a means of continuing to occupy Lebanese space while also being in New Bedford. Well after this interview, I became struck by the fact that at no point did Najeebeh say that sitting under the stairs makes her feel "as if" she is in Lebanon. She simply says that it makes her feel that she is still in Lebanon, and even more, so she says, it "takes her" to Lebanon.

Toward a Conception of Lenticular Reality

I have argued that inhabiting and being situated in a particular spatial reality always involve a series of relations with selected parts/points of our environment that are in a position of physical proximity to us. Forms of remembrance and forms of acquired knowledge allow us to relate metonymically to those nearby points and permit us to see in them an extension of the larger surroundings that we end up seeing ourselves as inhabiting. By rethinking the examples of Nahiyyeh, who is living in Montreal but, in the eyes of her granddaughter, acts "as if" she is living in her village in Lebanon; a man nostalgically evoking the memory of his village and its inhabitants while walking in Sydney; a woman making a Lebanese cucumber salad, also in Sydney; and another woman remembering the sentiment of being together with her family in Lebanon while living in New Bedford, I have shown that these modes of remembering are not cases of "as if in Lebanon" as they might initially seem; that they are not the opposite of actual inhabitance but a different form of inhabitance and situatedness. They share some fundamental similarities with the more matter-of-fact forms of inhabitance that we usually refer to as here as opposed to there, where we are as opposed to where we are not, and these forms are fundamental to diasporic discourse.[18] People like Nahiyyeh circulate in a landscape where, along with the material existence of Montreal, material traces of Lebanon abound. There are, of course, plenty of things around her to relate to that remind her she "is" in Montreal. But, as with the landscape we arrived at earlier by transforming Lambek's text, there are also enough Lebanese things to relate to metonymically to enable her to foster the feeling of being in Lebanon. She lives by inhabiting, and situating herself in, both spatial realities at the same time. We need to think through the significance of this multiple inhabitance.

One reason why it is difficult to analytically come to terms with multiple inhabitance is that, while easily expressed in a mundane way in public discourse, as with Jo's up-front manner of saying she is both in Vermont and in Lebanon, the idea of existing in multiple spaces and realities from a social scientific perspective continues to generate a "you've been smoking too many joints" reaction. At best, we get attempts to translate the idea into something more palatable to commonsense logic: "what you really mean is . . ." But isn't anthropology the discipline supposed to be comfortable facing experiences that make us uncomfortable, yet resisting the desire to translate them and reduce them to something palatable to conventional wisdom? While taking "inhabiting two realities at the same time" at face value is hardly like dealing with shamanic practices, it is nonetheless an invitation to widen our horizon of the meaning of "inhabiting a reality."

Let us begin by noting that we easily accept the idea that we can be in two spatial realities when those realities are superposed on each other but not necessarily coterminous. Thus, if Nahiyyeh while living in Montreal showed herself to be more interested in national Canadian than Quebeçois matters, Wendy would not say of her that she's in Montreal but lives "as if she is in Canada." The idea that one can inhabit a space referred to as Montreal or Quebec and at the same time inhabit another space referred to as Canada does not pose a problem. Nahiyyeh can relate directly to certain things in her proximity that are specifically Quebeçois and are metonymic of Quebec, such as French signs, and to other things that are more generally Canadian and metonymic of Canada as a whole, such as the Canadian flag. Indeed, such a double inhabitance, of occupying both a specific regional and a wider, more general national space, is a common mode of inhabiting nation-states. A dimension of this spatial superposition is akin to what Goffman calls "lamination," where a particular phenomenon is located within two frames, which are imagined here like two layers: the one "laminated" or superposed on top of the other.[19] But while lamination can help us analyze some aspects of the multiple situatedness we are aiming to think through here, it is, however, too epistemologically oriented. Multiple frames are multiple interpretive constructions rather than descriptions of a multiplicity of simultaneously inhabited spaces. Closer to what we are aiming for is Herzfeld's notion of "disemia," which tries to capture two different cultural systems coexisting within the same space. But Herzfeld's account needs a further ontological push to move us from his emphasis on coexisting semiotic systems to coexisting realities.

Because of this need for an ontological direction, a more obvious theoretical orientation here is the multi-realism associated with the ontological turn, not only because it is ontological but also, just as importantly, because it is constructivist. To be clear, while the dimension of the ontological

turn that has circulated most has to do with viewing the world as an entanglement of human and animal ontological perspectives or ecologies, another
part involves pluralizing the human modes of inhabiting the world and the
various coexisting realities that such a multiplicity of human enmeshment
with the environment leads to.[20] A "reality" from this perspective is not that
different from a "practical spatial environment" in that it is the product of a
particular enmeshment with the surrounding environment: multiple realities
are the product of multiple enmeshments, and every enmeshment includes
particular ways of relating to specific points of interest in our proximity.

In the field, I encountered a graphic example that can help us understand
how the production of this multiplicity works in a migratory context.

> *Paul is holding Chafic, his baby son named for his grandfather, in his arms and
> showing me around his new house in Boston. We get to the living room, where Paul
> has some modern furniture along with a large Elvis poster and some Elvis memo-
> rabilia that he, a great fan, got from Graceland. In one corner, however, he has a
> bar built with stones very much like the stones used to build traditional Lebanese
> houses—darker stones depicted an unmistakable Lebanese cedar. On the shelf are
> two* arghilehs *[water pipes], and on the floor next to the bar's entrance is a* jurn
> *[traditional stone mortar]. The whole thing is a festival of Lebaneseness.*
>
> *"If you look on this side, this is all Elvis, this is my America," Paul says. "If you
> look on this side, this is my Lebanon. Look—there's even a photo of the village here."
> At that moment, Chafic emits an unintelligible sound, as if understanding what
> his dad is saying. Paul turns to his son and says in baby talk, "Yes, America and
> Lebanon." Next, he lifts his son and turns him so he faces the room, then swivels
> with him a number of times so he can alternately face the Elvis-saturated part of the
> room and the Lebanese bar, saying, "See? America, Lebanon. America. Lebanon.
> America. Lebanon."*

This illustration takes us some way in exemplifying what I mean by the
creation and inhabitance of multiple spatialities. But, while graphic, it is
in another way very specific, in that the two coexisting inhabited realities it
allows us to see are much too neatly divided: America on the left, Lebanon
on the right. In general, the relational points that form the metonymic basis
for the creation of "Lebanon" and the points of attachment that create the
place where one has migrated to aren't so precisely partitioned.

When I became aware of the nature of the entanglement I was trying to
portray, I started to pay more attention to how various Lebanese objects are
dispersed within the immigrant houses I was visiting, particularly in living
rooms and kitchens where I had access: paintings of Lebanese landscapes,

photos of Lebanon and of kin, religious icons, Lebanese objects of aesthetic or practical value. These are permanent relational points, but there are others, such as accents, aromas, and food, as we saw earlier. In most houses, these are entangled with relational points metonymic of the space in which an individual is more practically situated.

Lena is speaking with me while we sit in her living room in São Paulo. Her daughter looks like her and thus helps situate her in Lebanon, but the daughter also has a very Brazilian accent, which firmly situates Lena in Brazil. The morning cup of Lebanese coffee they drink takes them to Lebanon, while the *pão de queijo* (cheese bread) situates them in Brazil. Thus, Lena can be relating to her daughter's looks, the smell of Lebanese coffee, a photo of her dad, and the Lebanese music playing in the background, all of which work to situate her in Lebanon, while at the same time her daughter's accent, the breakfast cakes, the bills on the table, and the tree outside position her in Brazil. This is not a stable division as in Paul's living room. The relations to her daughters' appearance, Lebanese coffee, and so on form a bundle of relationality that works to create a space metonymically related to Lebanon and situate Lena within that space. But this bundle is continuously intermingled with another that situates her in Brazil. The two spaces don't exist neatly separated from each other but are continuously refracting each other, as if in constant dialogue.

We have come now to the limits of how much ontology, as imagined within anthropology's ontological turn, can help us analyze the phenomenon we are facing. For while ontological perspectivism allows us to account for the plurality of the constructed spaces of inhabitance we are examining, the imaginary of ontology as a stable ecology dominating the ontological turn does less to account for this continuous "flickering between realities that are speaking with each other" that we are dealing with here. What is needed is something akin to Bakhtin's dialogism, which accounts for multiple logics intertwined and speaking with each other within one sentence. For the diasporic condition, we need to account for multiple realities speaking with each other: not dialogism so much as a di-ontologism. It's because of this need that I was attracted to the "lenticular" figure as a way of capturing interconnected flickering multiplicity.

The surfaces of photos printed using lenticular technology can reveal different photos when viewed from different angles. These are the well-known "flip" photos that change when one "flips" them. The flipping changes the angle of vision, which changes the photo being viewed. What's important from our perspective is that these photographic surfaces contain the potential for constituting two different images—or let's call them, to drive home our point, two different photographic realities. It's not one photographic reality that looks different depending on the perspective from which it's being viewed. The angle of vision makes one relate to different points within the total environment comprising the photographic surface, and this relation brings forth from that surface an actual photographic reality already potentially present in it. What's more, these are unstable realities that constantly shift according to the angle of vision (the mode of relationality). Thus, one photo is constantly intruding into the other, dialoguing with it as one is looking at the surface. Multiple inhabitance, a similar lenticularity involving a continuous flickering between existing in Lebanon and in the land where one has migrated, is the mark of diasporic reality, as I have been suggesting.

Lenticularity between the Migratory and the Diasporic

The village of Kfersghab is in the same part of North Lebanon as Jalleh, but further up Mount Lebanon. Many of the village's inhabitants have migrated to Australia. Most of them have settled in Harris Park, a suburb not far from Parramatta, a major city-suburb to the west of Sydney. To get to Harris Park upon arrival at Sydney's airport, one needs to take the long Parramatta Road, which links Sydney to its western suburbs.

At some point in the eighties, someone from Kfersghab pulled a Parramatta Road sign from somewhere along the route and took it to the village, where it was planted at a major intersection there. Since that time, all the villagers, from the moment they are born, have the "Parramatta Rd" sign as part of their village reality. The fact that it's an Australian road sign that has been brought to the village all the way from Australia helps us better understand the nature of a metonymic object, described above. To begin with, the road sign is Australian, not just in that it symbolizes something Australian, but in that it is an actual "bit" of Australia in Lebanon—or better still, an extension of Australia intersecting with/on Lebanese soil. To think of it as a metonymic object is to consider the ontological continuity between it and what it "represents." More than "representing" Australia, then, it *is* the beginning of a road that extends from Kfersghab all the way to Australia. Metaphor and metonymy are not an either/or matter, so the road sign might indeed operate as well as a metaphoric "reminder" of Australia's existence. I have nonetheless been arguing that acknowledging the metonymic dimension and experience of this sign, and many other objects like it, is particularly important when thinking about the diasporic condition.

Diasporic subjects construct through such an object not just a reminder of but the beginning of a road extending all the way to whatever distant spatial reality the object is considered a part. As with the Parramatta Road sign, on one hand, metonymic objects become intrusions of that distant spatial reality into the spatial reality where the subjects are more conventionally, geographically located; on the other, each is also experienced as an opening, a road, and a pointer to those faraway spaces. It is because of this mode of relating to and experiencing these objects that diasporic subjects can occupy and inhabit the distant spaces these objects point to, regardless of how far, geographically speaking, they are from such spaces.

Importantly, each of these objects is related to as the beginning of a road, regardless of whether the road is short or long, whether it is easy to travel on or difficult, and whether the subject has the capacity, such as the physical or monetary means or the necessary legal papers, to embark on such a journey. The fact that not everyone wants to or can take such a road does not make it less of a reality. A road's existence is not predicated on everyone's being able to take it. For an inhabitant of a Lebanese village, the road to the cedars can be blocked by snow, the road to Syria might be dangerous, and the road to Jerusalem is illegal to embark on. This doesn't mean that the villagers don't relate to those roads as roads that take them somewhere. The same goes for the roads that open when relating to metonymic objects.

It should be clear here that I am highlighting the Parramatta Road sign in Kfersghab for mainly heuristic reasons. I am hoping that the fact of its being a road sign has helped me further explain how objects operate as metonymic objects that in turn work to constitute a lenticular reality. Otherwise, the Parramatta Road sign is not different from any other objects that, because of migratory relations, have become part of the Lebanese landscape. I have in mind objects and social phenomena we examined earlier in the book—from accents, names, photos, music, and souvenirs, to villas, medical clinics, and sports venues named after overseas places of migration. All work to make of Lebanon's reality a fundamentally lenticular reality for its diasporic inhabitants.

Here lies another reason I am ending this chapter with the Kfersghab road sign. It helps me operate a geographic displacement of the problematic of diasporic lenticularity. Throughout this chapter, I have introduced and analyzed the lenticular condition mainly with the help of ethnographic material gathered among Lebanese people who have migrated and who are situated in the more conventional geographic sense outside Lebanon. I've shown how these Lebanese relate to Lebanese objects in such a way as to also situate themselves in Lebanon, thus producing various experiences of multi-situatedness and multiple inhabitance around the world. With the road sign in Kfersghab, I am making a point of examining the lenticular problematic as it is experienced by Lebanese villagers situated in the more conventional/geographic sense in Lebanon. Just as there are metonymic objects that help situate Lebanese migrants in Lebanon, regardless of where they are geographically located around the world, there are also metonymic objects that situate resident Lebanese in the world, even when they are geographically located in Lebanon. After all, the latter are part of a lenticular reality that comes into being as a result of transnational migration: people migrate, then return to Lebanon with objects from the lands where they have migrated, and these objects end up being constitutive of the lenticular reality that makes up modern Lebanon. While Lena's lenticular world that we examined above allows her to be situated in Lebanon while being geographically situated in Rio de Janeiro, her mother in Lebanon also experiences a lenticular world: the photo of her granddaughter, born and living in Rio; a little statue of Cristo Redentor (Christ the Redeemer) on top of Mount Corcovado (she knows the name of the mountain, because she visited Rio two years ago); and the Portuguese accent of her son, who has returned from Brazil—but also the television, which she always remembers was bought by remittances from Brazil. All of these work to situate her in Rio at the same time as in her village.

In geographically relocating the lenticular condition in Lebanon, I want to expand on what was the key starting argument of this book: the idea that the diasporic condition develops in Lebanon as the culture of Lebanese capitalist modernity before circulating worldwide as a result of migration. I believe this to be true also of the lenticular condition. Lebanese modernity, in being a diasporic modernity, is a lenticular modernity right from the start, before the migratory movements that globalized it. In this sense, the Parramatta Road sign, while helping us take the problematic of lenticularity geographically to Lebanon, does not take us far enough temporally. To do so, we need to highlight a more primary, pre-migratory lenticular experience. It is the lenticularity that comes into being at the very moment of the Lebanese diasporic subject's formation as a split subject. That we can understand this process of splitting of the subject as something that happens alongside a splitting of reality itself, so to speak, is already prefigured in how we analyzed the split subject as the coming into being of a split or a multiple illusio. For illusio, as Bourdieu invites us to think with it, does not just involve the process of constructing subjects that come into being through their pursuit of what they consider is worthwhile. That pursuit of the worthwhile is also the principle behind constructing the subjects' reality itself. Bourdieu sees illusio as a "principle of relevance, [leading] its owner to discern and distinguish features that are ignored or treated as identical by other principles of construction."[21]

Illusio, then, works as a principle of construction by selecting from a subject's environment what is important and what is not; what is worthy for one to be attached to and what is not; what is to be seen and what is not. As such, it becomes the principle of selecting what exists for the subject and what doesn't. Illusio points the subjects to, and makes them latch onto, what is important and meaningful to them in their surroundings; it is the principle of generation and distribution of the degrees to which the various elements of their surroundings actually matter to them. It directs them toward what exists for them and what doesn't when they are interacting with their environment. In this, it's like the way Jakob von Uexküll in *A Foray into the Worlds of Animals and Humans* famously conceived of the lifeworld's construction based on his experiments with ticks: "Just as a gourmet picks only the raisins out of the cake, the tick only distinguishes butyric acid from among the things in its surroundings. . . . We . . . do not ask how the butyric acid tastes or smells to the tick, but rather, we only register the fact that butyric acid, as biologically significant, becomes a perception mark for the tick. . . . Every subject spins out, like the spider's threads, its relations to certain qualities of things and weaves them into a solid web, which carries its existence."[22]

Perhaps we can say that for Bourdieu, what characterizes the "perception marks" of the human subject is, obviously, not only biological but also social, political, and affective. Further, rather than weaving one solid web, the human subject is always weaving a multiplicity of intermingling solid webs that "carries [his/her] existence." Diasporic reality forcefully highlights this multiplicity to us, making the phenomenon salient enough for us to see and analyze. Split into a seeking self and a home-oriented self, the diasporic subject weaves for these selves a home-oriented and an outwardly oriented reality, a personal construction replicated to become a social structure across and a characteristic of the totality of the Lebanese diasporic landscape inside and outside Lebanon.

The above is important. So far, in exploring Lebanon's diasporic culture at its point of emergence, I have examined what I am calling the internationalization of the space of viability, the permanent state of anisogamic comparative spatiality, and perhaps most important, the splitting of the diasporic subject into propelled-into-the-world and home-oriented fragments. I have shown these to be integral dimensions of the modern diasporic condition. All of them, however, describe and analyze diasporic conditions of subjecthood—that is, modes of being of the diasporic subject. To say that lenticularity is above all a mode of being of the totality of the Lebanese landscape is to highlight the fact that with it, we are dealing with something different from what we examined previously. We move from the analysis of the diasporic subject to a characterization of the subject's total diasporic reality, which also includes this subject. That is, we shift from analyzing the characteristics of persons and groups to analyzing the attributes of the milieu, or the lifeworld in which they are situated—which also means: of which they are constitutive components. In this sense, it can be said that the lenticular condition is the most encompassing of all in defining the modern diasporic condition we are analyzing. While an internationalization of the space of viability, or comparative consciousness, or even the split subject can exist on its own, lenticular reality can only exist insofar as it comprises all of these. Just as importantly, to think with the lenticular is an invitation to see, in all those subject "modes of being" we have examined so far, a cor-responding state of reality.

Lenticularity, then, is above all an ontological condition. Perhaps we can paraphrase the famous Maurice Godelier pronouncement about the nature of ideology to say that whatever the subject is, that subject is a mark of the reality that he or she is inhabiting.[23] For example, if the diasporic subject is ambivalent, it is because that person is inhabiting an ambivalent real-ity; if the subject is fragmented, it is because that person is inhabiting a fragmented reality. Diasporic subjects' ambivalence or fragmentation is a mark of their appreciation of the lenticular reality they inhabit and are part of, rather than simply some psychological traits that make them hesitant or fragmented subjects. In the next chapter, we will examine the significance of this ontological perspective on the anisogamic condition that we examined in chapter 3.

SIX

Lenticular Realities
and Anisogamic Intensifications

Diasporic anisogamy, as we examined it in chapter 3, is foundational to the diasporic condition. It involves a primal experience of loss and injury: a sense that the mere fact of being driven toward migration involves entering a relation of reciprocity with another people deemed superior—not in a modern racist hierarchical sense, but because unlike those propelled to leave their country, these people have precisely been kept in the fold by theirs. As I argued, this sense of belonging to "a country that lets go of its children because it cannot care for them" leads to strategies of compensatory valorization of one's country of origin long before people migrate. This is because the diasporic condition positions one comparatively in, and in a reciprocal relation with, the world from the time of one's birth—entailed by what I called "the internationalization of the space of viability."

To consider this anisogamy in conjunction with diasporic lenticularity is to note, first, that since lenticularity arises at the very moment of the fragmented diasporic subject's emergence, the multi-situatedness and multiple realities at its heart are anisogamically structured; and second, that anisogamy is not merely a process of differential valorization of cultures but also a process of differential situatedness and dwelling in a multiplicity of realities. That is, it is not simply about having a high opinion of the value of one culture over another but rather about a process of inhabiting one reality such as to make it more ontologically important than another.

With a little stretch of the imagination, I found it useful to think of anisogamic lenticularity as a temporally condensed version of Marcel Mauss's analysis of "double morphology" in Eskimo society.[1] Double morphology describes societies that have two different spaces of inhabitance. Usually, those are seasonal: one for summer and one for winter. What is also interesting is that many aspects of such societies change with the change of residence. If they are authoritarian and hierarchical when inhabiting their winter residence, they become permissive and egalitarian when inhabiting their summer residence. One can think of diaspora's anisogamic lenticularity as having such distinctive spaces: the affectively and intellectually satisfying space of home and the existentially driven space of financial pursuit. Except in our case, the inhabitance of these two spaces is not seasonal but simultaneous.

In the previous chapter, Nahiyyeh's multi-situatedness and her opting to live in one reality more than in another offered us a classic example of an anisogamic lenticularity. Valorizing her attachment to the Lebanese grocers, food, and language more than other things around her in Montreal, such that she appears to her granddaughter "as if" she is living in Lebanon more than in Montreal, is anisogamic. This became clear when I started chatting with her about her migratory trajectory. Nahiyyeh said:

> Maurice [her husband] wanted to come here, I never did. It's true that we were not financially well-off and we became much better off when we migrated, but I was happy in Lebanon. I was part of the first women's book club in the village. We used to meet and discuss all kinds of books. It remains the nicest thing I've ever done. All the time, people around us are going on about how lucky we are to live in Montreal. I never thought of myself lucky, and I disliked the superior looks the people of this country [*ahl hal balad*] gave us. I always thought: if only I could go back and relive those times. I always felt and I still feel a warmth take over my body when I think of those times. I used to hold on to this warmth especially in winter and look at the snow around me and say, "Why on earth am I here?" My sister used to make fun of me when I used to describe this warmth to her. She used to say, "Nahiyyeh is the only one who can walk the streets of Montreal in winter without a coat, because she gets warm just thinking about Lebanon."
>
> When we migrated, I stopped reading books. I started working in the shop with Maurice instead. I was too exhausted to read books by the end of the day, and I lost the habit for a while, but I never forgot how nice it felt to read a book. So when we finally retired, I started reading books again. I read a lot of Lebanese novels. Some of them, like the novels of Jabbour Douaihy, take me back to where I lived between Zgharta and Tripoli. . . .
>
> We don't have the shop anymore, and Maurice is now dead. I could go back and die in Lebanon, but I have children and grandchildren here. I am here for them. If it weren't for the fact that I'd miss my family more than I miss my country, I'd go back to Lebanon today, not tomorrow. What more is there to say?

Nahiyyeh's discourse contains oppositions inspired by a logic of anisogamic reciprocity under the negatively experienced gaze of *ahl hal balad* (the locals): sure, Montreal offers money, but Lebanon offers warmth; sure, Montreal offers work, but Lebanon offers literature—in this, she replicates the drama of Georges (chapter 4), who by migrating had to leave his desire for poetry and Gibran Khalil Gibran behind. But what's important to us here, and what I began highlighting above, is that this anisogamic logic is not simply about "talking up" Lebanon and "talking down" Montreal. Nahiyyeh's valorization leads her to dwell in Lebanon more than in Montreal, even if geographically she is in Montreal. In the process, Lebanon as a reality in which she is situated and that she is, in her own way, inhabiting and constructing takes on a greater significance. While lenticularity involves dwelling in a multiplicity of realities, these realities are not equally real, so to speak. Some are made more real than others, and physical proximity is not necessarily what makes them more real. What does this mean?

Strategic Lenticularity

In developing his conceptualization of illusio, Bourdieu connects it to what he calls "social gravity." In doing so, he plays on two meanings associated with *gravity*. The first has to do with gravity as seriousness: the stronger our belief in our life pursuits, the more we take them gravely/seriously. The second has to do with gravity as a force: the more serious we are about these pursuits, the stronger our attachment to them. This meaning includes not only how we become affectively attracted to our life pursuits but also how they, in turn, "suck us in," precisely in the way gravity does. It's this gravity that plays the important role of intensifying and making some realities "more real" than others. Thus, by being the principle behind social gravity, illusio is not only the principle behind what we "pick" and choose from reality—it's also the principle behind the variation in intensity in how we relate to what we chose. This is because, as we saw in the previous chapter, illusio invites us to see in those metonymic objects that we relate to in constructing reality not just different national "road signs" but also points of affective attachment. Our connection to these different points varies according to the variation in our attachment. In the process, we connect to objects with different intensities, which in turn gives reality itself different intensities. Intensity here, then, is not necessarily about proximity and physical impact, although it can also be those things. An intensely experienced reality is not the same as a "hard-hitting" reality. Intensity as understood from the lens of gravity has more to do with how much a reality is involving and affecting. The effect of a factory machine or a city street can be very strong on a migrant worker from a rural background, but we can't say that she necessarily experiences them intensely just because of their strong effect. An intense reality is primarily an intense relation in which the person's attachment to and involvement in reality are the main generators of the intensity.

Accordingly, along with a principle of selection/rejection of environmental elements like that of Jakob von Uexküll, Bourdieu offers us a conception of reality construction that includes a principle of intensification and de-intensification. We end up with a more complex conception of lenticular realities. A lenticular reality is not only a reality made of many intersecting different realities. It's also a multiplicity of realities that differ in terms of intensity. That is, it invites us to see the diasporic subject as being not only at the intersection of multiple realities but also at the intersection of realities of varied intensities. It's not that I am situated in Lebanon and Brazil and I keep being located interchangeably in both. The intensity of how Lebanon and Brazil are present to me also changes.

Along with inviting us to see lenticularity in terms of differential intensities, illusio, as all Bourdieusian categories do, invites us to see these intensities not simply as constructed but as strategically constructed: that is, we don't simply find ourselves in a lenticular reality comprising different realities with different intensities; there are willful politics of intensification concerned with which reality is, and which isn't, intensified. These politics can even extend to which reality exists and which reality vanishes, what Bourdieu calls the politics of "making and unmaking reality," as when a would-be immigrant looks at the Lebanese reality around him or her and tells me, "There is nothing here." It can be said that anisogamic intensifications begin from the very genesis of diasporic subjects, with their dual propelled-into-the-world and homely illusios. For, given the reality-making propensity of the illusio, this means that diasporic subjects find themselves amid a lenticularly intersecting propelled-into-the-world reality and a homely reality. The game of intensification begins at the very moment these two realities are formed. Indeed, the very question of whether to migrate becomes an anisogamic game of intensification and de-intensification, whereby home and the world come to the fore or recede according to one's fluctuating desire about whether to migrate.

Let us return to the case of Jameel, with whom we examined the foundational split of the diasporic subject in chapter 4. As we left him in the opening of that chapter, Jameel was preparing to migrate to Australia the next day. After years of telling me that there was "nothing here," meaning in his village of Jalleh, Jameel was suddenly acting as if a reality which hadn't existed for him for a long time had suddenly come into being. Not only had home reality come to the fore, but he was also mourning leaving it, expressing doubt at his farewell dinner party as to whether he should leave. He was looking nostalgically at his parents and his friends, and his nostalgia was already anisogamic and lenticular.

A dimension of this nostalgia can be explained by the fact that when diasporic subjects are about to migrate, propelled by their migratory illusio in the way we have seen, they often become located in the future and look at the present from the viewpoint of a time soon to come. I've heard one person actually say about his cousin who was about to migrate and who looked like he was daydreaming: *"Khalas. Shee enno ba'do hoan. Tlatt rbe'o saar be Amehrka"* (That's it. He's only minimally here. Three-quarters of him are already in America). But there is more to this.

It is also clear that during that process, Jameel was engaging in a classic game of strategic intensification of Australia and de-intensification of home. He was initially so focused on and consumed by his desire to leave Jalleh that this desire became the principle of classification and construction of reality: everything and everyone around him became, practically and emotionally, either something that helped him leave or something that hindered that effort, as when the migratory subject is still feverishly trying to get a visa and says "there is nothing here." Among other things, "there is nothing here" indicates that the subject can't afford to see anything here. In other words, the subject can't afford to be attached to anything here. The reason is that anything one gets attached to comes into existence. And everything the would-be immigrant becomes attached to enough to bring into existence "here" is perceived as getting in the way of the desire to get "there."

While all the above is true, it would also be true to say that the repressed homely reality, the feelings that "there is really something here" and that "the people around me are important to me," was never totally absent from Jameel's world. On the odd occasion, I had noted the intensity with which he embraced his mother after applying for a visa. It was clear, given the context of the embrace, that it was not just about seeking comfort while awaiting the application's outcome. In my field notes following a previous visa application (unsuccessful, though I wrongly presumed it would work out), I had noted:

Jameel must be confident that he will get his visa this time. He embraced his mother as if it were for the last time this morning. It was after he commented on how nice his mother's homemade goat labneh *was, and she replied, "Enjoy it; soon you'll only be having Australian breakfasts made by Chantelle."*

Chantelle is her Anglo-Australian sister-in-law; it had been taken for granted that if Jameel succeeded in going to Australia, he would initially live with his maternal uncle, as indeed he was planning to do now. The interplay between the breakfast of the mother and the breakfast of Chantelle shows that an anisogamic logic, grounded, as we have seen, in the opposition mothered by Lebanon/mothered by a foreign adopted mother, is continually hovering over the unfolding of the migratory process.

Once he obtained the visa he was seeking—that is, the capacity to leave Lebanon—Jameel had more room to be openly attached to what surrounded him. Like Raymond with his Canadian passport in the drawer (chapter 1), the visa in Jameel's hand already transformed the Lebanese space he had been inhabiting. It was no longer the prison he'd experienced it to be ever since his desire for migration emerged and began intensifying. Now that he acquired the capacity to leave, the people around him were no longer a reminder of his sense of imprisonment.

For the person eagerly awaiting yet failing to obtain a visa, a key reason home is felt to be unhomely is because it becomes experienced as a claustrophobic, suffocating enclosure. It's not surprising that the moment one gets a visa, home recovers some of its lost homeliness reasonably quickly. We can miss this moment's significance if, as argued in chapter 4, we fail to grasp the intrinsic importance of a sense of openness and opportunity as an integral component of the homely recipe.[2] As noted, when a person desires to leave a place and is unable to do so, the place and the people inhabiting it are looked at increasingly aggressively. They are fantasized as being in the way, if not actively stopping one from leaving. At the very least, they are a simple reminder of one's state of "stuckedness"[3] and inability to engage in existential and physical mobility. But the moment a person realizes that she can leave, those same people and places are suddenly looked at nostalgically, literally in a split second—with the added guilt of the about-to-migrate subject recognizing that she has been unfairly directing all her past aggression at her current surroundings. More fundamentally, then, the visa allows the about-to-migrate subject, who yearns to be propelled into the world, to reconnect with the non-migrant subject, who yearns for homeliness and kinship. For in a way, the essence of diasporic nostalgia is there: it is the propelled-into-the-world subject yearning for the homely subject it is constantly leaving behind.

So far in this chapter, I have aimed to highlight how the anisogamic processes of strategic intensification and de-intensification of a lenticular reality mark diasporic culture right from the start. In addition, I have highlighted that anisogamy and lenticular reality do not mean that diasporic subjects always intensify homely culture at the expense of the non-Lebanese cultures they are oriented to or that they have settled in. What is intensified and what is de-intensified vary from one setting to another and from one person to another, depending on several sociological variables. In what follows, I examine how this variation happens in the way people relate to news items about Lebanon.

The Intensity of the News

In *Sentiments filiaux d'un parricide*, Proust refers to what he qualifies as "the abominable, voluptuous act called 'reading the paper.'" Here was a practice, he writes, "whereby all the misfortunes and cataclysms suffered by the universe in the last twenty-four hours," from "battles which have cost the lives of fifty thousand men" to murders, bankruptcies, and divorces, are all "transmuted into a morning feast for our personal entertainment," making "an excellent and particularly bracing accompaniment to a few mouthfuls of café au lait."[4] Commenting on this text, Bourdieu sees it as the "the aesthete's variant" of the practice of reading the newspaper. It's not that there is something wrong with such a mode of reading the paper but more the fact that it's a very particular mode: such a "mediated, relatively abstract experience of the social world supplied by newspaper reading" is a variant of what he critically refers to as the detached, "scholastic" mode of interacting with the world. Instead, as his whole conception of practice implies, people have a variety of interests in reading newspaper items, "from the detachment depicted in Proust's text to the activist's outrage or enthusiasm." Thus, the various forms of attachment to the news make for a far more affective and affecting reading than the kind Proust is talking about. These forms of attachment vary, for example, as a function of whether the item is a piece of local news or international news. They will also depend on variations in social distance to the news, such as differences in the degree of political commitment.[5] While not dealing specifically with migrant subjects, Bourdieu's questions concerning the social and affective distance and the mode of attachment to the news take us right into the heart of the problematic of lenticularity and anisogamy that we have been developing here.

Indeed, very early in my research, and before having access to the language of lenticularity and anisogamy, I developed a keen interest in how the practice of reading/listening to/watching the news about *el blaad* (the homeland) emerged as an important element in Lebanese everyday life. My ethnographic observations of reading newspaper articles about Lebanon that I use here had been made before the advent of widespread internet and social media use, so reading newspapers was a far more important practice then than it is now. Nonetheless, as will be clear, the reflections elicited by the ethnographic material remain pertinent and apply well beyond the specificity of reading newspapers.

My first observations were recorded in 1990, the year, we now know, that the Lebanese Civil War ended. The war's intensity was still felt, and as it looked as though it had ended many times before, whether the war had "really" ended was unclear at the time. Consequently, news about Lebanon was something people yearned for and awaited, sometimes with great eagerness. As Bourdieu intimates, news about Lebanon being read by Lebanese diasporic subjects was hardly ever a passive experience. No one I encountered at the time read such news as "entertainment" with either their café au lait or their morning Lebanese coffee.

Lebanese people were clearly affected by the news, but just as clearly, they were affected by it in various ways and to differing degrees. It is in this context that the pertinence of Bourdieu's comments became particularly clear to me. Here was "news" from which people were equally distant as far as the physical Sydney-Beirut distance was concerned, yet clearly unequally "distant" as far as the social distance that separated them from it was concerned. That is, they experienced it with various degrees of gravity, hence various degrees of intensity. These degrees of intensity and gravity varied because people were differentially implicated by it.[6] As I will detail below, consuming news about Lebanon is a particular mode of inhabiting Lebanon. It is these two related ideas of the differential modes of being implicated by the news and the intensity with which one experiences the news in which one is implicated that I want to develop here. At that point, our understanding of lenticular realities and anisogamic intensification will be furthered.

Lebanese News and News about Lebanon

As with any migratory culture, news of family and friends as well as of the political situation in Lebanon is essential in sustaining the lives of Lebanese immigrants still affectively, socially, and sometimes economically connected to their home country. News items are subjects of discussion and sometimes of intense arguments, operating as classic triggers of nostalgic feelings. While for some, this news merely represents what is happening in Lebanon, there is no doubt that many relate to this news as being not merely "about Lebanon" but also a part or extension of Lebanon. Listening to the news can sustain a feeling in the listener that he hasn't totally left his home country, so he feels implicated by what is happening there.

In the early 1990s, when social media was hardly ubiquitous, local news of kin and friends was communicated in personal correspondence, while news about the political situation and other general social issues was communicated publicly by the media. Although there were several radio stations that people often listened to as well as various televised broadcasts in Arabic, my research was chiefly concerned with print media.

A newspaper article can be read metaphorically, as conveying a representation of, "news about," its subject matter, or metonymically, as "news emanating from," something that is part of, its subject matter. Whether the reader relates to the news item as predominantly metaphoric or more metonymic depends on the reading subject. But, as with other relational objects, reading the news about Lebanon metonymically is prevalent among the country's migrant diasporic subjects. It contributes to situating them in Lebanon rather than simply to "remembering" Lebanon—though, as argued in chapter 5, metaphor and metonymy are not an either/or matter. A relation to an object can fluctuate between the two or be both at the same time. There is another layer of complexity when dealing with news items, for it's nonetheless the case that the manner in which such items are materially presented makes them inherently more metaphoric or more metonymic. Each presentation style has a different implicating potential.

There are three types of newspapers from which news about Lebanon can be obtained: the mainstream Australian newspapers—that is, English-language local (national or regional) papers; the Australian Lebanese newspapers, typically Arabic-language papers produced in Australia; and the Lebanese newspapers printed in Lebanon.

News items about Lebanon read from the mainstream Australian newspapers are far more suitable for metaphoric consumption. Even though they still have the capacity to have a metonymic function, normally they're experienced by the Lebanese diasporic subject as alienating, even when nonetheless welcomed because of a scarcity of information about Lebanon in Australia. Such items are typically in the newspaper's world section. They are clearly intended for non-Lebanese; the very mode of reporting is by non-Lebanese for non-Lebanese. That this news is communicated in English on a page where many other items of world news are printed situates the reader in Australia, emphasizing the distance between the reader and the event being reported. Typical complaints by the Lebanese at the time of my research were that Australian newspapers "only have a news item on Lebanon when there is a bomb" or "since the war ended, Lebanon has become less interesting for them." Such negative reactions are often part of the endless politics of recognition structuring the migrant's presence in the host society. Thus, a question such as "Did you see the article on Lebanon in the *Sydney Morning Herald*?" is less an urging to read such news for its content and more a celebration of a moment of recognition by the dominant culture. This implicates the Lebanese reader in an Australian rather than a Lebanese reality, heightening the distancing effect of the news item.

News items in the Australian Lebanese papers function differently. Each has a greater potential to operate metonymically as a fragment of an imaginary Lebanon and as such brings readers closer to, or situates them in, the event being reported. The use of the Arabic language, the assumed knowledge of certain basics (there are no distancing statements such as "Prime Minister Hariri, the wealthy businessman who has been in power since . . . ," as found in non-Lebanese newspapers), and the fact that the Lebanese are the clear addressees of the text all work to create a feeling of continuity between the event and its reporting, along with a feeling of an imagined community between the reported event and the reader in Benedict Anderson's sense.[7] These feelings are especially pertinent since increasingly, the news item about Lebanon in the Australian Lebanese newspaper is nothing other than the reproduction, under a special agreement, of the same item appearing in Lebanon in one of that country's dailies, sometimes on the same day.

Even so, the Lebanese in Australia express a clear preference for reading the same text from the original Lebanese paper that produced it, because the paper is taken as a metonymic part of Lebanon. Another reason for this preference, taking us further into the complexity of the metaphor/metonymy classification, is that the Lebanese paper as a whole is a metaphor for Lebanon. That is, paradoxical as this might seem at first, it is because it is a metaphor that it can be so powerfully metonymic. This is due to the nature of the totality of the newspaper as a collection of texts, which takes us to an important aspect of reading.

What makes the same news item more popular in its "original" setting in a Lebanese newspaper from Lebanon is the context in which it is presented: how it stands in relation to the set of other items printed next to it in the newspaper. Though the article in the Australian Lebanese paper might be the same, it appears on a page next to an ad for a Lebanese bakery in an Australian suburb and an article about an Australian-Lebanese Liberal Party fund-raiser in Melbourne. The totality of what is on the page is a series of items that reproduce metaphorically Australian space but in the process also situate the reader metonymically in Australia, despite the article itself being about and from Lebanon.

Therefore, the availability of a constant flow of information notwithstanding, a person arriving from Lebanon is often quickly asked for a Lebanese paper, even if the news in it is usually two or three days old. The reading of a news item in this paper is a totally Lebanese experience, where belonging to the Australian physical space becomes immaterial and suspended. This newspaper doesn't just offer a genuinely Lebanese perspective on a topic; it positions the reader in Lebanon. As one is reading about the events of the day on page 2, next to the news item is an ad for a home decoration expo in a Beirut suburb. A woman reading the paper in Australia will turn to her husband and say, "ABC is having a sale," and he will nod. One can even read about what is happening in Australia as perceived in/from Lebanon. It is in this process that the Lebanese newspaper works metaphorically—in that the totality of the relations among its different articles becomes a metaphor for the totality of the relations constituting Lebanon as an imaginary nation—to allow the paper to work metonymically in situating and even transporting the reader in/to Lebanon. Through it, one manages to experience what Anderson refers to as unisonance at a distance.[8] One shares the "national" perspective, and in the process the distance between the report and the news event is seemingly abolished. In reading the newspaper, one doesn't read about the nation, one reads the nation.

What is clear from the above is that when reading a newspaper article, one doesn't relate just to the article being read. Readers at every moment are reading the whole newspaper as a system of relations among different news items, ads, announcements, and so on. This system of relations, as I have suggested, already positions the reader at a specific distance from the reported events and allows (but doesn't necessitate) him or her to experience them with greater intensity, depending on the extent of the personal investment in and attachment to such events.

But just because there is an inherent distance from the event and a mode of being situated in the event that is inherently facilitated by each type of newspaper, this doesn't mean that the reader passively accepts whatever intensity is being communicated by a paper. Readers are themselves capable of relating to news items in specific ways to vary their intensity. This is where we arrive at what I have referred to as strategic intensification.

Strategies of Intensification

Let me begin with two short ethnographic accounts.

I am watching Maurice reading the paper. He's sitting on a chair behind the counter of his dry cleaning business, which is located on the ground floor of his family home in Dulwich Hill, Sydney. For the last hour, every time there haven't been customers around, he has pulled the Australian Lebanese paper from under the counter and read. He knows I am "studying" his family. We're distantly related, and he's become used to me sitting in the corner of his shop, reading a book or scribbling in my notebook.

Maurice migrated from Jalleh to Australia twelve years ago. His wife is also from Jalleh, but they married in Australia ten years ago. When he first settled in Sydney, he worked for Australia Post. He bought the dry cleaning business the same year he married. He thinks the business is "slow," but he's been saying this ever since he bought it. Nevertheless, he's clearly not doing very well financially. His livelihood doesn't allow him to put his kids in a Catholic school as he would have liked.

Sometimes, Maurice gets to read the paper for one minute, sometimes for two or three. This time it's been more than five minutes since a customer came in, and he's become quite absorbed in his reading. He's also becoming visibly agitated, moving about on his stool.

"Yeh'rek deenak akhroot!" he mutters. He slaps the paper with the back of his hand. "Eh akeed! Lawayn baddak trooh? 'a Sooriyya! 'Tfehh 'alayk shoo wahteh." He looks at me. "Lebanon is finished," he tells me in Arabic. "If I was in Lebanon, I would spit on every single politician. Put this in your study," he jokes. Maurice was reading about the Lebanese prime minister going to Syria to consult with the Syrian government about the coming Lebanese elections. Like many Maronites, Maurice resents the way, since the civil war has ended, that Lebanese politicians have become dependent on Syria for running Lebanese affairs. His comments take the form of a direct conversation with the prime minister: "Of course! Where else are you gonna go? To Syria! Shame on you, you lowly thing."

During that period of my research, I had become quite interested in the mutterings and the bodily movements that accompanied Maurice's newspaper readings, already conceiving them as "strategies of intensification" although I wasn't working with a theory of lenticular reality.[9] If the news has an inherently implicating effect depending on where it is printed and how it is produced and distributed, readers also clearly have enough agency to further implicate themselves more or less in the news, hence to intensify themselves as a metonymic reality. People can intensify the news and the reality of which it is part in various ways. They can do so by being more attentive, by asking people around them to be silent, by how much time they dwell on the article they are reading, and many other strategies.

The act of slapping the paper with the back of the hand is quite common but hardly unique to immigrants. Lebanese people interact this way with their reading material even in Lebanon. In doing so, they could be bridging a symbolic distance and a sense of alienation and helplessness in relation to political processes they feel unable to really control. So intensification isn't specifically a migrant thing. What gives it its migrant specificity is that it's an intensification that aims to bridge a geographic distance. What gives it its diasporic specificity, meanwhile, in line with our argument that diasporic subjects aren't necessarily migrant subjects, is its articulation of an aniso-gamic dynamic. This is made clear in an interaction I recorded two months after Maurice's slapping of his newspaper.

> It's lunchtime on Sunday. Maurice's brother, Lucien, a reasonably successful business-man, is visiting, and so is Maurice's Lebanese next-door neighbor, Raymond, who runs the corner store. Both men have come with their families. The lunch is almost a ritual, with the same people gathering in Maurice's backyard monthly and sometimes fort-nightly.
>
> After lunch, Maurice is sitting on the lunch table, having a coffee and reading the Australian Lebanese paper. Others are also having coffee, chatting with each other, or playing with kids. Maurice starts muttering, "Yeh'rek deenak akroot! [Damn you!]" He turns to Raymond. "Did you read this!? It says that Assad [Syria's president] expressed to Hraoui [Lebanon's president at the time] his displeasure with the infighting within the government. And now where is Hariri gone? 'a Sooriyya!!"
>
> Lucien's wife, Amal, looks smilingly at Maurice and says, "I don't know why you get so worked up about it. They obviously can't govern on their own. Maybe we should be thankful that the Syrians are intervening; otherwise, they'll spend their time fighting each other and nothing gets done."
>
> "Listen to her! Well, why doesn't Assad declare himself the president of Lebanon and forget about this masquerade."
>
> Raymond nods in agreement. "This way it will become clear who is ruling us. Maybe then people will wake up to what is happening and start resisting."
>
> Lucien shakes his head: "You're eager for a new war, are you?"
>
> "Anything is better than this."
>
> "Maybe you've forgotten what it was like."
>
> Maurice folds the newspaper and slaps it on the table. "Oh, you get off it, Lu-cien! You don't really care anymore what happens there! What was it like? It was better than what it has become like now. Everyone is getting poor now, and the Syr-ians are stealing everything."
>
> Raymond agrees. "I'd rather fight than allow this situation to go on. At least, we need to get rid of this lousy government."
>
> "If I was in Lebanon, I would spit on them one by one," Maurice exclaims.

Lebanese immigrants discussing the news about Lebanon during the war and soon after hardly ever discussed it with people from "the opposite side" of the Lebanese sectarian and political divide. Most arguments, such as the above, are what discourse analysts refer to as pseudo-arguments. Arguing over the news is a strategy of intensification in continuity with practices like slapping the newspaper with one's hand, slapping it on the table, shouting at it, and so on. Indeed, in examining the above segment one is of course struck by the marked correspondence between Maurice's utterings on the two occasions. In a sense, it's irrelevant whether he is talking to himself or "having an argument." Or, to put it differently, we can say that the argument is merely a means for Maurice to use his personal technique of intensifying the implicating nature of the news and his situatedness within a Lebanese reality.

In the above, one might think that the reason for wanting to be implicated in such a way is evident: Lebanese migrants feel "distant" from events occurring in Lebanon, and their strategies of intensification are part of a wider range of strategies in which they try to deal with this geographic distance. This is clearly demonstrated in Maurice's direct expression of such a desire for proximity—"if I was in Lebanon"—and in how he turns his comments about the prime minister into a direct conversational mode as if he were right "there" with him. But, as the above shows, such a desire is not equally felt among diasporic subjects.

Indeed, the "argument" above stages two sides and "opposing parties," Lucien and Amal versus the rest of the gathering. What differentiates the two sides is precisely an unequal wish to intensify the news event and be implicated by it. This is evident from the degree of affect, and one is tempted to say "objectivity," characterizing the statements of each side. Lucien's and Amal's comments appear far more reasonable and detached than the highly charged "let's have a war again" discourse of the others. Maurice's comments and mutterings are infused with affect made clear by his very bodily demeanor while interacting with the news item. His affect is also made clear by his choice of words, his swearing, and his metaphors ("Damn you!"; "I would spit on them"). Maurice's exclamation to his brother reveals to us what is perceived to be at stake throughout the process of intensification: "You don't really care anymore what happens there!"

For the person engaging in intensification, the wish to be affectively implicated by the news event is perceived as being the result of caring. For Maurice, caring is thinking that what's happening in Lebanon is important and is worthwhile being part of. It's possessing what I have called a homely illusio. In the context of the highly conflictual space of Lebanese politics, which demand that one take the side of one's community, detached observations become constructed by Maurice as an indication of not caring.

A subjective relation is established therefore between various elements mentioned above: caring, illusio, being implicated, intensity of reality, inhabiting reality. To care about a reality is to share in the illusio that it's worthwhile being part of it or being implicated in it; and the more one becomes implicated in a reality, the more one feels it intensely. This is, at least, how the wish to be more implicated by the news is experienced by those intensifying it. The question I have asked, however, remains to be answered: why do some people care and want such an intensity more than others? To answer this question takes us into anisogamic territory. As I will argue, strategies of intensity are strategies of managing conflicting belonging, opting for one or another according to an anisogamic logic.

Anisogamic Logics: Migration, Guilt, and the State of the Debt

One of the most important theories linking the degrees of being implicated by reality with the intensity of this reality is Marx's theory of alienation. Marx conceives our implication in social reality in general along the model of, and as causally related to, our implication in production. For participation in society to be a genuine participation—that is, for it to generate for the participant a feeling of being part of society and implicated by it—the participant must feel in control of the process of production (not only of goods but also of the total social reality encompassed by the production process). Among its many important facets, Marx's theory of alienation is precisely a theorization of how the lack of control over the production process leads the social reality to become less intensely experienced by the worker. Reality's diminishing intensity is a fundamental aspect of estrangement.

Marx already understood that reality was not experienced by all with the same intensity. And intensity was not for him a question of how hard-hitting capitalist machinery was, for example, but of how implicating it was: the degree to which the worker related to it affectively as part of what constitutes his or her being. To a certain extent, Marx posited a normative intensity, which he saw as particular to human beings, and argued that capitalism leads to a dehumanizing relation to reality, such that humans stop experiencing it with the intensity they ought to be able to experience it with. Because of the alienating nature of work, the intensity of life becomes located in the home that people experience only intermittently. There is certainly a sense in which this relation between home and work is replicated in the opposition between home country and host country, whereby living in the land of migration is merely a means to an end. The immigrant suspends the intensity of life and reserves it for his or her affective attachment to the homeland. But clearly this can't remain true forever, and it's the case that the longer that person has lived in the land of migration, the more living within it is likely to be intense. Yet at the same time, there are many cases where lack of economic success easily leads the migrant's attachment to the home country to increase regardless of how long he or she has been living away from it. This dynamic is clearly at work in the above. But notwithstanding the importance of this production-based understanding of one's implication in social reality, there is also another important understanding located in the experience of migration as an anisogamic reciprocal exchange, as we examined earlier.

In his *Genealogy of Morals*, Nietzsche comments that

> the community, too, stands to its members in that same vital basic relation, that of the creditor to his debtors. One lives in a community, one enjoys the advantages of a communality (oh what advantages! We sometimes under-rate them today), one dwells protected, cared for, in peace and trustfulness, without fear of certain injuries and hostile acts to which the man outside, the "man without peace," is exposed—a German will understand the original connotations of Elend—since one has bound and pledged oneself to the community precisely with a view to injuries and hostile acts. What will happen if this pledge is broken? The community, the disappointed creditor, will get what repayment it can, one may depend on that.[10]

Communal life, we can read Nietzsche as saying, is a gift that the community expects its members to reciprocate. This is similar to how, in certain religions, the life of an individual is perceived as a gift from God. Consequently, with those religions, such as Roman Catholicism, individuals will see their lives as marked by an original guilt associated with their state of indebtedness to God. Most important for us, they conceive of living in a religious manner—that is, of religiously guided participation in life—as a mode of repaying the debt. To be implicated in life in a religious way is the mode of repaying the religious debt.

In much the same way, Nietzsche is pointing out that social/communal life is also perceived as a gift. If God gives us the gift of life as such, it is our community that gives us the gift of social life. And if in being religiously implicated we repay the gift of life, it is in being socially and communally implicated that we repay the gift of social life. Being a family member is a gift from the family. Being a national is a gift from the nation. We repay this gift through a lifelong participation in the family and community or whichever communal group we feel has provided us with that gift of communality. The sublime element of dying for one's nation must partly lie in the debt-free state that nationalist martyrs acquire in this process: the nation gave them the gift of social life, and they gave their life back to the nation. Generally, however, we remain in the debt of the community, repaying it in slow installments through a lifetime of participation.

We can see from the above why migration can be a guilt-inducing process. To leave the communal group to which we are indebted is precisely to refrain from repaying the debt. It is important to remember, though, that there is no necessary communal entity we feel indebted to. Not all migrants feel indebted to their nation, for example, but most will feel indebted to their family. This guilt-inducing state of indebtedness is most apparent in times of crisis when your family, your village, or your nation is going through a hard time and you—the subject organically related to the community through the original debt of social/communal life—are not there to help. When you do not share the fate of the collectivity which gave you social life, you are guilty of letting others pay alone for a debt you're collectively responsible for.

I think that among Lebanese migrants, it's in this sense that the desire to be implicated to intensify reality must be located. Strategies of intensification are guilt-ridden moves within a general moral economy of social belonging. That's why they are permeated by an affective language. They are modes of repayment: the more intense the mode of being implicated, the more "debt" one repays in this symbolic-moral economy.

So far, to emphasize the process I was introducing, I have drawn a picture of what can be called an elementary form of social indebtedness: one community member indebted to one community. The empirical situation in which everyone finds her- or himself is clearly far more complicated than this. Most important, feelings of indebtedness aren't restricted to one communal formation. Someone can belong with equal or varying intensity to several communities. Furthermore, the gift of social life is not offered to individuals only by being born in a specific community. One can incur the debt of communality by voluntarily becoming part of a community that accepts one in its midst. This, of course, can be the case in migration, to which I want to return now.

If migrants leave their home country in a state of debt and with guilt-ridden feelings of having left without repaying the debt, no sooner do they settle in a host country than they incur a new debt. Even if at first the host country doesn't offer the same sense of communality found in the home country, it nevertheless offers hopes of a better future, an important ingredient in any kind of life. This creates a complex situation in which participation in the host community can be seen as repayment of the debt of belonging to it, while this same participation can accentuate feelings of guilt toward the original community. Thus, it's not uncommon for migrants, especially in the early stages of migration, to refrain from showing excessive enthusiasm toward the host country in front of their "original" compatriots, even if they genuinely feel excited about the social and economic opportunities it's offering them. Such enthusiasm can be constructed as a form of social treason: a sign that one has forgotten about one's original debt.

Matters are complicated further by the fact that the development of a moral obligation to a country offering the gift of a new life is also linked to how this gift is offered. Here the whole subtlety of gift exchange comes to the fore. The gifts that create the greatest moral obligations are those offered most graciously. If the giver of the gift keeps reminding the recipient of his or her state of indebtedness or if the gift is given ungraciously, then the moral obligation, while always present, becomes nevertheless reduced. Thus, comments such as "They treated us like beggars" by Lebanese migrants who have nevertheless received an Australian entry visa imply a badly offered gift (by the Australian Embassy!). Here the whole politics of a country's immigration policies and how its national discourse constructs migrants become implicated in this moral economy. It's interesting how the more a country hardens its immigration policy and treats its migrants "like beggars," the more the discourses demanding migrant adherence to the nation abound, betraying an implicit recognition or fear that the manner of offering a new life does not carry with it the moral obligation of adherence.

To conclude these reflections, I would like to mention an important factor determining the state of indebtedness, though by no means the last one, and that is the degree of social and economic success one experiences in the host country. The feeling of satisfaction generated from a sense that one has achieved something in migration is also a sense of how much the host country has offered and is clearly of great importance in determining the relation of indebtedness to it. Notably in the case of the "argument" we examined above, Maurice's brother and sister-in-law are far more successful economically than he or his neighbor. To a certain extent, we can say that excessive attachment to one's original country is a strategy of compensation for one's life not turning out as hoped for.

SEVEN

The Lebanese Transnational Diasporic Family

As I noted in the preface, right from the start of my stay in Jalleh and Mehj, families with members living in various parts of the globe quickly captured my research imagination: What is a transnational family? How does it manage to maintain itself as a family? How does transnationalism affect kinship relations? How do the various class, generational, and cultural differences manifest themselves within that family? Later, as I was refining my theoretical framework, I also became interested in how the lenticular experience and the anisogamic dynamics that constitute the diasporic subject manifest themselves in a familial framework.

The idea of researching two families, one from Jalleh and one from Mehj, who have members living in the various international geographic locations where most migrants from each of the two villages have settled instantly seemed like a good idea. But while finding such families was relatively easy, finding those whose various members around the world would agree to have me stay with them was a much more difficult ethnographic space to find and research. It took several failed attempts before I ended up with the two families that became the focus of my attention. The family from Mehj had members living in Lebanon; London; New Bedford, Massachusetts, and Vermont in the United States; and Gatineau in Canada. The family from Jalleh was in Lebanon, Cabudare in Venezuela, Boston, and Sydney. But then, after one year of international travel struggling for some semblance of contact with all the members of each family in all the various parts of the globe, working with two families proved impossible, physically and ethnographically. My fieldwork became far more centered, as is this chapter, on the family from Jalleh. For comparative purposes, however, I will still introduce some dimensions of the family from Mehj.

The Neefa Family from Jalleh

I met members of the Neefa family for the first time in 1992 while researching multiculturalism in Sydney. As I noted in the preface, I had paternal relatives in Jalleh, which facilitated recruiting some of the Neefas for my research purposes at the time. In 1994 I interviewed Hoda and her husband, Sa'd, for a project on multiculturalism. I stayed in touch with them throughout the nineties, as I was engaged in a variety of research projects that involved working with Sydney's Lebanese community. We've already met Georges and Waheed in previous chapters.

The Neefa family was, relatively speaking, among the most well-to-do in the village. With its honorary Ottoman title, it was even perceived as quasi-aristocratic. Historically, it had owned both the silk factory and the olive press in the village. It also owned and operated Jalleh's private school. But clearly, even when the olive press was still operating, the profits weren't enough to support everyone in the family, so its migration to Venezuela began in 1920; its migration to Boston began in the 1940s. The Neefa family suffered further during the Lebanese Civil War, when in 1976 the whole village was attacked and burned to the ground by fighters from neighboring Muslim villages. This led to another round of migration. The generation of Neefa family immigrants that became the center of my attention moved principally to Cabudare, Boston, and Sydney because of that late migration. These immigrants are parents Jameeleh and Ya'koob; their three sons, Lateef, Waheed, and Mario; and two daughters Maya and Hoda (boldface names and lines in figure 2).

Jameeleh's brothers, Antoon and Georges, had migrated to Cabudare in the 1950s and, after owning a store for many years (see chapter 4), had become reasonably successful rice farmers in areas around Cabudare. Her sister's son, Ameen, migrated in the 1960s and bought his uncles' store as they moved into rice farming. So when the village was destroyed in 1976, Jameeleh and her husband decided to move to Venezuela. At the same time, her sister, Jeannette; her brother-in-law, Robert; and their three sons migrated to Boston, where Robert's mother's family had been born and raised (see figure 2). An unforeseeable event happened at Beirut Airport, however. Jameeleh's husband, Ya'koob, was totally petrified of the plane and refused to board it. There and then, the family's entire migratory trajectory was changed. Rather than a total and final migration as planned, Jameeleh decided on the spot to leave Ya'koob behind and settle some of their children in Venezuela before returning to Lebanon.

After six months in Cabudare, it was decided that Hoda (the eldest daughter) and Mario (the youngest of the boys) would return to Jalleh with

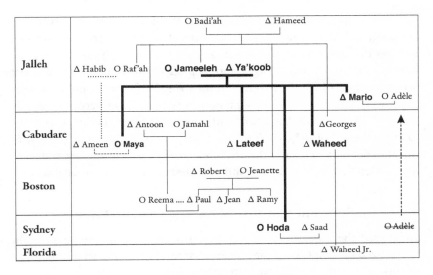

Figure 2. Jalleh family tree.

their mother. A couple of years later, Hoda married Saad, a man from the village who had migrated to Australia ten years earlier and owned a restaurant in Sydney. She went to live in Sydney. What's more, when Saad came to the village to marry Hoda, his cousin Adèle, born and raised in Sydney, came with him. She and Mario fell in love and married, and Adèle ended up staying in Jalleh. Around the same time, Paul, Jeannette and Robert's eldest son who had migrated to Boston, married his cousin Reema, the daughter of his maternal uncle Antoon, who had migrated to Venezuela earlier on, creating new kinship ties between the Boston and Cabudare branches of the family. We've already encountered Paul and his son, Chafic, while he was showing me his Elvis living room and his Lebanese bar (chapter 5).

Ya'koob died of a heart attack seven years after the initial migration. Theoretically, Jameeleh could have moved to Venezuela at that time, but a few circumstances made her remain in Jalleh. First, by that time the village had been rebuilt, and Jameeleh had rebuilt the private school where she invested a lot of her time and was now the director. Second, both of her other sons were already doing quite well in Cabudare, each owning large rice and sugarcane farms. Lateef, in fact, was on the way to becoming by far the most financially successful member of the entire family, further investing in his cousin's businesses in Boston. Third, both brothers desired to maintain the family's land and were even purchasing new plots that Mario, the brother who had stayed behind with his mother, was responsible for looking after.

These people, then, constitute the family that I took as my fieldwork site: Jameeleh and Mario's family in Jalleh; Jameeleh's sons Lateef and Waheed and her daughters Maya and Hoda, along with Jameeleh's brothers, early immigrants Antoon and Georges, and their respective families in Venezuela; Jeannette and Robert, their sons, and their sons' respective families in Boston; and Hoda and Saad and their family in Sydney. There were other family members living in São Paulo and in Montreal that I visited briefly just to get to know them, but they aren't so much part of the transnational family, in that they don't participate in the extensive circuit of people, money, and communication that constitutes the family as a transnational/communal space.

Culture and Structure of the Transnational Family

To be sure, the various family members around the world share a certain generalized Lebaneseness. Many forms of decoration mark each household's relationship to the homeland: mirrors in the shape of Lebanon; wooden or metal carvings of the Lebanese cedar, a major cultural symbol; photos and statues of Lebanese saints; and of course, photos of Lebanese relatives. At the same time, however, what is shared is not just "Lebanese culture" in the abstract but family-specific Lebanese forms and habits that give the Neefa family not only a cultural but also an aesthetic commonality. These most markedly reside in how certain common Lebanese dishes are made and consumed. I noted that whenever a large festive meal was prepared, some family-specific aromas would emanate from the kitchen regardless of where in the world I was.

There are also family-specific ways in which Lebanese dishes are served. *Kibbeh nayyeh* (raw meat crushed with wheat and herbs), for instance, is a Lebanese national dish, which, like any other dish, varies regionally in how it is both made and served. But the Neefas had created their own variation on the regional dish. They all like to spread the kibbeh very thinly on a large plate when it is served. A Venezuelan Neefa will go to Boston, and when she or he is served *kibbeh nayyeh*, the *kibbeh* served in this manner reinforces his or her sentiment of being among family. In addition, the thinly spread kibbeh became a signature dish at the Lebanese restaurant that Hoda's husband ran in Sydney and where she became the principal cook.

Moreover, the Neefas have certain ways of saying Lebanese words that are specific to the family. I noted very early that a Neefa never fails to say *"Yalla!"* (come on!) with an extra emphasis on the *l*'s, such that the word sounds like *Yall-lla!* Everyone was clearly aware that this is their family's own mode of uttering the word, using it as a way to reinforce a sense of familial commonality. No one could tell me the habit's origin, except that they all remember their parents saying *Yalla!* this way.

A particular family phenotype, some common facial features or a more general and vague mode of faciality that the Neefas recognize as existing among them, is equally visible to an outsider like me. This visual commonality is associated with certain gestural similarities, a certain way of moving one's head, of turning, of looking, of walking that indicate remnants of an inherited common habitus which has long been fractured and continues to exist in fragments here and there. There is, then, a multiplicity of recognizable features that work at making the family distinguishable by its members as well as by outsiders.

These common features are not just the source for a *representation* of what each family member experiences as having in common with other family members; they also work to constitute a space where family members experience their individual existence as dissolving within a wider mode of familial existence. The Lebanese denote social closeness by saying of a person, *hayda minna w'feena*: he is "from us and in us." This phrase is not used about someone just because that person is biological kin. It must denote a kind of existential kinship. While the idea that someone is "from us" is common enough as indicating that someone is "issued from us," the idea of someone being "in us" takes us into the domain of mutuality analyzed by Marshall Sahlins.[1] Thus, when a man from Boston visits Sydney, looks at his nephew, and recognizes a family resemblance, he recognizes a commonality but also a mutuality: "I am in you." Mutuality, then, is not so much an "all for one and one for all" as an "all in one and one in all." It is a collective and affective mode in which the family exists and is experienced for its members as both interconnected but also interpenetrated. This experience is reinforced by how the family shares its transnationality.

On my first visit to Venezuela, staying at Maya's house, I noted a map of Australia, carved from wood with a golden clock in the center and with a miniature Tasmania dangling from the mainland by a golden chain. I noted it because the same clock hangs on the wall of the family's home in Jalleh. A week later, I noticed it also on the wall of Jeannette and Robert's home in Boston. I made a note to myself to take a closer look, on my next trip, at how each household marks its transnational connections with similar items: non-Australian households all have besides this clock an assortment of kangaroos and koalas, and one Venezuelan household has a didgeridoo; the Venezuelan households have a lot of American baseball memorabilia, some in the living room and some in the boys' bedrooms—and sure enough, there was an obvious bias toward the Boston Red Sox. Even in

Sydney, one of the boys has in his bedroom a poster of Ted Williams, the famous Boston Red Sox hitter. In Lebanon, however, true to the popularity of basketball in the country, Mario has a poster of the Boston Celtics logo next to his desk. Only one Boston household has a Venezuelan item, however: a poster of the Salto Angel waterfall, although in the Jalleh household there are several wood carvings of Spanish greetings and home blessings that were made in Venezuela. Arguably, these common cultural items are at the same time common attachments, making for a common lenticularity. Not only do these items make the whole family exist in a similar field of fluctuating multiplicity of situatedness, but they also constitute the transnational familial space as another space of situatedness to add to this multiplicity. This is particularly so since, as noted above, the family is not only constituted by shared commonalities. It's also formed by an intensive field of multilayered social, moral, economic, and affective relationality, which gives it different modes of existence.

In 2001 I asked all members of the Neefa family to keep their detailed phone bills so that I could have a sense of the flows of communication between them. Figure 3 gives a sense of the nature of these flows based on the number of telephone calls, the average duration of the conversations, and the average cost of a call made from any of the key international locations where the family is present. This flow of communication, as we shall later see, is not just a feature of the familial space but an essential form of communicative labor that keeps the parts of the family together. It is made more crucial in the absence of physical proximity. Figure 3, especially when viewed concurrently with the circulation of people (fig. 4) and the circulation of remittances (fig. 5), also gives us a good sense of the family as a space of circulation and exchange of communication, people, and money.

At one level, the family operates like a transnational mechanism of production and distribution of social viability to its members. At that level, it comes across as a socioeconomic functional whole, with a Durkheimian organic solidarity. The Venezuelan members, being the most successful economically, are responsible for distributing a small but still substantial portion of their wealth to others when needed. It should be noted, for instance, that remittances not only go from Venezuela to Lebanon, as would be expected. They also flow from Cabudare to Sydney, where the least financially well-off part of the family lives. In addition, the Venezuelan Neefas are generally very generous with gifts they give to all the children in all the locations.

The Bostonians have helped the Venezuelans make a small business investment in the United States. They also offer accommodations and more generally "family space" to their transnational kin's children aiming to get a

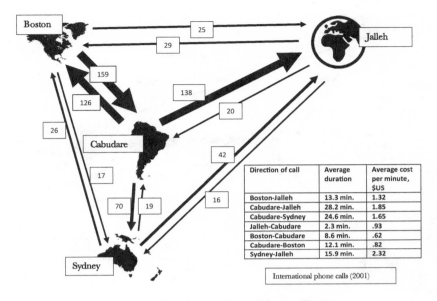

Direction of call	Average duration	Average cost per minute, $US
Boston-Jalleh	13.3 min.	1.32
Cabudare-Jalleh	28.2 min.	1.85
Cabudare-Sydney	24.6 min.	1.65
Jalleh-Cabudare	2.3 min.	.93
Boston-Cabudare	8.6 min.	.62
Cabudare-Boston	12.1 min.	.82
Sydney-Jalleh	15.9 min.	2.32

International phone calls (2001)

Figure 3. Jalleh family's international phone calls, 2001.

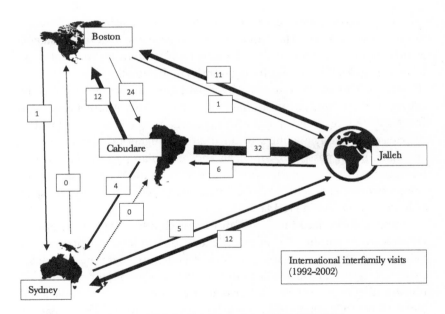

International interfamily visits (1992–2002)

Figure 4. Jalleh family's international visits, 1992–2002.

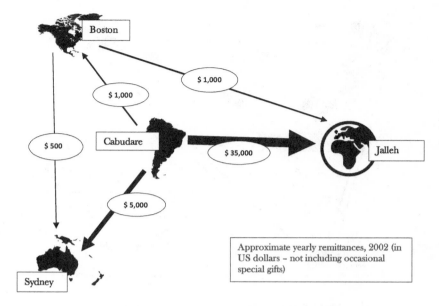

Figure 5. Jalleh family's international remittances, 2002.

"good education": three Venezuelan children attend colleges and universities in the Boston area. The Sydneysiders also have one Venezuelan staying at their home and attending the University of Western Sydney. But these Neefas are generally seen as offering—and actually do offer—the other family members a base for tourism. This makes Australia the most visited by others of all the family's various international locations. Another important functional service provided by the Sydneysiders and the Bostonians involves offering other family members, through various migratory and matrimonial strategies, better passports: American and Australian passports allow better freedom of movement internationally than do the Venezuelan and the Lebanese ones. This is how Waheed managed to get an American passport to look after his son in Florida.

These relations feed into and transform each other. Sometimes one relation leads to another. For instance, education can lead to marriage: one Venezuelan who went to study in Boston ended up marrying his cousin there and staying. I have also encountered one example of touristic relations transforming into business relations. At one point while in Venezuela, Lateef took me to his office in the middle of the sugarcane fields near Barquisimetto. When I entered, I was struck by the number of Australiana posters on the walls: kangaroos, koalas, and the Barrier Reef. I said to Lateef, "I know that your sister lives in Australia, but this seems a bit excessive. Why all this?" Lateef explained to me that when visiting his sister in Sydney, he and Waheed went on a trip to Queensland just for tourism. There they met a local tractor manufacturer with whom they ended up forming close business ties. They buy lots of tractors from that firm, and its technicians often visit the farm. "We've put the posters up for them," Lateef said. I tried to argue with him that this wasn't necessarily what the Australian technicians would want or expect, but ten years later he still had the posters on the wall.

A distribution of roles helps make the family into a structure of functional/organic solidarity, as demonstrated by Mario agreeing to remain in the village to look after Jameeleh. He had been asked almost formally by his brothers to forego migration in order to take care of their mother. As Waheed's and Lateef's businesses continued to improve, their commitment to Mario's family and its needs increased. Their commitment is regarded as what the whole family owes Mario for foregoing migration and "looking after Mum." He is also looking after various family properties and interests in Jalleh. But his is not just any role, and he shoulders a special responsibility.

Transnational families have a certain directionality or orientation. This orientation is formed by several variables and changes with time. The Neefa family is oriented toward Lebanon. A quick look at the global maps of phone calls made by the family in 2001, of visits, and of remittances (figs. 3–5) shows that the largest flows of communication, visits, and money are directed to their home village of Jalleh.

One can easily lapse into instinctively normalizing this situation, considering it obvious: "Of course, Lebanese diasporic families, like Lebanese immigrants, are oriented toward Lebanon." However, this doesn't have to be the case. The family from Mehj noted earlier, which I researched for a while until I could no longer do so, is a case in point. A look at a similar map of communication (fig. 6) shows clearly that this family is oriented toward New Bedford. This is because the head of the family (*Raas el Ayleh*) had left Mehj and moved to that Massachusetts city. The family still had a house and property in Mehj and visited it often, but nonetheless its orientation to its home village is far less pronounced than that of the Neefa family.

That the Neefas are as oriented as they are toward their village has to do with the fact that they are relatively recent immigrants and that Jameeleh, who is the head of the family and its nodal point, has remained in Lebanon. But there is a further investment behind this directionality that offers a window on what I have termed the family's other mode of existence.

Despite all the talk about Mario's "looking after Mum," Jameeleh doesn't really need looking after in the classic sense of the word. This is not a case

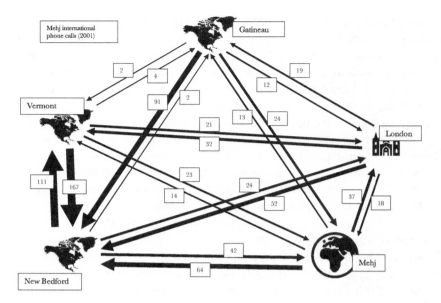

Figure 6. Mehj family's international phone calls, 2001.

of "transnational caregiving for the aged," as analyzed by sociologists and anthropologists.[2] Jameeleh is a healthy, strong, and somewhat domineering woman. Throughout the time I was conducting my research (from the late 1990s until 2011), she was still the director of Jalleh's private school, which the family owned. Many in and around the village refer to her, with reverence, as Madame la Directrice or simply Madame. If anything, it is she who sees herself in the role of the transnational carer, without whom her family would fall apart, and she freely makes all kinds of decisions on behalf of both the immediate family in the village household and the family scattered overseas. She has a say in the global management of the Neefa finances, particularly when it comes to questions of distribution. Jameeleh's opinion matters in determining how much money needs to be sent from Venezuela, to which location, and for what purpose. Moreover, she is often obeyed in a matter-of-fact manner. She is a transnational matriarch.

Thus, the idea of "looking after Mum" has more of a symbolic than a practical value. This transnational family has a considerable investment in its status in Jalleh as a kind of village aristocracy. By having Jameeleh stay there and someone like Mario able to migrate and yet refraining from doing so, the family asserts to other villagers that it has overcome the logic of economic necessity that governed its initial departure. It doesn't need to migrate; it now simply lives in more than one place.

Consequently, there is a Goffmanesque dimension to the Neefa family's transnational being: a transnational mode of the presentation of the familial self in everyday life. In this familial mode of existence, the village operates as the stage on which the family presents itself, where it deems it important in terms of status and honor to do so. On the other hand, the entirety of the international family travails, businesses, labor, and so on operates backstage, secondary insofar as the economy of prestige is concerned.[3]

In both its Durkheimian mode of existence as an international mechanism of socioeconomic viability and its Goffmanesque mode of existence as a village-oriented mechanism of symbolic viability, the Neefas as a transnational family present themselves as a socially and culturally homogeneous totality. However, the family is also ridden with various class, gender, and national/cultural divisions and tensions, which coexist with its more homogeneous dimensions. These tensions surface every now and then, and they can even come to dominate certain periods in the family's life. In what follows, I examine how they manifest themselves aesthetically.

Distinction: The Aesthetics of Interfamily Differentiation

Just as there is a culture and an aesthetic of commonality that foreground the family's unity, so there are features that highlight its internal differentiation. The family is most notably differentiated along national (the country they have migrated to), developmental (degrees of rurality, urbanity, and cosmopolitanism), educational, and class lines. These make for an aesthetic domain of perceived differences as the Neefas' households and members develop styles reflecting their national, socioeconomic, and cultural positioning. In addition, there is a domain of conscious strategic and competitive deployment of this difference, what Bourdieu defines as the space of distinction.

Class differences are often consciously and unconsciously exhibited, giving rise to what we might call aesthetics of diasporic success hardly specific to the Neefas or to the Lebanese more generally. These aesthetics are exhibited in the type of houses people live in, the clothes they wear, and the cars they drive. But one of these is a tradition more or less specific to northern Lebanese, particularly Christian immigrants: success is measured by the label on the Johnnie Walker whiskey bottle placed on the lunch or dinner table.

At some stage in the history of Lebanon's modernization, whiskey replaced *arak* as the alcoholic drink people have with food, for those who saw in it a mark of Westernization. Like *arak*, it is drunk with ice and mixed with water. Johnnie Walker became by far the most successfully marketed whiskey in the country, with its ads becoming part of the Lebanese landscape. Very quickly, drinking "Black Label" became a way of distinguishing one's middle-class stature. This tradition was continued in the diaspora at the same time that awareness of Johnnie Walker's label varieties expanded to Gold Label, Blue Label, and others. Among the Venezuelans, having several bottles of Blue Label on the table is de rigueur at festive meals and is very consciously used to differentiate themselves from less successful immigrants inside and outside their family.

Other obvious domains of differentiation include those features that symbolize the integration of each family member in his or her country of settlement, such as a native Venezuelan rug in a Venezuelan house, an American flag in a Boston house, or a Ken Done print (a popular Australian artist) in a Sydney house. At one level, this type of household decoration as an aestheticization of the home is no different in its function from any other non-diasporic household decoration. Nonetheless, there is a specifically diasporic dimension here, without which one fails to fully capture its significance for various family members, and which gives these decorations something I will call a diasporic *style*, after Roland Barthes. In a little book titled *What Is Sport?*, Barthes defines *style* while reflecting on the art/sport of bullfighting: "What is style? Style makes a difficult action into a graceful gesture, introduces a rhythm into fatality. Style is to be courageous without disorder, to give necessity the appearance of freedom."[4]

It's difficult not to extrapolate from bullfighting to life in general here. Insofar as life is a struggle that tends to imprison us in the order of its necessities, style is precisely that aesthetic dimension we manage to give our lives in order to transcend and sublimate this order. In much the same way, I want to suggest that diasporic style is that dimension of life where diasporic subjects struggle to inject things like grace and freedom into the domain of necessity governing the migratory process. Accordingly, there is always an anisogamic dimension to this aestheticization of the migrant household, as these features—their placement in the household, their prominence, their number, and so on—denote not only the difference between each of the national cultures of the countries of settlement but also different degrees of integration, different desires to integrate, and different levels of willingness to be seen to integrate.

One thing that drew my attention when I began working with Lebanese immigrants is how bare of decoration immigrants' homes are when they first move to a new country. With this image in mind, it's difficult to see a decorated household without seeing it in relation to this quasi-foundational state of bareness. In that early stage of home dwelling, an almost pure functional/instrumental reason seems to be behind the households' internal furnishing, as if it is nothing but the homely externalization of the realm of necessity. Slowly, I came to understand that there were several reasons behind this bareness and functionality. First, there is the issue of poverty and the recency of arrival. Second, it's a matter of belief in the transience of one's presence away from the home country. Most immigrants and people working with immigrants know for how long this belief is maintained against all odds. But finally—and it's here that the anisogamic dimension materializes most clearly—the refusal of decoration is partly an attempt to delay the sentiment of betrayal of the "mother country" some immigrants feel when settling in a new one. To decorate is to say that one is moving from the domain of necessity to that of enjoyment. By not decorating, immigrants are saying that they are "here" because they have to be: paradoxically, then, there is at this stage an interest in dwelling in the domain of pure necessity. The moment immigrants decorate—that is, the moment they begin to create such a purely aesthetic space—is the moment they begin to carve out for themselves a space that's not governed by the domain of diasporic necessity.

Early in my research, I noted that a person who had recently arrived from Jalleh—he had been living in Sydney for only two years—hung a Matisse print on his wall. It was the first time I saw such an object of pure art in his apartment. I said something like "Ah, you're starting to make yourself at home here." He looked slightly perturbed and replied, "*Mish hal add*" (not that much). It was as if there were a sense of embarrassment associated with the idea of making himself at home in Australia. Hanging a painting for pure visual pleasure on his wall means a desire to settle. And the moment an immigrant indicates a desire to settle, he's also saying to his country of origin: there's room for enjoyment here in settling in this new country; I am not going to live my life thinking that the good life can be lived only in Lebanon; there's more to life than this. To be clear, then, it's not that the immigrant is immediately shamed for settling, but an honorable settling has its temporality: it's dishonorable to show yourself settling "too soon."

The first time I noted a competitive nationalist edge emerging among various members of the Neefa family was during an email exchange among second-generation Australian, American, and Venezuelan members. It degenerated into a form of competitive tourism, in which members were each highlighting their own nation's touristic sights as the most beautiful and worthiest of visiting.

Often, such strategies of distinction are acted out in the absence of those from which the practices are aiming to distinguish the practitioner: those Neefas in Boston, for instance, always feel the presence of the other members of the family in Lebanon, Sydney, and Cabudare. They are part of the general imaginary of the family even when not physically present. On rare occasions, the strategies of distinction occur in an interactive space. Such an occasion arose in 2004.

Lateef, who is, as indicated above, the most financially successful member of the family, had four girls. He desperately wanted a boy, but after the fourth girl arrived in 1999, he had given up. In 2003 he and his wife, Christina, decided to give it a last try, and toward the end of that year Christina gave birth to a boy they named Jacobo (the Spanish rendition of his grandfather's name). Lateef decided to christen Jacobo back in Jalleh and invited relatives around the world (including me) to come to the village for the ceremony. Given how much having a boy had meant to him, it was clear that this was going to be a big occasion of the family regathering in their home village.

It was during that christening that I witnessed a few interesting instances of interactive interfamilial strategies of diasporic distinction. It's important here to recall the Goffmanesque structure of the family, in which the village is the very place where symbolic accumulation is displayed. Usually, these strategies of accumulation, when they happen from afar, aim to maximize the family's symbolic capital. But with all the family members present in the village, differences between them become far more visible.

At the christening's church ceremony, the Venezuelan Neefas were wearing very expensive and formal designer-label clothes. The Bostonians, who aren't as rich the Venezuelans and on the whole can't as easily afford such clothes, generally opted for a less formal style: they tried to compensate for their relative lack of wealth by showing themselves to be worldlier. It is a common theme among the Bostonians that the Venezuelans "never migrated": they'd moved from one rural area to another. The Bostonians think that while the Venezuelans have made a lot of money, they have nevertheless stayed villagers at heart, exhibiting their wealth in the way villagers do. They lacked the kind of cosmopolitan style that one acquires by living in a middle-class part of Boston.

On the other hand, the Australians, who live in a working-class part of Sydney, are by far the least financially successful of the family. At the christening, the younger generation among them didn't even bother to dress up. Instead of playing up a worldliness and a cosmopolitanism they couldn't afford, they played up their Australianness. Explanations like "We in Australia, we don't care about things like this" and "We have an easygoing egalitarian culture" were used when I raised the question of who is and who isn't dressed up.

It's interesting to note here that claiming to be Australian at the expense of one's Lebaneseness is not a claim the Australian part of the family could or would make in Australia. Many of them, with few exceptions, would feel that they're betraying their Lebaneseness by doing so. At the same time, the politics of identification in Australia is such that there are always people questioning the extent that Lebanese Australians can be Australian. Thus, no Lebanese can make that claim without being wary of that potentially hovering "real (White) Aussie," always present in the imagination of the racialized, who will come and say, "No, you're not really Australian." Interestingly, then, Lebanon becomes the only place where the family's Australians can feel liberated to act "fully" Australian without worrying about either homeland guilt or racist doubters. The same goes, but in different degrees, for the Venezuelans and the Americans. Consequently, the village becomes an interesting site of shameless strategies of national distinction. Nonetheless, in those very strategies of distinction the family in its totality, like a multicultural collector, continues to project to the whole village the richness of the diasporic culture that composes it.

Throughout this chapter so far, I have aimed to show the many ways in which the Neefa family presents itself to its members. These tactics also represent different familial modes of existence that, as I will now show, constitute the family as a lenticular intersection of multiple realities. In this final section, I want to examine a transnational family conflict that brings to the fore how various interests can make various members of the family dwell more in one or another of the realities that constitute it. I trust that this analysis can enrich our understanding of lenticular forms of diasporic existence.

The Case of the Poorly Offered Cup of Coffee

It was a day in June 2002 during my stay in Cabudare that the sequence of events I am examining here began. On that day, a serious family conflict erupted. I was at the home of Maya and her husband, Ameen, where I always stay when in Cabudare. Maya's house is the space for family gatherings. Her brother Lateef is married to a Venezuelan Lebanese who, everyone agrees, is "not good at Lebanese cooking." Her other brother Waheed is considered single, even though he has a son from a relationship with a Cuban American in Florida who sometimes visits Cabudare. The idea of her preparing a

Lebanese feast isn't even discussed. So Maya has become the upholder of the social and culinary traditions of the Neefa family and those of Jalleh more generally. It's at her house that the family meets for lunch every Sunday and for most special occasions, such as christenings and graduations. It was rightly decided, when I was negotiating my fieldwork with the family, that this would be the best place for me to stay. Maya's children were boarding at university in Caracas, so she had a spare room. What's more, her husband was semiretired and could spend time with me and drive me around.

On that day, I had just woken up and was heading to the kitchen. Usually, Maya is already there, waiting for me to have a morning coffee with her. But this morning she's on the phone, screaming at somebody. I retreated to my room. When I reentered the kitchen ten minutes later, she was smoking a cigarette in front of her cup of coffee. Hacera, the Indigenous live-in domestic servant, gave me a complicit look, shaking her head slightly. Very early in my research, she had developed a sense of complicity with me, as if to say, "You and I are on one side, and those crazy people are on the other."

"I'll make you your coffee," Hacera said. Like most northern Lebanese villagers, Maya and her husband drink their coffee excessively sweet, and I drink it with no sugar. So Hacera made me my coffee separately. And while she made coffee for everyone as part of her job, this allowed her to make mine as if it were a way of consolidating "our team." There are many ways of making, serving, and drinking a cup of Lebanese coffee, and this is at the heart of the transnational familial conflict I am about to relate here.

"Did you hear me scream?" Maya said.

"Well, yes," I said. "It was hard not to."

"I was screaming at Lateef."

"What happened?'

"He had an argument with Mario."

"What about?" I was surprised. As far as I knew, Mario is the most easygoing, laidback person around. He's happy helping people, socializing, politicking, and roaming around the village and its surroundings in his Mercedes or his BMW, both provided by his brothers as part of the "looking after Mum" deal. So usually, no one in the family ever has arguments with Mario.

It was a long story. Two days earlier, Maya explained, her mum, Jameeleh, had phoned. This was unusual, as she often waits for Maya to phone her because of the expenses involved. She wanted it to be known that she was "very upset," because Adèle, Mario's wife, had been rude to her. Adèle was serving her a cup of coffee, and she put it in front of her "rudely." Maya made what she put to me as "the mistake of mentioning this to Lateef." Then Lateef apparently proceeded to phone his brother and blast him for not looking after their mother properly. This made Mario phone Maya and tell her off for reporting Jameeleh's version of events without consulting him, prompting Maya to phone Lateef and have an argument with him, because "surely he knows that it is not Mario's fault . . . as if he doesn't know what it is like living with Mum."

"But how 'rudely' did Adèle put the cup of coffee in front of your mum?" I asked, not even trying to hide my smile.

"Mum said, '*Khabatito iddehmeh w'iddehm el kell*,'" Maya replied, conveying the way her mum had expressed it—meaning "She banged it in front of me and in front of everyone else to see." Maya laughed despite her genuine anger. The situation was indeed tragicomic. And it became even more so later, when the whole family got involved. The rudely served cup of coffee made a man in Venezuela accuse his brother in Jalleh of not assuming his familial responsibility. But as the "bang" started to reverberate across the world, becoming a truly international incident prompting interventions from Sydney to Boston and back to Venezuela and Lebanon, it soon became clear that not everyone has the same idea of what *responsibility* means. And with all the different and conflicting but equally valid conceptions of *responsibility* that were expressed came different and conflicting but also equally valid conceptions of the kind of entity the family itself is. In fact, while all the members inhabit the family as a lenticular space of multiple modes of familial existence, their different interests mean that they dwell in one part more than others. Consequently, in the case of the coffee incident, they were implicated and had a sense of responsibility more in line with the reality they occupy most.

After the incident, I had many opportunities to casually raise questions with various family members concerning the significance of the events and their unfolding. Never in the form of a direct interview, these questions took the form of "by the way, I am interested in what happened on that day, do you mind telling me?" People didn't mind. After ten years of working with the Neefas, I was in many ways a member of the family, and they were invariably happy to give me their version of events. As a way of understanding the competing conceptions of responsibility that emerged as the conflict unfolded, I will begin with how the tension between Adèle and her mother-in-law was experienced by Adèle herself.

Looking After Mum

Let us recall that Sydney-born Adèle, who had fallen in love with Mario and married here, did so knowing that Mario had been bound by a deal with his brothers to remain in Jalleh and look after their mum. Many people in the village talk about Adèle with admiration when noting how well she has adapted to village life given her urban Australian upbringing. Let us also recall that far from needing someone to look after her, Jameeleh is the family's respected matriarch.

The first layer of tension between Adèle and Jameeleh emerged precisely because of these circumstances, when it became clear to Adèle that Jameeleh makes many of the crucial decisions affecting the household. This hasn't affected Mario as much, since he's more preoccupied with looking after the olive orchard attached to the house and engaging in local politics. At the time, he was also being financed by his brothers to run for municipal elections and had been elected the village mayor, which took up a considerable amount of his time. Indeed, he was hardly at home. Adèle, however, was at home all the time and often experiencing a sense of being dominated and overlooked by her mother-in-law, even concerning matters affecting her daily life.

The second layer of tension that made things particularly difficult between Adèle and Jameeleh emerged when Adèle and Mario's daughters became teenagers. As the girls grew up, they were spending more of their summers with their uncles in Sydney and constantly dreaming of leaving the village and doing their university studies in Australia. Adèle and Mario were unwilling to be separated from their daughters and therefore were unwilling to let the girls go. They want to go and live in Australia as a family, but clearly they can't do that. So now it was no longer just Mario, or Mario and Adèle, who are foregoing migration. Increasingly, it's the whole family being condemned to stay in the village to assume responsibility for "looking after Mum." "Stuck here looking after someone who really wants to look after everybody," as Adèle unceremoniously put it to me.

The night before Adèle banged the cup of coffee in front of her mother-in-law, Jameeleh had put her in a bad spot by not allowing "the girls" to go to "the city"—Tripoli, Lebanon's northern capital—at night, even after their mother had given them permission. As was often the case, she didn't do it in a blunt way as if to say, "No, you can't go." As Adèle explained to me, her mother-in-law said that she would be worried if the children went, as there was a soccer match on, and hooligans could be roaming the streets. So Adèle had to choose between telling her girls that they could no longer go, upsetting them and undermining her own sense of authority over matters affecting them, or sticking to her original decision and "showing disrespect" to Jameeleh. She decided on the former, which made her even more resentful toward her mother-in-law. It is in this context that the rudely "banged" cup of coffee must be understood from Adèle's perspective.

As can be seen so far, from this perspective the crisis appears as a break-down in the distribution of responsibilities affecting the functional Durk-heimian mode of the family's existence: what was initially viable for Mario and Adèle to take on as their responsibility was no longer so.

Clearly, as we have already seen, this Durkheimian mode of existence wasn't the only one. Particularly in relation to the question of "looking after Mum," there was another, Goffmanesque mode of existence at stake. We can begin to access this different mode of existence by noting that when Ja-meeleh phoned Maya about Adèle's behavior, she wasn't upset just because Adèle had been rude to her. Many things she had said publicly, or to me personally, clearly showed that she's conscious of, and understands, Adèle's resentment. She understands that for Adèle and her daughters, being stuck in the village with her isn't the best of life's options. Nonetheless, she thinks that the tension between her and her daughter-in-law is unavoidable, pro-duced by the very nature of the family as a diasporic entity. Self-servingly, perhaps, she thinks that it's the price that Adèle and Mario must pay for being part of the family. That being the case, she expects to be the recipient of some antagonistic behavior on Adèle's part. What Jameeleh was upset about, however, was that Adèle had exhibited her resentment *in front of oth-ers*. This was where she failed in her responsibility. Recall the description of the event that Jameeleh gave Maya and that Maya in turn gave me: "She banged it in front of me and in front of everyone else to see." *Everyone* here means "visitors." Jameeleh's house is the village's open house par excellence, and a continuous stream of village people occupy the family's living room from early in the morning till late at night.

The key issue here is how the family appears in the eyes of other villagers. As noted earlier, even if "Mum" doesn't really need to be looked after, it's crucial for the Neefa family's prestige and reputation in Jalleh for its mem-bers to appear as if they were looking after her. While the first conception of the family as an organic transnational totality emphasized its members' responsibility for the internal functioning of the whole, here the idea of responsibility emphasizes the responsibility of family members in manag-ing how the family is seen by others. This would be no different from the responsibility of the members of any entity to uphold the entity's appear-ance in the world—except that for this family, appearance matters most in the village, and a lot has been invested in upholding this appearance. It was clearly the dimension that dominated Lateef's concern when he phoned his brother after Maya had told him what happened. As he later said to me, "Well, what I told him was obvious. I told him, *'Ayb walaww'* [This is shame-ful], what will people say about us?" Lateef's traditionalism has always been very clear, extending to his patriarchal belief that Mario has failed to assume his responsibility, even if it was Adèle who had banged the cup of coffee, for it is up to him to control his wife.

Indeed, this conception of the world as divided between the space of migration, perceived as a space of pure labor where it doesn't really matter what people think of you, and the place of origin, which remains the only space where prestige and honor count, was a common mode of fragmenting the self, as we have seen. This was particularly so for first-generation immigrants from a rural background. For such immigrants, it might be shameful to work as, say, a garbage collector in the village, because one has the responsibility of upholding one's honor. But there's nothing wrong with working as a garbage collector in the place where one has migrated to, for there, one's responsibility is to make money. This localized conception of honor is very much at play here and is compounded by the family's status within the village.

We can note that although there's a difference in the imaginary global geography of the family between its conception as a spread-out, transnational functional unit in which each member is responsible for the internal reproduction of the whole and its conception as a village-oriented, honor-seeking assemblage, both realities are grounded in a similar idea of responsibility as the performance of a task directed toward the collective functioning of the whole. Still, there is a certain tension between the two conceptions that is played out between Adèle and her mother-in-law. It is also played out elsewhere. For example, the whole Boston part of the family, who often see the Venezuelans as too traditionalist, were critical of Lateef defining responsibility too much in terms of what people in the village thought. They felt, as noted earlier, that by migrating to a rural part of Venezuela, Lateef and the others "have not migrated at all," as one Bostonian put it to me. They, on the other hand, see themselves as far more "modern"—a term they use. And it's true that some of the Bostonians, particularly the younger generation, clearly have no sense of the family as a village-oriented honor-seeking apparatus. This isn't true of the younger generation in Cabudare. Thus, while for the Bostonians, failing one's responsibility is more a transnational failure of duty that generates "rational-modern" blame, for the Venezuelans the failure of responsibility *also* generates quasi-feudal shame.[5] Nonetheless, they all share a conception of responsibility as a division of tasks, and all have a solid conception of the transnational family as a functional unity.

There was, however, a different conception of responsibility voiced by various people throughout the conflict, one associated not so much with performing a task as with administering degrees of care. It delineated an experience of the family as a moral rather than a mechanical totality. This conception comes to the fore most clearly when examining what is at first glance an unrelated phenomenon: how claims concerning the importance of one's own contribution to the family are intertwined with claims of being in a position to judge the value of the contribution of others and to evaluate whether they are assuming their responsibility properly.

Money Isn't Everything

The conflict between Lateef and his mother on one side, and Mario and Adèle on the other, at one level involved competing valorizations of their contributions and responsibilities. Lateef valorized the fact that he is giving Mario "anything he needs and more," and he aimed to valorize his financial responsibilities and his contribution as a distributor of money wherever money is needed within the transnational familial space. Mario and Adèle valorized the fact that they must "endure" the practicality of living day to day with Jameeleh, which everyone acknowledged "was not easy." At one point Adèle, criticizing Lateef, said to me (with a somewhat more Sydney-sider ethos than a village ethos), "Lateef hardly ever interacts with his mum except when he comes here for a two-week vacation and is treated by everyone like a king. For him, Mum is 'Mum' [raises both hands]; for us, she is a pain in the arse." It's always implied that Lateef bought distance from practical and affective responsibility with his money, and it's this distance that allows him to idealize his mother.

Clearly, however, the conflict was triggered transnationally, not because Lateef wanted to make a claim concerning the value of his contribution compared with that of Mario and Adèle, but because he felt that his financial giving grants him the right to judge their contribution. His wealth, backed by his mother's authority, allows him to preside over not only family business but also the circulation of transnational remittances (see figure 5).

Therefore, the competition between different valorizations of different dimensions of the family and different corresponding responsibilities also turned into a dispute over who has the right to judge others and assume the position of "distributor" of responsibility. Because of this, at one stage Mario exclaimed about his brother, "If he thinks that by offering money, he is suffering so much that he can judge me, let him come and look after Mum himself. I'll go and make money and suffer instead of him, and then I can judge him." The son of Lateef's aunt (his mother's sister) from Boston also reported to me that his mother said something like "Paying money is no substitute for interaction. Lateef doesn't even bother to make a phone call, so why does he think it is up to him to tell Mario what to do?" Hoda, Lateef's sister who lives in Sydney, was apparently more direct in blasting him. She told him that it's become a habit of his to treat people with disrespect just because he makes a lot of money. "And what is a family where people do not know how to respect each other?" she said.

What I want to highlight in this debate is how, from the idea that the distribution of money does not give one the moral high ground to judge others, a different nonfunctional conception of responsibility starts to emerge. To be sure, this generalized critique of Lateef's money is not without a hint of jealousy and is certainly not disinterested. Hoda, for instance, is the least financially successful member of the family—indeed, she's a recipient of remittances from Venezuela. Nonetheless, this discourse marks a mode of existence of the family different from its experience as a mere mechanical totality aiming for transnational efficiency and an honorable presence in Jalleh. And it is through Maya's experience of the family that this different familial mode of existence comes to the fore.

The Family as a Moral Reality:
From Responsibility as Duty to Responsibility as Debt

While expressing to me yet another critique of Lateef's valorization of money, Maya made a comment that nonetheless clearly pointed to the different mode of existence referred to above. "Money," she said, "is not a substitute for care. Caring is a lot of work, and you don't do it by distributing money and visiting someone a couple of times a year. Surely you owe people, and you owe the family more than this." What stands out in this statement is an understanding of responsibility that brings together three important concepts: care, work, and "owing." While at first glance this appears to be an endorsement of Mario and Adèle through highlighting the notions of care and work that they tend to valorize, in fact it is not. Maya isn't speaking about the value of "caring for Mum through labor," as Mario and Adèle do. For her, care is the extent to which one cares about the family—that is, how much the family *matters*—which in turn is linked to how much it is perceived as the source of one's well-being. It is here that the notion of responsibility as duty is upstaged by the notion of responsibility as debt: a debt to other members of the family that is at the same time a debt to the family as a whole. For Maya, one can only try to repay this debt by "work," which means working at maintaining family relations. Here it can be seen

Table 2. International phone calls per Cabudare household

	Cabudare to village (138)	Cabudare to Sydney (70)
Maya	87	49
Waheed	22	10
Lateef	18	8

how one moves from the family existing as a functional mechanical whole to the family as a Maussian domain: a space of exchange laden with moral value where everyone owes everyone else and where, in trying to repay what one owes, one reproduces the family as a transnational moral assemblage.

It's not by chance that this familial reality is highlighted by Maya or that, within it, she gives herself the right to claim the high ground and to judge others. She is, and is recognized as being, the most responsible for keeping the family connected, largely through endless communicative labor. It can be clearly seen from the map of telephone flows that Venezuela is the communicative center of the transnational family. But, as table 2 shows, most of this communicative labor is done by Maya herself.

This kind of labor is often feminine and devalorized. Maya's husband would often go on about how she is "always on the phone." But I have also seen him ask her to contact a relative in Boston about a financial transaction, taking for granted that the relation exists as if Maya's communicative labor had nothing to do with that. Maya herself, however, has a clear sense of the reproductive power of her labor. That's why she allows herself to make authoritative claims about what responsibility to the family entails. These claims compete with Lateef's economically based authority. But, unlike the competition between Lateef's financial contribution and Mario and Adèle's practical contribution, the competition between Lateef and Maya, between financial power and communicative labor, denotes two different modes of existence of the Neefa family.

In this concluding section, I have tried to emphasize how particular experiences of responsibility by certain family members are integral in producing the transnational family's modes of existence. To be clear, it is not claimed that each person therefore has his or her own family reality. All these modes of existence are shared by all family members. Certain experiences, however, allow someone to dwell in one reality more than in others. In this sense, responsibilities are modes of investment in one's surroundings that intensify some realities at the expense of others. Accordingly, familial conflicts, as in the case of the rudely served cup of coffee, aren't so easily "solved," because they aren't a matter of agreeing or disagreeing with some-one's "point of view"; nor are they the product of an always overemphasized clash between modern and traditional "values."[6] Rather, they are a matter of colliding worlds, all of which are constitutive of the cosmos that is the transnational family.

EIGHT

Diaspora and Sexuality: A Case Study

Adel was born in 1956 in a village near Mehj. When I met him, he had been living for the past eighteen years in a town not far from New Bedford, Massachusetts. He is a close friend of the Mehj family that I was research- ing there. He's often present either at family-organized events or in certain "boys only" outings to bars and strip joints that he particularly enjoys. For a while, Adel himself became a major source of information about his rela- tion to, and perception of, the family. After two years of knowing him, we gradually became close, as he assigned himself an "I'll be your spy while you're away" role on my behalf. The incident I am about to describe hap- pened during my 2003 visit to New Bedford.

After a night of heavy drinking at a suburban strip joint, Adel wasn't in any shape to drive. Having maintained myself in a state of relative sobriety so as to continue indulging in my anthropological voyeurism, I ended up taking him home in his own car, planning to stay at his place for the night. I had done so on several previous occasions, and I've come to know his wife, Lamiya, and children well. During the drive home, I noted that Adel was unusually silent. As I stopped his car in front of his house, he didn't make any move to get out of the car. I looked at him, somewhat puzzled by both his silence and his immobility, and thought that maybe he was even drunker than I realized.

But then Adel turned to me and said hesitantly, "Docteur . . . I want to ask you about something." Somewhat dramatically, he made me prom- ise "not to tell anyone." Next, he told me that for some time now, he had been getting very anxious about his capacity to perform when about to have sex, leading to erection and ejaculation problems. He explained that his difficulties began to happen when he was having sex with his wife, but now he has the same problems "even with prostitutes." (Adel had disappeared with one of the women during our long stay at the strip joint, so I wondered whether he'd had a fresh experience of his problems that evening.) Finally, he asked me whether my knowledge of "this 'analysis of feelings and soul' [*tehleel'l el ehsehs wil nafs*] you talk about" could help cure him. He meant psychoanalysis.

During my fieldwork, I am repeatedly asked the question, But what is it exactly that you do? I usually interact strategically with queries of this sort. I reply by providing information that I hope will make those asking the question more comfortable with why I ask them the sort of questions I ask.[1] It is in that spirit that, during a previous visit, I tried to explain to Adel the significance of the psychoanalytic orientation of some of my work and the kind of issues and approaches that psychoanalysis entailed. Since then, he has asked me about psychoanalysis on a few occasions. But it took his disclosure of his sexual performance problems that night to make me aware that his interest, which in retrospect seemed somewhat odd, was not born out of pure curiosity.

Something else began to make sense that night. Although, as I said, Adel and I had become close, he's always insisted on addressing me with the classic French Lebanese hybrid title "el-docteur." Some of my informants use "Docteur" or "Doctor" occasionally, often to gain a form of symbolic capital by association when introducing me to others. Adel, however, uses it all the time. That night I began to strongly suspect that Adel's "docteuring" me had to do with more than my PhD.

I told Adel that I wasn't qualified to deal with his problem, and I casually asked him whether he tried Viagra. He obviously had been contemplating it, for he had accumulated a considerable amount of folk knowledge about the drug. He said that he was too scared to take it, mentioning "three-day-long erections that you cannot hide," heart attacks, and a host of other things that the drug was supposed to cause. I said that he could go to a psychotherapist for counsel but that he should probably see a physician first. Adel replied that he would be ashamed to see anyone in New Bedford and that if anyone around him knew, he would be dishonored: "I cannot tell anyone here . . . neither a Lebanese nor a foreigner[2] . . . I can only tell you."

He then started telling me how he has always confided in me because he's noticed that I was "not like the others." He said that he was struck by the fact that I don't gossip about people "like the other Lebanese," or judge and "say bad things" about anyone when we're talking about them. He informed me that he noticed this especially during my last visit, when we were discussing Nabil's sister.[3] He said that he had thought about telling me about his problem then, but he couldn't muster enough courage. Adel reiterated that he trusted me and that he was certain that what he told me would remain between us.[4]

I experienced Adel's noting that I do not judge as a small anthropological victory, as I often work hard to project that Spinozist aura of "do not condemn, do not laugh, do not hate, just understand." And although initially I couldn't understand why he wouldn't tell a "foreigner," I also felt victorious about his confiding in me, given his stated inability to tell either "a Lebanese [or] a foreigner." I think that to him, I was in a category between "both a Lebanese and a foreigner" and "neither a Lebanese nor a foreigner." I often found this position to work well for me.[5]

I asked Adel how Lamiya, his wife, felt about his sexual problems. His face changed, and he replied as if struck with fear: "I hope you're not going to talk to her about this." I said that he very well knew that I wouldn't, but that I just wondered whether she suggested that he do something about it. He said that he simply doesn't talk with her about it.

I continued stressing to Adel that notwithstanding his position—"honor or no honor," as I somewhat flippantly said—he simply must get some medical advice about his problem. He insisted that he couldn't. But he then told me that when he was in Lebanon three years earlier, he had made a special visit to Mar Charbel,[6] seeking a miraculous recovery. He even maintained that it "helped a bit" at first, but when he was back in New Bedford his problems resumed.

Suddenly, Adel shouted, "Fuck migration! [*Ayreh bil gherbeh*]. It's all got to do with me being here." I was surprised by the abruptness and the force with which he delivered his self-diagnosis. I asked him what he really meant by this. He said that he was "one hundred per cent sure" that his problems were completely related to his migrating to New Bedford. And then he said, "You should know this better than anyone, *ya docteur*, migration smoothly fucks you through the heart" (*El hijrah bit neek 'el 'alb 'al neh'im*)—a Lebanese colloquialism denoting destroying and grinding someone without their even noticing. I replied that this might be so but that I couldn't see what it had to do with his sexual problems. Adel told me that he "could see it coming five or six years ago." He explained that this was when he went through a phase of having a strong urge to return to Lebanon and began reflecting on his life in the United States. At this point, he "realized" that his migration was "one long and big mistake" (*ghalta taweeleh 'aridah*). Then his troubles "all happened at once." He became depressed, dissatisfied with everything, and along with that he started experiencing sexual problems. Adel concluded by saying to me in English, "I know I have wasted my life."

I replied consolingly that this surely can't be the case, emphasizing that he has a nice family and a good job. But Adel broke into a full-on depressive rant about his social and family life in New Bedford. He told me that his job stinks, that "after twenty years of hard work" he can't have a single day off without having to plan it way in advance, and that he can't even afford to go to Lebanon when he wants to. Not like Nabil, he pointed out, who goes whenever he likes.

Adel continued, saying that he also began comparing his wife's work as an accountant, where she deals with "high-status people" (*'aalam zaweht*), with his, where he constantly deals with "*'aalam 'aayfeen rabbun.*"[7] He said that this is why no one really respects him, not even his kids: "Kids don't have respect for their parents in this country even if they are Einstein, let alone someone uneducated with a lousy job like me. And anyway, you can't control kids here." While the Einstein bit was a specific Adel addition, the "no respect . . . no control" was a classic first-generation migrants' theme when speaking of their children everywhere I went around the globe. Although it had been four o'clock in the morning by the time I was alone in the spare room of Adel's house, I spent the rest of the night writing both the content of the conversation and my notes about it.

When I woke up the next day, it was almost midday. Adel and his wife had already gone to work, and his kids had gone to school; but he left me his keys and a note saying that I could use the car if I wanted to. I couldn't wait to see him again. I phoned him and said that I was driving to his work-place to join him for his lunch break. Straightforwardly, I informed Adel that I had been thinking about how he has come to see his perceived failure to succeed as a migrant as the cause of his sexual problems. I said that I would like him to talk with me about how he felt about his sex life—not only now but also before he left Lebanon and in the early stages of his migration ("as much as you are willing to reveal, but you can leave out the pornographic bits," I joked). I reiterated that this conversation would have nothing to do with curing him. I told him straight out that I didn't think that the connection he made between migration and his sexual per-formance was correct, but that I was nevertheless interested in the fact that he made that connection.

Here I must admit that when Adel told me about his problems that night, I hadn't precluded the possibility of a causal relation between his migration and sense of loss of social power, and a metaphoric dephalli-cization that ends up translating as "erectile dysfunction." But even by the next morning while thinking a bit more about it, I felt that the idea was rather far-fetched, and in any case I wasn't equipped to investigate it. By any standard, Adel leads a very unhealthy lifestyle. He's overweight, never exercises, chain-smokes, consumes a lot of alcohol, and has high blood pressure. As I learned later when I avidly started reading the medical literature on the subject, many of these factors are suspected as correlating with erectile dysfunction. Furthermore, erectile dysfunction can itself be the cause of low self-esteem rather than vice versa.

Nevertheless, I strongly suggested to Adel that although what I was asking him to participate in had nothing to do with curing him, his situation might become clearer to him, and he might feel better by talking with me about it and reflecting on the issue. I feared that now that he was no longer in a drunken state, he might refuse to talk or would take his time before agreeing to. But to my astonishment, he agreed on the spot. He clearly felt a strong desire to discuss his situation. Consequently, I began a series of informal interviews with him that took place during three visits to New Bedford over two years (2003–4). Also during that time, I visited his village while conducting fieldwork in Mehj and had various conversations with his friends, his elders, and other people who remembered him.[8]

I used the information that I managed to gather to understand significant elements of the history of Adel's experience of his masculinity as well as his socioeconomic history. In so doing, my primary aim was to examine the relation between Adel's diasporic trajectory and his conceptions of his own sexual viability. I tried to explore how this relation was transformed by the social locations and the various cultural milieus he has occupied along this trajectory. Throughout, I was also concerned with how much my emerging understanding of the diasporic condition could make sense of Adel's experience. Even though in my early analytical effort to understand this relation and these transformations I had not begun to think systematically with the concepts of lenticularity and anisogamy, once I did, they turned out to be helpful for a nuanced appreciation of Adel's experience.

A Short History of Adel's Diasporic Trajectory

When viewed from an economic perspective, Adel's migration appears to have been successful, as it led him to achieve a lifestyle far better than many from a similar background. At least for an outsider looking at the evolution of his economic lifestyle and capabilities, it's very difficult to understand the depressive reaction he has to the experience.

Adel was born in Lebanon in a Maronite village near Zgharta, the main Maronite town in the north. He attended primary school in the village. For his secondary schooling, he was first sent to a private Christian Brothers school, the well-known Frères of Tripoli (the capital of North Lebanon and at the time about an hour's drive from his village). But he stayed there for only two years, as his father, who owned their village's only grocery store, could no longer afford the fees. Adel tried to continue his education in a public school, but according to him "it was disastrous," so he left school after he received his certificate marking the end of middle school (year 9). He then joined a technical school, where he studied *méchanique*. In 1971 he began work in the mechanical repairs section of the Shekka cement company—a large employer of industrial labor in the north of Lebanon, and about an hour's drive from his village—but continued to live at home. Then in mid-1975 he lost his job. The Lebanese Civil War had already started, and in 1976 he became a full-time Phalangist militiaman.

Like most Phalangist militiamen in North Lebanon at the time, Adel was implicated in the forces that had assassinated the northern Christian leader Tony Frangieh in 1978 and so had to leave his village.[9] Like many of his military comrades, he moved to the Christian coastal town of Jbeil, where he lived between Phalangist barracks and his paternal aunt's house. Then in 1980 he had a disagreement with members from a militia subgroup closely affiliated with Samir Geagea, the leader of the northern Phalangist forces. Adel was relocated to the Christian suburb of Achrafieh in Beirut. There he remained with what became the Lebanese Forces, serving with a group led by Elie Hobeika, a key leader of the militia. He was slightly injured in the bomb blast that assassinated Bashir Gemayel, leader of the Lebanese Forces and Lebanese president-elect.

Soon afterward, Adel's maternal uncle managed to bring him to New Bedford in late 1983. Adel worked as a truck driver, delivering home construction lumber (for doors, windows, etc.) for his uncle's company for about one year. Next, he ran the company's truck repair shop for another two years. Finally, he separated the shop from the company and moved it to new premises that still serviced his uncle's business while servicing many other companies in the area.

Adel's parents had aspired for their son to be upwardly mobile through education. However, though they briefly managed to give him a taste of elite education, they were financially unable to keep him in a middle-class school. He ended up with a certificate in *méchanique*, something commonly perceived in Lebanon as giving access to a semiskilled working-class job. In speaking about his youth and his education, Adel shows that he has experienced them as an economic failure. And yet he has internalized both a desire for upward social mobility and a resentment of upper-class people. Adel says that he had tried to migrate before the Lebanese Civil War but couldn't.

But the imminent war opened an alternative path to minor upward social mobility: joining a militia.

More than migration, Adel's joining a militia allowed for the coexistence of his desire for some upward social mobility and his resentment of the upper classes. This was especially the case in the culture of the Phalangist Party, which accentuated among its members at the time, particularly the militia, a modernist individualism opposed to rampant forms of political patronage in Lebanon (often referred to as political feudalism), on the one hand, and on the other a form of petit-bourgeois class resentment, heavily laced with envy, toward the wealthy. Adel has openly admitted his resentment of the Lebanese upper classes, who, as he put it, "made us fight a war to protect their interests." He also quite candidly detailed his involvement in stealing jewelry from rich people's chalets and bungalows after a major military operation aimed at disarming a rival Christian militia, Dany Chamoun's "Tigers" of the National Liberal Party. The operation involved a raid on two middle-class beach resorts, Safra Marina and Tabarja Beach, where Dany Chamoun and other leaders of his militia were located. Attacking those chalets symbolized for Adel his combined hatred of the upper class and aspiration to mimic them: "I bought myself a BM [pronounced in French *Beh Emm*, as BMWs are affectionately known in Lebanon] and was partying with lots of beautiful Achrafieh women for a while," he said. After the assassination of Bashir Gemayel, and because he was injured in that bombing, Adel said that his economic situation started to deteriorate again. Fortunately for him, his uncle finally managed to sponsor him to migrate to New Bedford.

Adel's migrating to the United States and having his own business soon afterward is, in many ways, a dream come true—something hard to associate with a sense of failure, let alone a failure that could have had a metaphoric dephallicizing effect on him. A more obvious sense of disempowerment emerges in how Adel achieved his economic success. This takes us into the domain of anisogamic marriage, since Adel's relative economic success in the United States was largely because he had married his uncle's daughter. Indeed, by Lebanese standards Adel "married well," in that his maternal uncle's family is considerably wealthier than his own. His marriage is therefore anisogamic at this basic socioeconomic level. As noted in chapter 3, anisogamic marriages depend on a certain amount of symbolic labor of co-valorization for their success, without which they degenerate into their opposite—what I termed an infernal dialectic of put-downs and devalorization of the other compensated for by over-valorization of the self. Unfortunately, this latter situation was precisely where Adel and Lamiya's anisogamic relation was when I met them.

Articulations of Kinship and Migration

No doubt, Adel and Lamiya's marriage is a loving one. Both have made a point of speaking about love when talking about when they met. Lamiya said that when Adel arrived from Lebanon, she hadn't been interested in him. However, she explained, "there was something about his presence and the way he looked at me that I found increasingly attractive, and before I know it, I fell deeply in love with him." When talking about meeting Lamiya, Adel used a well-worn cliché, but one that seemed totally heartfelt: "I loved her from the day I arrived in America." In watching them interact with each other, I could tell that these feelings seemed to continue to exist, and they surfaced here and there. At the same time, however, I saw that the relationship was swimming in a sea of negativity, bitterness, and sarcasm. This was especially true on the part of Adel, who seemed now to speak of his wife, her brother, and her father with the same kind of resentment he exhibited when speaking of "rich people" in Lebanon. He had become totally alienated from his wife's family and spent most of his time with the Mehj family I was researching, which is where I met him.

As far as Adel is concerned, part of the problem began precisely because he married Lamiya and was made to feel by his father-in-law, mother-in-law, and brother-in-law that they didn't approve of the marriage because he wasn't good enough. Adel seems to have had to continuously manage claims of superiority on the part of some of his wife's family and sentiments of class inferiority on his part. Of his father-in-law, the uncle who had brought him to the United States, he said, "Every time he's helped me, he's made me feel like an underserving beggar rather than family." It is of course hard to know whether this is actually the case or whether Adel is himself exceptionally oversensitive, but there's no doubt that this was how he experienced the help he was given.

Adel also felt forms of class resentment toward his own wife, who is much better educated than he is. After their children grew up, Lamiya returned to university and resumed a career as a reasonably successful accountant, working continuously for her family's company in that capacity. Adel saw this work as allowing her to mix with a "better class" of people, unlike the truck drivers with whom he's been forced to mix. This was clearly expressed the night he started talking with me about his medical condition.

Adel's real bête noire, though, is Georges, Lamiya's brother, who according to Adel made a derogatory comment "that I will never forget" about his family's lifestyle in Lebanon. According to my Mehj informants in New Bedford, Georges, who is married to a German American woman and considered by his own family as "too American," holds Adel in contempt. Georges, by far the most educated and the most cosmopolitan of the family, finds his brother-in-law vulgar. Another member of the Mehj family who is a friend of Lamiya's said that Georges thinks that Adel is "all looks and nothing else" and apparently said so to his face. To Adel, as he unceremoniously informed me, "Georges was a wimp" who is jealous, because "no woman would bother looking at him when he is walking down the street." The men are barely on speaking terms. At the same time, Georges's disapproving gaze, as I was to discover, had been internalized by and constantly hovers around Adel, working nonstop to inferiorize him. In a kind of aristocratic logic that emphasizes those who are superior by essence rather than by achievement, such a gaze clearly works by reminding Adel that the very conditions of possibility of doing well out of a marriage are precisely to be not doing so well originally. Adel often made comments about Georges as if his brother-in-law were watching what he's doing.

There is no doubt that the totality of this anisogamic experience dented Adel's sense of patriarchal authority within his own family. He often expressed, as he did on the night I drove him back home, the sentiment that his children didn't respect him enough. He also expressed resentment over what he saw as "losing" his children to his wife's family, even though he recognized that this was inevitable, given that his own family is in Lebanon. All this was bound to generate a sense of domestic disempowerment for someone as traditionally patriarchal as Adel.[10] This domestic disempowerment not only increased when his business stalled in the mid-nineties, but it was also superimposed on a wider social disempowerment resulting from how he lived his Lebaneseness, particularly his traditional Lebanese maleness, in New Bedford.

At one point when speaking with Adel about his sensed loss of control over his family, I began to note something interesting: he continuously created a correspondence between his relation to his uncle's family and his relation to the United States. Just as he was concerned about losing his children to his wife's family, so he was also always concerned about losing them to the United States. Because of his already damaged and brittle sense of patriarchal power, Adel perceives the US state as a competitor for the domination of his familial realm as patriarch. He is genuinely haunted by the thought that "you can't even slap your kid here," which he repeatedly mentioned when describing his life in the United States, although his wife and kids said he has never been violent or ever had the disposition to slap the kids in the first place. Nonetheless, he experiences all state laws designed to empower women or children within the domestic space as an "intrusion" into what he sees as "his" domain.

Talking about his father-in-law, Adel said, "The way he treats me is no different from the way Americans treat most Lebanese. They think that because we come from a background where people have less money and are uncomfortable financially, we are less worthy human beings." Similarly, he said, "He and all of America might have a lot of money, but I am not going to respect them just because of that. If you want to be respected, you need to respect people. He acts as if he has given me his daughter or something archaic like this, and he conveniently forgets that she fell in love with me."

At another point, he sharply criticized something his brother-in-law said to marginalize him: "So when do you stop being the one who married into the family and become just part of the family?" This remark reminded me of the thankless dynamic of integration in which immigrants are always "trying to be" American, Australian, and so on but never fully becoming one in the eyes of the established population, which nonetheless expects them to keep on trying. Indeed, in the same way he has aspired to upward social mobility while resenting upper-class people, Adel also aspired to American modernity while hating the Americans he thought embodied it. In that sense, he is, paradoxically, an assimilationist. While he complains that life in America is inferior to life in Lebanon because of drugs and homosexuality among the youth, and says that one can be "too American" (which is "bad"), he also states unequivocally that the West and America are "modern" and "superior" in everything else. Adel is highly committed to the idea of "American democracy," where you don't follow someone "just because they are from family so-and-so." To him, to be more *moderne* (the word is always used in French) means above all to have more money, more education, a nice (i.e., new and big) house, and more goods. In this, he is no different from many Christian Lebanese migrants from his class and rural background. And as with many of them, his excessive enthusiasm for their specific version of Western modernism translates into racism toward Muslim Lebanese, who are perceived as bringing the collective Lebanese down in the struggle to achieve modernity. He proudly displays Jewish American newspapers in his shop to make sure that "no Palestinians or Muslims do business with me."

Adel's overemphasis on "marrying for love" also indicates this modernistic aspiration, as he uses it to demarcate himself from, and express a sense of superiority over, the Lebanese who engage in arranged marriages. But because of his low stock of modernistic cultural capital, his trying to be Western/modern always generates the sense of anisogamic inferiority common among those who are furiously "trying to be" while the gaze of the other is always telling them they are nowhere near their goal.

In this paradoxical state of intercultural relations reminiscent of those described by Frantz Fanon, Adel comes to dread any contact with the very middle-class Americans he so idealizes, as they put him face-to-face with his "trying to be" self.[11] His sensitivity about going to an American physician for his sexual problems, which I initially thought was rather strange, is better explained by this positioning of the middle-class American as the ultimate example of modernity and, more important, an object embodying his own superego—an imaginary severe judge always out to evaluate how "modern" others can be and someone always ready to condemn them for their failure to be modern enough.

It was because of statements and experiences such as the above, and a number of others like them, that it slowly dawned on me that in fact, Adel's anisogamic imaginary of American-Lebanese relations was therefore very close to how he imagined his marriage. Both were seen as negative anisogamic relations that were in fact articulated to, and reinforcing, each other. They were relations in which the party that thinks itself superior (his wife's family and "America") is constantly trying to make the other party forcibly acknowledge that superiority, and the other party (Adel himself) reactively refuses to acknowledge any gratitude for what he has received, because he feels it has been badly given; this whole ensemble propels the relation into a destructive dialectics. At the same time, we should note that because of the sense of "stuckedness" in this anisogamic sea of negativity, there is also a desire to see things improve. Of his relation to Lamiya, after listing a litany of problems, Adel said, "What can I do, he's my uncle, she's my wife, and we've got children. If only we can go back to getting on a bit better than this." Of his relationship with the United States, Adel also said at one point, "Leaving is not an option. I don't like saying it, and I wish it weren't the case, but our future is here."

Thus, in an important sense Adel feels stuck in a situation where he is experiencing a sense of social, economic, and patriarchal disempowerment. That this experience can be expressed as a form of symbolic castration isn't hard to see. It's at the risk of being banal to note here that in many masculine forms of domination, "having what it takes" to be the legitimate holder of patriarchal power within the family and society is captured with phallic metaphors. The literature on migration is full of allusions to phallic loss in describing how migrant males lose their culturally specific patriarchal power in migration. Words that suggest symbolic castration, such as *effeminization* and *emasculation*, are often used to describe this.[12] *Castration* itself is also used, of course. These words are often borrowed from an earlier usage, in describing colonially subjugated Third World males.[13] From this perspective, Adel's phallic experience is expressed as if it were merely a continuation and another version of his social experience of symbolically not "having what it takes" to be a dominant male, whether it is a lack of money, a lack of prestige, a lack of "modernity," or a lack of patriarchal authority.

Pointing to this experience of metaphoric and symbolic castration might seem satisfactory in helping us understand how Adel ends up connecting his experience of erectile dysfunction to the negative dimensions of his marriage and settlement. That is, the story goes something like this: it's not purely by chance that Adel suffered from a sense of social and patriarchal disempowerment at the same time that he experienced some form of erectile dysfunction. Thus, it was easy for him to see the two as related. In an extension of the common folk association of social power with phallic symbols, Adel comes to associate not being able to do something social with not having what it takes to do something sexual. His own language is full of metaphoric usages of the penis.[14] However, as I was interviewing him I was also visiting his village and investigating as best as I could the male sexual culture within it. I quickly started to appreciate an important dimension of the performative aspect of male sexuality among the Lebanese male villagers of the same area and the same class as Adel. One thing stood out: there was far less of a metaphoric link between this masculinity and the phallus as actual penis than what Western theorizations of the phallic nature of masculinity allowed for.

Penis-Centered Masculinity in a Lebanese Village

What follows is a slightly edited version of a couple of paragraphs I wrote in my notebook after talking with Adel in mid-2003. They can still serve as a good introduction to the questions preoccupying me then and in this book:

(1) In the West, the penis's social/public value as a symbol of masculinity in everyday life has markedly decreased. Those who valorize their masculinity through a valorizing of their penis are perceived as immature (teenagers) or vulgar (working class). Perhaps it is because of this that it has become common today, especially under the influence of Lacanian literary studies, to speak of any patriarchy as "phallocentric" and "phallocratic" but implying that this is always metaphoric or symbolic, to the point of vacating the actual imaginary of the penis from the metaphor.[15] (2) However, this actually stops us from differentiating between "actually phallocentric" and "metaphorically phallocentric" masculine cultures. (3) There are certain cultural milieus where there is nothing metaphoric about phallocentrism and phallocracy. It seems increasingly so to me that for Adel, as for several Lebanese males from his age group in the villages, phallic

power is above all just that: the power of the penis. And phallocentrism also means above all just that: all power is centered on the penis. (I say "above all" because even then there clearly remains a lot of room for metaphoric phallicity.) (4) In this kind of phallocentrism, the penis itself becomes the site of a condensation of all that signifies patriarchal masculine social power, whether in the realm of the sexual (men's domination over women), the familial (men's domination within the family), or the social (men's domination within a society). Thus, the penis comes to embody social power, not just signify it. This raises some important anthropological and theoretical questions:

—Am I right in thinking that this masculinity is at the intersection of cultural forms that are, in turn, specifically Mediterranean, rural, and class based—upper-working-class/lower-middle-class types?

—Also, it seems quite clear that the process of "civilizing" masculinity (as in Norbert Elias's conception of the civilizing process) involves its increased detachment from the biological phallus. And, therefore, is this penis-centered masculinity a sign of a primarily "Third World" and "underdeveloped" masculinity? Or is there another way of seeing it?

—Maybe just as racist discourse in the West today (which we may want to call advanced or civilized racism) has discarded biological difference in the name of cultural difference between "races," civilized patriarchal discourse likewise increasingly discards the biological as the site of sexual difference and domination?

It is from this perspective that Adel's formative years in his village, where he lived until he was twenty-two years old, acquire their centrality. Analyzing the village's male sexual culture, particularly among people of Adel's age and class background, makes it clear that it is there that Adel acquired the disposition to see in his penis this condensation of sexual, familial, and social viability I refer to above as the mark of "real" phallocentrism.

One doesn't have to stay in the village long to note that "the social order functions as an immense symbolic machine tending to ratify the masculine domination on which it is founded,"[16] as Bourdieu argues on the strength of his Kabyle ethnography. But Bourdieu still sees the male's lived "phallicity" as metaphoric: "The phallus, always metaphorically present but very rarely named, concentrates all the collective fantasies of fecundating potency."[17] Michael Herzfeld's Greek ethnography also relies on a relation between masculinity and metaphoric phallicity. For example, in analyzing the male physical posture, he, like Bourdieu, sees the men in the village as walking with bodies that are erect like the phallus.[18]

I suppose what I am aiming to describe are men whose masculine posture is not primarily manifested in being erect *like* the phallus but rather in standing in such a way that they make sure that it's their *actual* phallic region that is perceived as the key part of themselves. Masculine posture here is the art of arching the body in such a way that the crotch is obviously protruding and confronting. That is, what we have is a male sexual culture where the penis, even if always "clothed," is an important part of, to mobilize Goffman, the "front" in the masculine "presentation of the self in everyday life." The male body in its interaction with women evolves in a cultural milieu that gradually makes its whole *hexis* pivot around the penis. We can speak of a discursive and practical construction of a penis-centered worldview that internalizes its priorities in the male body, arching it accordingly.

In Adel's village, appreciative penis talk directed at boys begins very early in life. Both men and women while pampering and playing with male babies employ, very often publicly, comments like *Te'berni zabertak* and *tislamli hal anburah*, both roughly signifying a kind of submissive love of the boy's little penis and aimed at anthropomorphizing it. This play can and often does include catching the penis between the fingers, wiggling it, and in some cases kissing it while uttering the appreciative words. The "catching" of the penis continues well beyond toddler stage and up to the age of six or seven, though "checking up" on the public status of a boy's penis becomes by then an entirely male affair. An uncle or a close friend of the family can publicly take off a boy's pants and check the child's penis or simply pinch it without taking the pants off, saying *"Farjeeneh wayn sernah"* (Let us see where we're at) but just as important associating its state with other forms of social power: *"Shawfeeneh hal anburah. Saar feenah neflah?"* (Let me see this penis. Are we ready to plow the field?) This kind of play is internalized by boys, and one can see it resurfacing in teenage boys' play, which periodically involves melees in which they try to pinch each other's penis and make derogatory comments about it. I observed such interactions only recently, and it's likely that they were more pervasive in Adel's time. But perhaps no ethnographic detail can capture this early centering of the penis as well as a (rather exotic) quasi-ritual that Adel ended up telling me about somewhat indirectly.

From his late teenage years until he left his job, Adel was, by his account and those of others in the village who were his friends at the time, "very popular" with women. One older woman said to me that he is *mitl el-amar*—"like the moon"—commonly used to describe people considered physically beautiful. A close friend of his still in the village said, "We used to spend our time after work and on the weekends *am 'n nammer*" (literally "playing a number," which means showing off in front of women), adding that Adel was *"malak el tenmeer"* (the king of the show-offs).

As I was discussing this with him, I said to Adel jokingly, "So you clearly weren't shy with women." He enigmatically replied, "How can you be, once they've made you do *a'sit el-dabboor* [the sting of the wasp]?" Here is the rest of the taped conversation:

G: What is that?

A [*Smiling*]: You've never heard of *a'sit el-dabboor*?!

G: No. Sorry!

A: When you are very young . . .

G: How young?

A: I don't know, five or six years old. Anyway, someone among the elders [*el kbaar*] takes your pants off.

G: Wait . . . who do you mean by "the elders"? [*My mind, unrealistically, had started ticking in the direction of Herdt's* Guardians of the Flute.][19]

A: Well, your father, an uncle, or one of their close friends . . . but your father must be there, or no one would do it otherwise.

G: OK . . . and then?

A: Well, they take your pants off, and they put you behind a girl your age, and they keep pressing you and rubbing you on her until you get a little erection.

G: Are you serious?!

A: Yes.

G [*With a genuine sense of having missed out on an important Lebanese cultural tradition*]: I can't believe it. I've never heard of anything like this before . . . [certainly hasn't happened to me . . . Wait, before you go on. I've got too many questions. Let's see . . . uh, I'll come back to the questions]. Whoa, what happens next? After you get an erection?

A: That's it. They all start clapping, often some of them wiggle the boy's penis or pat him on the back while saying things like "Bravo *'aleik* . . . *'emella a'sit al dabour* . . . *aah ya Malak*" [rough translation: Good on you, he's given her the sting of the wasp. Oh, you king!].

G [*Laughing*]: I still find this unbelievable. But what about the girl? What do they tell her?

A [*Frowning*]: Nothing. Everybody is laughing and shouting, so most of the time she just thinks it's fun and she laughs too. Though I remember a couple of years before I left the village, we were doing it to the son of George with the daughter of Samira, and she [the daughter] started crying hysterically even before the rubbing started and we had to give up!

G: Tell me about when it happened to you. Who was present and who was the girl?

A: I only remember vaguely, but definitely my father and my paternal uncle were there. I still have an image of them in my mind, laughing their heads off when it was happening. I can't remember who the girl was.

G: But I am intrigued . . . I mean, presumably, she is the daughter of a friend of
   your family or something.

A: I don't remember . . . It must have been the daughter of a friend we have
   stopped seeing since, because otherwise people would have continued reminding me of who she was. But yes, usually she would be a friend of the
   family who just happened to be there on the day. And, of course, her father
   would be there. You wouldn't do it without the parents knowing. It is never
   planned; it usually happens after a lunch or dinner party, and lots of people
   are around . . .

G: And do you remember any one of your friends to whom it was done?

A: Hmm . . . actually . . . no, I don't remember this. I only remember it with other
   boys later, when I was older.

G: Tell me . . . did you do it to your son?

A: You've got to be kidding. Can you imagine what el Madame [the title Adel uses
   sarcastically, in its French-Arabic combination, to refer to his mother-in-law]
   would say if this happened to her beloved?

G: But you don't have any objections yourself. You'd do it?

A: Yes, of course I would. I think it would be good for him.

G: OK . . . your daughter . . . if you're around, would you have let this be done to
   your girl if you are around?

A [Smiling]: Yes. Why not? Let her get used to it. This is how it will be in life.

I asked around the village and in several others for accounts of *a'sit el-
dabboor*. The practice doesn't seem to have been as known outside the village. Since I first detailed this practice, a number of people have disputed
that it exists. They argue that it must be the product of Adel's imagination. I
doubt this is the case. When I asked around, only a handful of people from
other villages, one fairly distant from Adel's, knew about it. But all have
independently detailed it to me in much the same way Adel did. In Adel's
village, however, several older men confirmed the practice, though they said
that no one does it anymore. But it was clear that the practice had not been
widespread. In addition, it was looked down on by the village's "aristocracy" as "what the peasants do." And not surprisingly, it was disliked by
the women. Also unsurprisingly, none of the few people I asked could find
me a female villager who would share her childhood experience of it with
me. An older woman told me that women used to leave the room when
"it" was happening and, as one of them put it, "leave the men alone to play
this disgusting game." With a number of her relatives, men and women,
sitting around her and laughing at what was clearly the telling of a ritually
recounted story, another woman told me the story of Afifeh, who didn't

allow her daughter to be "sacrificed." She had said to her husband, "You let this be done to your daughter and you'll never get to rub your own penis except on the fig tree outside!"

Besides being a festival of penile phallocentrism, what was also interesting about *a'sit el-dabboor* were the words uttered to the performing boy once he proves himself capable of having an erection: *"Bravo 'aleik, 'emella a'sit al dabour. Aah ya Malak!"* They roughly mean "Good on you, he's given her the sting of the wasp. Oh, you king!" This pronouncement delivers a clear association between the possession of a well-functioning penis, the capacity to dominate girls, and the capacity to rule within society, which is at the core of this "real" phallocentrism I've been describing.

The frequent touching of and direct and indirect remarks about the penis slowly create a fusion of the social and sexual male viability and the ultimate male posture of the protruding crotch. Flaunting the crotch is particularly emphasized during the traditional *dabkeh* dance, where the male arching of the body, accompanied by the display of various forms of physical prowess (the males are said to engage in *'ard adhalat*, muscle exhibition), stands in contrast to the female undulating bodily movements. But the male-female posturing and interaction at such parties actually offer us another important dimension of this phallocentrism: the penis is itself party to men's classification of girls according to their suitability for marriage or sex.

I initially didn't give it much attention when someone from a village neighboring Adel's joked that "men here think with their penis." I took it to mean what it ordinarily means, that they follow their sexual instincts. This is because I heard another person say in the same vein that when it comes to girls, the men of the village don't use their brains, they just "go where the tip of their penis guides them"—which always gets them in trouble with the men of the villages where the girls they're chasing come from. But I noticed that the mode of deploying one's crotch was actually an intrinsic part of how men categorize women.

On one hand, this system is very simple: women are classified as "for marriage," a category usually reserved for the girls of the village,[20] or they are for flirting and "showing off" with. Exhibiting your crotch to the latter is fine but to the former is vulgar. It's considered rude to come on like a stud to village girls, in the sense that it's rude to be too sexual toward women you may potentially marry. To such women, you exhibit the social traits of your masculinity (gender without sex, so to speak): toughness, rationality, dependability, and so on. You emphasize your sexual/physical masculinity only to those outside the "official" marriageable realm. This behavioral code partly extends the logic of the arranged marriage, whereby marriage decisions are not supposed to succumb to the irrational flows of desire but instead must be rational, businesslike decisions. The code also extends into a division between women who embody reproductive sexuality and the others who embody sexuality for fun.[21]

Of course, the loves, great and small, that many village boys experience with village and non-village girls perturb the neatness of these domains. Furthermore, witnessing the kind of male-female interactions that go on during various "parties" and festive gatherings clearly indicates that these neat categories are continuously subverted even when the appropriate behavior appears to be reasonably maintained. Most males, for example, do not assume that the marriageable women of the village aren't interested in their penis exhibitionism. What they do in effect is displace their sexual exhibitionism: they play the stud with the strangers, but they hope that the women of the village are watching, for this is really where they want to establish their reputation and that of their penis. Indeed, the boy/man who proves himself *fahl* (basically, a stud) does so outside the village. But it's within the village that he is perceived as a holder of a social prestige that can be converted into real social power: for example, he attracts a group of other males around him who are akin to admirers, along with those trying to establish their own reputation by rubbing shoulders with him. If he's willing and able to play such a game, he may gain access to the position of middleman for a particular patron, which in turn allows him to have his own clientele.

Even when a phallic culture is penis-centered, however, masculinity still depends on a whole series of metaphoric phallic symbols that work to prop up the penis. That is, males within penis-centered patriarchies still rely on an array of phallicized cultural forms they claim to monopolize. For instance, the thick handlebar mustache was the village's supreme phallic symbol for a long time. Various items of clothing monopolized by males have also functioned this way. One example is found in John Gulick's early 1950s ethnography of a northern Christian Lebanese village not far from Adel's own. To be sure, Gulick's text has little to say about patriarchy and male domination. Yet in a section dealing with clothing, the anthropologist describes how "younger women, especially those who work in the city, follow modern European styles." "However," he continues, "the western practice of women or girls wearing slacks or shorts has been completely rejected." One of the reasons for this rejection mentioned by Gulick is that "the men regard the practice as a usurpation of a symbol of masculine status."[22] Nonetheless, in the above I have tried to give an account of the penis-centered nature of the masculinity Adel internalized during his formative years in the village.

By all accounts, including those of his friends and contemporaries, he not only was part of this culture but also was a reputed performer in it. This, I think, can help us understand even more the link he has made between his erectile dysfunction and his loss of social power.

When thinking through Adel's case, I came across a puzzle whose solution turned out to be crucial for apprehending the depth of his sense of dephallicization. It's good to finish this chapter with it, as it gives us a further sense of the complexity of the anisogamic dynamics constituting diasporic life.

After examining the material I had collected about Adel, I was reflecting on how he yearned for bourgeois life but hated bourgeois people, yearned to be educated but hated educated people, yearned to be American but hated Americans, and most generally yearned to be modern and hated those whom he perceived as too modern. Yet there was only one domain of life where Adel did not appear to aspire to more modernity and where we would say he was resolutely archaic. This was precisely the domain of male sexuality. In line with the penis-centered masculine culture in which he had spent his formative years, one would have expected Adel to at least yearn for a more refined display of male sexuality. But he didn't.

It's hard to think that this had to do with not having been exposed to such a different sexual performativity. In fact, when I asked Adel about his first relations with women when he moved to the United States, he replied that these hadn't gone well, as lots of women thought he was too pushy. Also, in a story Adel told me in too vague a manner for me to retell it coherently here, there were hints that one of the breaking points in the relation between him and George had to do with his telling George that he was too effeminate in how he behaved with girls and that he needed to act more like a man. Clearly, unlike in the domains of wealth, education, and style, Adel didn't feel that he lacked anything in the domain of sexuality compared with George. He firmly refused to dwell in a lenticular array of possibilities and was entrenched in the one and only form of male sexuality he had inherited and developed in his village. The reason behind this was not obvious, and it was revealed to me rather indirectly.

In the few visits where I spent time with Adel and Lamiya and her family, it was always clear that while Adel had plenty of things to say about every member of the family, Lamiya's parents never referred to him, positively or negatively, in my presence. So the one time that they did stood out for me. I had come to Adel's house to pick him up, but he was still getting ready. Lamiya was sitting with her mother and father, having afternoon coffee and cakes. The parents were talking about celebrating their upcoming fiftieth anniversary in Greece. Lamiya's father said, "I forgot to tell Adel that I am going to invite Hind [his sister, Adel's mother] to join us." Her mother replied, "And Youssef [Adel's father]." Then she turned to me and said, "Adel is very sensitive about his father." Nothing else was said about it at the time, but it was obvious to me that this sensitivity was an ongoing issue.

Sometime later, from what I gathered upon hearing various people knowledgeable about the situation speak about it, it became clear that in contrast with Adel's experience, Lamiya's family did not see themselves as the ones who had initiated the negative anisogamic cycle with him. Rather, they saw Adel as constantly boasting about the importance of his paternal side of the family—so much so that his in-laws began feeling that this over-valorization of the paternal side was a devalorization of their family. As for his maternal uncle, Adel was being doubly ungrateful. He wasn't showing any gratitude for all the work his uncle had done to help him obtain a visa and migrate to the United States, nor was he showing any sign of gratitude for all the financial help he has received from him since marrying his daughter.

For a time, I thought that Adel's valorization and sensitivity regarding his father comprised a classic anisogamic sensitivity about uncovering his less favorable class background. But something happened when I was in the village that allowed for an important and until then hidden process to work its way through the whole anisogamic web of relationality and strategies in which Adel was captured. As noted earlier, Adel is recognized as good looking by many in the village. Yet two people from the father's side of the family independently commented about Adel's appearance in a way that stayed with me. There was a clear implication in how they said it that Adel is "too good looking," implying a feminine quality. Something clearly unpleasant was in their tone, and it struck me that it wasn't a subject that Adel would want to discuss. But I finally did bring it up. And his reply was a very angry one: "Who are these sons of a whore who talked like this?" He didn't wait for my reply. "I bet you it's . . ." To my surprise, he immediately and correctly guessed which cousins had spoken about him in this way.

Adel proceeded to reveal to me that the core of this issue was that he looks too much like the maternal side of his family. Indeed, he does look very much like both his father-in-law and George! And I immediately understood what the problem was. In a wonderful example of an imaginary genetic "power struggle," the Lebanese male villager experiences his child's birth, without the aid of a microscope, as a fight for control between his genetic lineage (his blood, his stock, etc.) and that of his wife. To have a boy rather than a girl is not just to secure the paternal lineage, it's proof that his maleness has prevailed over his wife's femaleness in the making of the baby. But to have a boy that resembles the father rather than the mother is further proof of the vitality of the male's stock. Therefore, the son's lack of resemblance to the father becomes a signifier of an imaginary genetic "defeat" of the paternal lineage, which reflects negatively on the father's phallic power. The father then resents the son as an embodiment of his own genetic weakness. In turn, the son, being dominated by the genetic lineage of the mother, is perceived as effeminized. In Arabic, the maternal uncle is called *khal*. When a man looks like his mother's side of the family, he is said to be *m'khawwal*, which means looking like his *khal*. It has been pointed out to me that in Egyptian Arabic, the term *khawal*, which must have the same roots, is used for and is the equivalent of the derogatory *poofter* or *faggot*, both of which denote a form of effeminization.

Adel told me that his father never failed to remind him that he looks "too much" like his mother's side of the family. "When he was angry with me, he would always say, *'Tali' la khalak Jameel'* [You take after your maternal uncle Jameel]. Of course, he would not mention my other maternal uncles, who are all successful. He just mentions Jameel, who is known by everyone to be a weak man with many problems. I hated him when he did this." Nonetheless, it was very clear that Adel aspired to truly belong to his father's lineage. I couldn't help thinking that here was another space, indeed perhaps the foundational space, where the same pattern emerges as before. Adel both aspires to fully belong to his father's lineage and hates his father's lineage. But this also leads us straight into the classic psychoanalytic structure of penis envy and castration anxiety: "Like my father, I have a penis; therefore I am the patriarchal inheritor of my father, except that my penis might be too small, and therefore I might be undeserving as an inheritor." I suspect that Adel's unambiguous hypermasculinity is a mode of compensating for a life that is, because of his maternal phenotype, constantly haunted by the specter of effeminization.

Interestingly, it's hard to avoid seeing how foundational this is in understanding Adel's problem with his mother's family in New Bedford. Lamiya's father and brother clearly stand as a reminder of the constant dephallicization he has endured within his father's family because of his looks. His presence there intensified the specter of effeminization, triggering a further intensification of his attachment to his hypermasculinity. Adel's matrilocal mobility added a further anisogamic dimension to his migration that reverses the order of superiority and inferiority. If economically his migration and marriage to his uncle's daughter signal an alliance with a higher-status group and upward social mobility, a downward social mobility in migration is symbolized via accrued symbolic capital within a patriarchal, patri-phenotypical, patrilineal, and patrilocal order. This downward mobility is experienced as a form of matrilocalism that has made him now even more separated from the paternal side of his family. It has "locked" him with his dephallicizing maternal "look-alikes." It's is hard not to see in this experience of matrilocalism one of the bases of Adel's feelings of dissatisfaction and disempowerment.

I hope that this chapter has conveyed the complexities of the anisogamic processes that are part and parcel of the diasporic condition. At the same time, there is an important analytical lesson here. The anthropology of diaspora should never take for granted that when people experience mobility through international migration, the move from one national culture to another is the most important change they endure. Nor should it be what necessarily monopolizes our analytical imagination.

NINE

Diasporic *Jouissance* and Perverse Anisogamy: Negotiated Being in the Streets of Beirut

Despite the absence of shared public spaces, the serious environmental problems, and the lack of centralized urban planning that characterize it—and despite the recurring political violence that marks its history, Beirut's inhabitants of all classes, though in different ways, often speak of a quasi-mysterious but nonetheless tangible "buzz," a sense of "quiet pleasure," a type of urban *jouissance*, woven into the texture of the city's everyday life.[1] What is more, this jouissance is seen as closely entangled with rather than in opposition to the sense of chaos and uncertainty that the city can produce in people. Lebanon's semichaotic social life partly mirrors its economy. Someone, long ago now, defined the nation's *laissez-faire* capitalist economy as *laissez-tout-faire*, so bereft it is of any government regulation. The economic anarchy—which allows investors and developers to pursue profit with little regard for the social, urban, or ecological consequences of their investment—is replicated in how religious communal organizations, political parties, and groups as well as individuals behave socially and politically in everyday life: pursuing their interests with little regard for their effect on the collective. This conduct is often viewed as exasperating and is part of what gives Lebanon's periodic civil wars and uprisings their particularly chaotic form. *"Shoo hal fawda b'hal balad!"* (What a chaotic nation this is!), *"Ma fi nazam b'hal balad!"* (There is no law and order in this nation!), or *"Ma fi dawleh!"* (There is no state!) are commonly heard exclamations and lamentations. But it would be a poor ethnographer indeed who didn't notice that—without diminishing in any way the general sense of exasperation that these cries contain, or the fact that they point to real, often encountered problems—they nonetheless contain a mischievous enjoyment of the very chaos they are bemoaning.[2]

I refer to this enjoyment as jouissance because of its mischievousness, but also because it is experienced as a state of the body just as much as a state of the mind. Of course, like everywhere else, people in Beirut spend their time bogged down in the grind of everyday life, worrying about practical and financial realities. And more than just anywhere, they will be crankily caught up in an impossible traffic jam or trying to negotiate a transaction with the state bureaucracy. Yet despite and alongside all this, people can express a certain joy in maneuvering through these very difficulties. And more predictably, on a quiet evening alone or with family and friends, walking on the Corniche, having an *arghileh* (water pipe) in a café by the sea or simply having a smoke and a coffee with the concierge and a few others sitting in front of one's apartment building, or having a *man'ousheh* (Lebanese thyme flatbread) in the morning and taking cover underneath someone's balcony as the rain starts falling, people will readily tell you that "there's something about this place."

A fisherman near Beirut's *manara* (lighthouse), who began by relating a variety of personal and financial problems he encounters daily, finished by telling me, "Life is hard, but every time my friends come and we play a game of cards by the sunset here, all my problems disappear; even the traffic behind us [which I had been complaining to him about] seems like a nice traffic. I have the best of friends, and this must be the most beautiful sunset in the world." "Where else in the world have you seen a sunset?" I asked somewhat naïvely, genuinely wanting to find out. He hesitated for a second before turning his head and replying, "I haven't been anywhere." I had inadvertently embarrassed him. "But it must be one of the most beautiful sunsets in the world, don't you think?" he asked with a sense of pleading. I agreed: "The most beautiful sunset and the most beautiful traffic." Being after all a Beiruti at heart, I deeply believed what I said.

While it is important to keep in mind that almost everyone expresses these feelings every now and then, it's also the case, for obvious sociological reasons, that the more unburdened people are from the dismal local wages, the uncertainties of the future, the effect of pollution, and the weight of class, patriarchal, racial, bureaucratic, sectarian, and clientelist arbitrariness and domination, the more willing they are to be effusive about this "something," this "mellow and yet intense feeling at the same time," in the words of a man I was chatting with on the Corniche. Thus, it's not surprising to note that middle-class Westerners who come to live in the city for extended periods have often expressed similar feelings. The Australian journalist Catherine Taylor, in her book *Once upon a Time in Beirut*, describes living with her husband, Matthew, in Beirut for a few years while working as a Middle East foreign correspondent for an Australian newspaper. She reflects:

Matthew and I would often talk about why we liked Beirut so much. After all, it was polluted and chaotic and noisy. Don't even start on the traffic. The politics was turbulent and sometimes dangerous. . . . And . . . it was quite an expensive place to live. . . . It was the little things, we decided, that we loved. The upside of chaos was that regulations were sporadic. We could drink cocktails hanging off the edge of a tower block with a view of the ocean; drive the wrong way down a highway when all other routes were closed and break the speed limit (what speed limit?). The pace of life itself was slow and rhythmic, soothing, and full of things to like. . . . We would wonder out loud to each other if perhaps it was simply that Beirut's extremes exaggerated everything, made every moment seem alive.[3]

There is also a whole genre of light touristic journalism, regularly appearing in the international press, which celebrates how Beirut keeps being a city of enjoyment despite war and chaos, though these accounts are not based on long-term experiences of life there. Radical activists and academics often bemoan this type of journalism and the clichés it circulates. They rightly see it as mystifying the serious problems Lebanon is facing (which have led to several social movements and uprisings over the years). The way they criticize, however, ends up itself being so absolute that it negates how this reporting does point to a jouissance experienced by many. After all, mystificatory and lightweight though they might be, these same journalists do not write the same touristic things about every single city. What's more, they are hardly the only ones who inflate their experience of this Beiruti enjoyment. Indeed, no one expresses this jouissance with as much conviction as returned immigrants, particularly (but not only) middle-class returnees, who carry with them the economic and ontological security they have internalized elsewhere in the world and who come to Beirut with a nostalgic desire for an imaginary Beirut where the enjoyment of anarchy and chaos is a, if not *the*, central feature.

It is this lenticular experience of entangled order and disorder experienced by a group of returnees that will be the main empirical focus of this chapter. It should be clear from all the above that I don't see this enjoyment of Beirut as specific to the culture of returned immigrants. Indeed, I will argue that it's a feature of the lenticularity of Lebanon's diasporic modernity, as we have analyzed it throughout this book. What is specific to the experience of the people I am working with here is the clarity and intensity with which this enjoyment presents itself, allowing us to better understand the phenomena in question. At the same time, if Adel in the previous chapter exemplifies a rural person with low educational, cultural, and economic capital who experiences himself as constantly subjected to multiple lenticular and anisogamic orders that constrain the viability of his life, the subjects of this chapter offer the opposite case: people who are playfully, and perversely, constituted as strategic subjects who enhance the viability of their lives within such a lenticular and diasporic reality.

The urban anthropology of Beirut has been, like the anthropology of diaspora as I characterized it in the beginning of this book, more sociological and explanatory in its intent. It is worth noting in this regard that with the exception of the thorough doctoral work of Kristin Monroe, which explores the role of capitalism, corruption, and patronage in shaping the informal and unplanned character of urban space, some of the best critically and theoretically informed, sociologically oriented, and ethnographic studies of Beirut's urban culture is the work not of sociologists or anthropologists but of academics working at the intersection of architecture, urban design, and politics.[4] In this chapter, I want to continue the kind of critical anthropological quest for alterity with which I am approaching diasporic culture, now also including Beirut's urban culture in this approach. Though not concerned with radical alterity as such, the work of AbdouMaliq Simone offers, in a general sense, a similar direction.[5]

When confronted with the expressions of urban jouissance such as those briefly mentioned above, it would be easy to see in them merely an individualized libertarian enjoyment of an excess agency, akin to the urban Dionysian experience described by Ulf Hannerz but magnified by the absence of any systematic law-regulated forms of sociality.[6] But to be clear, we are not dealing with mere chaos here. For one thing, state laws in Beirut are never completely absent. They're just selectively or incompetently implemented in terms of where and on whom, and with what degree of tenacity and intransigence. Thus, what we have is a legal culture that reproduces the lenticular nature of diasporic culture. Second, and just as importantly, even when the state's capacity to implement the law was at its weakest during the Lebanese Civil War, Beirut, except perhaps in its war zones proper, never descended into pure chaos. Indeed, while it is more customary to speak of how unruly and chaotic Lebanon is, the more astonishing though less dramatically experienced fact is how lawful and disciplined it remains, despite all the wars and uprisings and the state's seeming inability to adequately govern and uphold the law. Everything continues to function: services, shops, traffic, schools, everyday social life, and so on—not wonderfully, indeed often very badly to the point of collapse, but functioning without collapsing nonetheless. It is this capacity of society to continue being one—to offer possibilities of everyday forms of relationality, coexistence, and considerate interaction in the shadow of the state, as it were—that invites us to consider the presence of *another* mode of sociality outside the law that allows for urban social life's continuity, which the experience I am analyzing here helps highlight.

Anthropology, more than other disciplines, has always had to come to terms with forms of sociality that are not based on state regulation of law and order. As James Scott notes, "Until shortly before the common era, the very last 1 percent of human history, the social landscape consisted of elementary, self-governing, kinship units that might, occasionally, cooperate in hunting, feasting, skirmishing, trading, and peacemaking. It did not contain anything that one could call a state. In other words, living in the absence of state structures has been the standard human condition."[7]

And in particular there's a long lineage of anthropological work highlighting the "horizontal" sociality of the gift in opposition to the "vertically mediated" sociality of the state. The contrast between state-based and gift-based forms of social relations is already well explored in Marcel Mauss's classic work *The Gift* and after him by Claude Lévi-Strauss, who saw in reciprocal sociality the "elementary" organizing principle of kinship.[8] This lineage continues via the work of Pierre Clastres as well as Marshall Sahlins's masterly analysis of Mauss's work in *Stone Age Economics*, where he argues that "where in the traditional view the contract was a form of political exchange, Mauss saw exchange as a form of political contract."[9]

In this chapter, I want to contribute to this anthropological lineage, arguing that it is to such outside-the-state forms of sociality, what I'll call "negotiated being," that the jouissance introduced above points us to. I will also show that this negotiated being is a form of sociality specifically adapted to the lenticularity of Lebanon's diasporic modernity. To begin to explore these points, we need to bravely enter the world of Beirut's traffic, for nowhere is this sociality more present than in the way people must negotiate the city's streets.

Driving Inside and Outside the Law in Beirut

In scenes with which inhabitants of many major Third World–ish cities are familiar but with a touch of Lebanese specificity, cars, pedestrians, and scooters circulate in the streets of Beirut in ways that produce a clear sensation of chaos for the uninitiated. One can never take it for granted that traffic laws will be obeyed. Cars don't necessarily stop at red lights unless a policeman is there directing the traffic. On the other hand, they can stop for no apparent reason at all, right in the middle of the road, sometimes because the driver has noticed a friend along the footpath and wants to say hello. Turn signals are hardly ever used, and cars can use any lane to turn right or left, cutting across traffic. In any case, lanes are often meaningless. While traffic lane markings have been retraced since the Lebanese Civil War, most motorists don't take them into account; if they do, it's to line up the markings with the middle of their car. That is, one drives on the lines rather than along them. On top of that, it's optimistic to think that these motorists will drive in a straight line. This is especially so with the "service" (pronounced in French)—that is, cars that function like minibuses—which use the road to engage in giant slaloms wherever potential customers make an appearance.[10] Moreover, while concentrating on avoiding the anarchic movement of cars, drivers also have to worry about pedestrians who can "pop up" seemingly out of nowhere. More worrying still are the scooters that operate by moving into any open space between cars, regardless of the direction of traffic. It's this kind of scene, which can be the source of extreme anxiety for newcomers and stress for many locals, that many Lebanese drivers also find quite exciting, priding themselves on their ability to maneuver their vehicles in such an environment.

Though outsiders have often commented to the contrary, such Lebanese motorists, particularly young and middle-aged men from Beirut and its suburbs, like to claim themselves as the world's best drivers. "If you are in Europe, people assume that if you are facing a green light, the others are facing a red light and will stop. Often accidents happen because people think: it's a red light, so people will stop. A Lebanese driver will never make that assumption. They never trust anyone obeying the law. That's why they don't have as many accidents at intersections as others," someone said to me with clearly no research whatsoever to back his claims, other than his firm belief in the truth of what he said. But it's true, as these Lebanese contend, that to drive in Beirut you must always be aware of everything and everyone and can't rely on any predictable driving by others. Cars, pedestrians, and scooters, not to mention the occasional ambulant fruit and vegetable vendor pushing a cart, can come at you from any direction. So you must learn to drive by constantly "keeping a 380-degree watch," as someone joked, or by heeding the same idea expressed differently by another person: "You have to keep your eyes on everything, and don't forget the rest." It's this scene that the returning diasporic subjects I am concerned with find, in the words of one returnee, "positively exhilarating." One of them explained that driving in Lebanon feels like being in a *Star Trek* movie navigating the USS *Enterprise* through a field of meteorites.

To be sure, not all people and not all returned immigrants express this sense of exhilaration when it comes to driving in Beirut. Many immigrant returnees feel the urge to uphold what they consider to be Western standards of behavior as if they were on a civilizing mission: one is always certain to meet an immigrant trying to act "more civilized than the locals" by decrying the chaos, or the rubbish, or the decimation of the mountain forests, or the racist way the Lebanese interact with their Sri Lankan, Filipino, or African maids. But sometimes the very people expressing exasperation with the chaos also express a sense of enjoyment of it, and vice versa.

In his memoirs, Abbas El-Zein, a Lebanese professor of engineering at the University of Sydney and a novelist, writes: "Shortly after returning to Lebanon in 2000, I made a startling discovery. Beirut was possibly the only city in the world where stopping at a red light was a subversive act."[11] El-Zein decided for a while to make a stand for Western civilization by insisting on stopping at red lights, heroically enduring the abuse of the locals. "It was my civic duty, I believed, to promote a Western-type traffic civilization in a city that was not generally interested in regulations, traffic-related or otherwise," he writes. But he goes on to say that "nevertheless, there was something appealing about the fact that abiding by these rules was a matter of choice rather than compulsion. A few months, heatwaves and traffic jams later, I relaxed my own rules and, when I felt I had to, I parked along a double line and, more rarely, I drove the wrong way down a one-way street."[12] Indeed, El-Zein finishes by noting that despite the endless Lebanese comments about the lack of law and order, he could detect another sentiment: "Sometimes I suspected that everyone, deep down, was happy at the chaos and that such comments were no more than lip service to uptight, over-Westernized returnees like myself who had a predilection for excessive management of public space and a strange penchant for straight lines."[13]

What distinguishes the group of young, cosmopolitan returnees and locals I am working with here is the opposite of a predilection for excessive management. If anything, they exhibit a kind of excessive management fatigue or, even more generally, a kind of Western civilization fatigue. They have a firsthand, routinized, and internalized experience of how "ordered" and lawful the traffic can be in other cities, and they have also fully internalized a Western sense of law and order. Indeed, one can say that they are the Lebanese variant of the transnational cosmopolitan middle class one meets everywhere around the world. They are all well aware that reaching a "level" of law and order such as what one finds in the West (particularly the English-speaking West) is widely considered by people around them as a higher stage of civilization. Yet having the experience of Beirut seems to have provided them with a comparative critical edge, allowing for an equally critical mode of inhabiting Western spaces. For this reason, they make a point of not sharing the general enthusiasm toward what they see as excessively overregulated spaces that constitute an attack on their sense of well-being.

For such people engaging in a kind of playful cosmopolitan "anticolonialism" the Lebanese who live in such semichaotic situations are not missing out on anything. Rather, Westerners are missing out on having Lebanese-like situations. And driving through Beirut's chaotic streets is seen as a case in point. Rather than lamenting the chaos, driving in Beirut is "fun." Just as importantly, many people I spoke with take great pride in their capacity to negotiate the chaos. They see it as a skill that people who live in ordered cities or, in the words of one informant, "those who moronically stop at a red light at three AM in the morning when the streets are empty" have lost. In a kind of perverse form of anisogamic strategizing, they reverse the widespread belief that the Lebanese minimal lawfulness on the road is indicative of Lebanon's underdevelopment. People who try to obey the law in a way that seems absurd are mocked as being too Westernized, and the Lebanese way of driving is held to be superior, with an implication that Westerners obeying the law have a passive sheeplike mentality. When I "inadvertently" stopped at a red light though there were no cars to stop for (sometimes my Australian driving habitus does take over), I saw the driver behind me slowly steer his car around mine, stop next to me, roll down his window, and say very calmly, "Have you just come back from Paris or something? Forget this type of behavior here!" He said, "Forget this type of *harakeht* here." The word means "affected behavior." This implies that if you're acting this way to appear civilized and superior, forget about it—no one is impressed. The best example of this attitude that captures the playful mood behind such stances comes from my informant Jihad.[14]

Les Trottoirs de Paris

For five years, Jihad lived in Chicago, where he studied design. During that time, he developed a strange mode of address, which has nothing to do with Chicago as far as I can tell, that involves inserting "my man" in every other sentence. He went on to marry Monette, a Paris-born Lebanese woman, and they lived in Paris for three years. When I met them, the couple had returned to live in Beirut and had been there for eighteen months. By now they had a one-year-old son. They were also constantly arguing over whether to remain in Beirut, with the argument often centering on what would be better for their son. Monette wanted to return to Paris. Jihad believed that having a family network and domestic servants made life with the child easier in

Beirut. Monette recognized that this was true but argued that their son was missing out on many other things. On the day that the conversation I relate below happened, the couple had been arguing the pros and cons of leaving Beirut for a good ten minutes in front of many visiting friends. At one point, Monette asserts that she has had it with Lebanese footpaths. They are full of cracks and holes, and, what's more, motorists and motorcyclists park on them and block them. It's basically impossible to push a stroller along them, and therefore she can't walk around their neighborhood with their child. She says that the footpaths are what she terms *anti-femmes*.

Jihad has already had a couple of beers and is in a very playful mood, so he looks at me and starts raving in the characteristic Lebanese cosmopolitan mode of speaking, which involves constantly moving between Arabic, French, and English: *"Ah! Les trottoirs de Paris. Comme ils sont lisses les trottoirs de Paris"* (Ah! The footpaths of Paris. How smooth they are, the footpaths of Paris). *"Ye'hne shoo baddeh illak?"* (I mean, what can I say to you?) *Les trottoirs de Paris* [he switches to English] are Western civilization's gift to humanity. And now, to make them even more sacred, I've just been made aware that the *trottoir* is a feminist issue as well. One thing I can tell you, my man, I don't miss any smooth sidewalks. They don't mean anything to me. I like my sidewalk cracked and full of holes. It stops you from going to sleep while you are walking." Then he looks at me again and says, "I bet you have real smooth footpaths in Sydney. Do you miss them?" My reaction is to give him an amused blank look. So he reacts to my silence. "What? Oh no! *Yaa haraam!* (I pity you!) You like *les trottoirs lisses* de Sydney, do you? You're lost, my man!"

Finally, I give him a tongue-in-cheek response. "Well, you have to give me some time. I have not encountered a footpath-based opposition to Western civilization before!" To this, Jihad quickly replies, "No. No. Don't get me wrong. I am not opposed to Western civilization. It's more like . . . you know . . . I am over it, my man. . . . Kind of been there, done that, you know!"

A similar paradigmatic moment is offered to me by Jeannot, who's visiting Beirut from Toronto, where he works in finance. In this instance, he's vehemently opposed to the very civilized Western practice of queuing.

> I can't bear the thought of standing in a line, idiotically waiting for my turn to buy a sandwich tasting as bland and sterile as the people who are queuing to buy it. I know how to queue. I don't want to queue. I know saying this is not supposed to be "civilized." I don't want to be civilized. I love rubbing shoulders with everyone, trying to squeeze myself in all the way to the

counter to buy my *man'ousheh*. I buy it and it just tastes so good, like I've earned it. I've never heard of anyone returning home without having bought what they came for just because people push and shove a little bit instead of queue. Queuing is for assholes who don't need much to think of themselves as refined and "advanced."

But neither the traffic nor the queues are the absolute obsession of people with such an opinion. Smoking is.

Healthy Smokers

The increasing incidence of bans on smoking in public spaces in the West, including restaurants, cafés, and parks, is typically perceived by Lebanese returnees as nothing short of the beginning of totalitarian rule. Upon their arrival back in Lebanon, they generally enjoy telling stories à la "In my office, they sacked this woman because the worker next to her complained that there's a smell of cigarettes always emanating from her." Many a conversation about smoking turns into a form of competitive storytelling aimed at showing who has encountered the most absurd smoking ban or case of antismoking behavior during their time in the West. When these talks were recorded (2002–3), the fact that hardly any space had an enforceable smoking ban in Lebanon was perceived as cause for celebration—the campus of the American University of Beirut was the exception then.[15]

I am having dinner with a bunch of returnees in the "downtown" area of Beirut, where the pedestrian zone is full of restaurants and cafés, and hundreds of people are sitting and smoking either cigarettes or an *arghileh* (water pipe). The question of smoking bans emerges yet again. Nayla comments about a supposed Lebanese health department campaign stressing that smoking one *arghileh* is equivalent to smoking one hundred cigarettes. The health minister becomes the butt of her joke: "He probably spent a week in New York and came back saying, 'Oh my God they are so healthy!'" Jeannot (of anti-queuing fame) says, "Pity he didn't notice they're so busy being healthy they have no time to talk to each other."

But Nayla's boyfriend objects.

I don't know about this. Where will the minister see healthy people in New York? Have you ever seen healthy people in New York? [*Laughter*]

But no, seriously, I never meet people in New York and think: "Wow! they are so healthy!" I mean, look around you here [*points to the people dining and smoking nearby*]. You want healthy people. Here are healthy people. They look happy, healthy, and fantastic, and they've all just had [*said mockingly*] "one hundred cigarettes." They all look much healthier than all these people you see jogging around Central Park, if you ask me.

"Yes, joggers in Central Park look seriously unhealthy . . . pale and like they're about to die," agrees Ziad, who is from New York. "We should set up an *arghileh* shop in Central Park, and everyone will become healthy again!" At this, they all burst out laughing.

Negotiated Being

It's quite clear that when people like the above speak about enjoying chaotic traffic or freedom from smoking bans, they do so playfully in a space that invites the listener not to take their remarks too seriously. They are engaging in what the Lebanese call *ta' hanak*, which literally means "clicking your jaws"—the implication being that one's jaw goes through the motions when one talks, but nothing worth saying has been said. Another word used to refer to this is *ja'daneh*, which means mindless chitchat and trivial joking. Thus, everyone involved in this chatter knows that they are bracketing certain taken-for-granted truths. Indeed, they would argue themselves that smoking kills, that the state of the footpaths is unacceptable, and so on, when in a less playful mood. This is tacitly understood among them and, in fact, is part of what makes their comments even more playful. What's more, it is a particularly anisogamic playfulness dependent on reversing the correspondence between positive/negative, civilized/uncivilized, and order/chaos and positing that the uncivilized and the chaotic comprise the positive side of the opposition.

As argued in the beginning of this chapter, enjoying the chaos of Beirut is amplified for people who, like these returnees, aren't trapped in the city's perennial traffic and other problems. While situated in this chaos, they have one foot firmly and securely grounded in the law of the Western state they belong to and the protections it offers. Accordingly, Beirut's oppressive dysfunction does not weigh on them in the same way it does on locals. But the emphasis here is on "in the same way." The lenticularity generated by having one foot in chaos and the other in the law is experienced more intensely by those middle-class returned migrants. But it's the intensity and the degree of enjoyment, not the lenticularity, that are specific to their subject positions. In being integral to the diasporic condition, lenticularity, as argued throughout, does not depend on migration as such. It is generated by Lebanese society and the state itself. Consequently, all Lebanese citizens have one foot in chaos and the other grounded in the law. That is, Lebanon's legal culture is an extension of its lenticular modernity. Just as there is plenty of rationality and plenty of emotions, plenty of money-seeking behavior and plenty of poetry, there is also always plenty of law and plenty of chaos entangled together on the streets. Thus, while experienced more intensely, the returnees' enjoyment still points to experiences shared with locals.

Indeed, especially with regard to driving, the returnees' discourse takes a nationalistic turn: they present themselves as natives returning home to enjoy the cultural specificity of their country of origin in a way that only natives can. That is, not only is the chaos identified as specifically "Lebanese" but so is its enjoyment and the capacity to maneuver oneself within it. All of this is part of what the local Lebanese themselves also see as a quintessential Lebanese ethos referred to as *shatara*. This literally means being clever and skillful at maneuvering oneself inside and outside existing structures and regulations, be they related to the traffic or the bureaucracy or even kinship conventions. At the same time, *shatara* involves a certain form of maneuvering among the various realities that make up the lenticular culture, such as knowing how to move between legality and chaos at will. It also means a certain know-how in navigating unforeseen situations and dealing with others competitively to come out a "winner" from a difficult situation. In the case of driving, for instance, it involves knowing how to maneuver when facing a traffic jam without confining oneself to lawful forms of driving, such as driving on the footpath, driving the wrong way in a one-way street, and so on. Just as important, one should come out of the whole thing with a sense of "I made it."

While the whole exercise is highly individualistic, it would indeed lead to chaos if there wasn't a particular built-in form of being fully aware that you exist on the road with others, especially others who might be doing the same thing as you. You go up a one-way street—but you do not do so without having quickly ascertained that you can move out of the way of a car going in the "right" direction. You compete with the other motorists for who is the "cleverest" in maneuvering in the traffic and getting ahead—and there is a sense that you are out to get them and they are out to get you; but if you go against the traffic and manage to block the road completely, then people will be upset with you, and indeed a violent interaction might ensue, which is always a potential part of the equation. People will be upset, not because you are breaking the law, but because you are showing that you don't know how to break the law. You may hear someone say, "They don't know how to drive *bi 'aks el seyr* [literally, against the direction of the traffic]. They see no one but themselves." A common and similar reproach is *"Khedna b'helmak."* This is understood as "Include us in your daydreaming." Thus, it is made clear that driving outside the law is not only a matter of narcissistic celebration of freedom, it is also a skill involving seeing more than oneself. That is, it is a skill involving knowing how to relate to others outside the law. It is a form of relationality and sociality. This is what I want to refer to as "negotiated being." While all societies have an "outside the law," where such negotiated being takes place, I want to argue that the lenticularity of diasporic culture makes for the special prevalence of this form of sociality.

There being no laws or guidelines concerning what others might do, drivers must negotiate each other amid their encounter. Clearly, they don't negotiate *with* each other, which is hardly possible in an encounter between drivers. Rather, they negotiate each other: each person must be able to read the field of potentialities and probabilities emanating from the other's presence to be attuned to whatever can possibly emerge from the encounter. A dimension of this negotiated being is reminiscent of what Henrik Vigh calls "navigation," to capture his young informants' capacity to operate in an unstable and continually shifting situation.[16] There is also a close resemblance between *shatara* and certain features of Michael Herzfeld's description of the Glendiots' "poetics of manhood" on the margins of the law.[17] This is especially so in how it's an individualized and competitive performance of selfhood. Indeed, there is an exclamation that the Lebanese utter after a successful performance of a feat of *shatara* that is exceptionally close to the Glendiots': "I am he, alone, and no one else but me!" (*Ana huwweh, wahdo, w ma hada ghayro*). As mentioned by Herzfeld, the cry is "I am [the one who matters], and no one else [*Egho ime, če čanis alos*]!"[18] What differentiates negotiated being from Vigh's navigation and Herzfeld's *eghoismo* is its intersubjectivity, its permanent state of awareness of the possibility of an encounter and the desire to coexist with others operating in the world in the same way as oneself. In this outside-the-law relation to the other, jouissance comes to the fore.

Dyadic Jouissance

Over a morning coffee and a couple of days after his "Western civilization . . . been there, done that" outburst, I'm checking with Jihad whether he agrees with my rendering of what he said, which I had written down from memory later that evening. I begin by explaining to him, in a more serious mode, what had interested me about his irreverent take on the "trottoirs de Paris." As the conversation evolves, I tell him that in my experience, many Lebanese immigrants are highly ambivalent about the rule of law. On one hand, they often think that the rule of law is the best thing that ever happened to them in migrating. They see it as a liberation from the clientelism that mars their everyday experience of the state in Lebanon. Among the many statements I heard is "It is so good to be able to access your rights simply because you are a citizen, not because you know so-and-so." But on the other hand, they find this very impersonality of the law hard to take when, for example, they are unable to "reason" with a traffic officer trying to book them: "It makes no difference whether you're booked by a camera or a policeman here," someone said to me. Another remarked that she found "the anonymity of the law scary."

As the discussion continues, I mention to Jihad a piece I had written long ago about a Lebanese migrant who was mentally ill and in his illness developed a fetish for the pedestrian crossing painted with broad white stripes in his street. In Australia, drivers must stop for people in such zebra crossings. Jihad says he'd like to read the article, so I send it to him. A few days later, he comes to me with the article after having underlined a couple paragraphs. They read:

> There are of course a multitude of ways in which pedestrians and drivers negotiate a pedestrian crossing. There are drivers who would simply stop for the pedestrian no matter what—except maybe if they are taking someone who is seriously injured to a hospital. There are drivers who see crossings as a place to compete with pedestrians over who gets to cross first. There are drivers who stop in a matter-of-fact manner and drivers who expect to be thanked. But of course the same driver can behave at a crossing differently according to the mood they are in, if they are in a hurry or not, if they slept well or not, and maybe according to their previous experiences of stopping at pedestrian crossings. For, of course, just as drivers stop in different ways, crossings are also crossed in many ways by pedestrians. There are pedestrians who express gratitude and pedestrians who cross arrogantly. There are pedestrians who cross absentmindedly and those who are very conscious of the traffic. There are those who cross treating cars as enemies and those who cross trying to cause minimal disruption to the traffic.
>
> But this plurality of modes of interaction, in all its richness, should not conceal the underlying—and by far the most important—aspect of the phenomenon: a pedestrian crossing is an ethical structural fact. It is a space where the dominant mode of occupying and circulating on roads, driving, is requested by social law to yield to a marginalized form of road occupancy, walking.[19]

Jihad claims that these paragraphs "said something about me," because I left out the most prevalent way in which people use the zebra crossing: "Cars stop, pedestrians cross, and nobody even bothers to look at anybody." So "why is that ethical?" he challenges. He has drawn my attention to the fact that although there is no respect for pedestrian crossings in Beirut, nonetheless in crossing the road people must interact. Indeed, upon further reflection, I felt that Jihad was pointing at precisely what I have called negotiated being, of which crossing the road in Beirut is a very apt example. As he more than intimated, this pedestrian crossing is a festival of interpersonal interaction, in which one must permanently engage with others, look drivers in the eyes, and either squeeze an ethical moment out of them by appealing to their better side and making them stop for you, or, even more competitively, adopt an "it's you or me, pal" attitude and aggressively aim to make them stop—with the chance that they might, equally aggressively, succeed in disallowing you to cross. It's a permanent state of first contact in which nothing can be taken for granted except precisely the sociality inherent to the encounter. This takes us to what is perhaps the most crucial dimension of negotiated being and sociality that differentiates it from state-guaranteed sociality.

Negotiated sociality is a face-to-face "horizontal" sociality that is not mediated "vertically" by the law as a third party. By the same token, it does not benefit from the "pacifying" effect of the state, which requires citizens to divest themselves from the means of aggression and violence. This, in fact, is something that Sahlins has highlighted as a quality of all gift-based sociality. As he puts it:

> The gift, however, would not organize society in a corporate sense, only in a segmentary sense. Reciprocity is a "between" relation. It does not dissolve the separate parties within a higher unity, but on the contrary, in correlating their opposition, perpetuates it. Neither does the gift specify a third party standing over and above the separate interests of those who contract. Most important, it does not withdraw their force, for the gift affects only will and not right. Thus the condition of peace as understood by Mauss—and as in fact it exists in the primitive societies—has to differ politically from that envisioned by the classic contract, which is always a structure of submission, and sometimes of terror. Except for the honor accorded to generosity, the gift is no sacrifice of equality and never of liberty. The groups allied by exchange each retain their strength, if not the inclination to use it.[20]

Yet we need to be careful here and note that being "horizontal" does not make the laws of reciprocity and gift exchange outside the law. There is a big difference between being outside the law of the state and being outside the law as such. When gift exchange is institutionalized, it means that it is regulated by various laws of exchange. These are not the same as state laws, but they are laws, nonetheless. Indeed, the lawfulness of institutionalized exchanges, which is what constitutes them as social facts, is precisely what was analyzed by Mauss as well as by Lévi-Strauss. Thus, we need to be clear that the encounters and modes of existence of interest to us are not only outside the law of the state but outside all societal laws.

In many places in the world, the exchange of greetings is reasonably lawful. As with the famous Lévi-Straussian exchange of wine in working-class eateries, one knows what to expect.[21] In Parisian shops, for instance, it is quite ritualized to enter and offer a greeting, and you know you can expect to be greeted back. Likewise, when you leave: "au revoir monsieur, au revoir madame." This is not the case everywhere. As a keen jogger, I've jogged in many parks around the world. When jogging in Central Park in New York or in Australia's Centennial Park or the Jardin de Luxembourg, it is very hard to know whether you should offer a greeting: whether the people you encounter want to be greeted or whether, when greeted, they will greet you back, and so on. You're in a situation akin to first contact: you don't know what to do. You can decide not to have an encounter, of course. But if you decide to initiate an encounter, you must proceed carefully, living one second at a time, because there is no possibility of knowing what will happen next: you might start to offer a timid greeting but realize that there is no interest in such a greeting whatsoever, and you discontinue what you started. You might start a greeting and realize, as is often the case in my experience, that people do indeed desire to be greeted but have the same fears that you have. In such situations, you initiate the process, and you find people almost racing to make up for the fact that they weren't the initiators: they utter their greeting back before you even finish yours. With time, you learn how to engage in this encounter that must be lived through a moment-by-moment evaluation of the situation. Even when there are some predictable and rule-filled dimensions in such situations, they never become ritualized and are destined to forever be nongoverned by any law or etiquette and to contain a fair degree of uncertainty as to where each step will lead. Thus, what we have here are clear instances of negotiated being.

Negotiated being has echoes of Derrida's "unconditional hospitality," which is critically directed precisely at the Kantian rights-saturated discourse of cosmopolitan hospitality, which presupposes the existence of a third party: the law into which the asylum seeker is welcomed.[22] What Derrida is seeking instead is a hospitality offered without the sense of dominance that comes from the knowledge of being the one with the power to offer it;

a hospitality where it is not unthinkable for the other to dictate me inside my realm. Indeed, by offering a gift without knowing whether it will be returned, we can say that the ethical moment of such an exchange is our ability to put ourselves at the mercy of the other. It is a sociality where one is constantly exposed to the threat of the other. The jouissance that partakes of negotiated being is closely related to this "buzz" of living with the threat of the other. It is a Nietzschean overcoming, the community of those who can still hurt each other but refrain from doing so as opposed to the community of those who can't hurt each other anyway as provided through submission to state law. What further intensifies this sense of enjoyment is that such a sociality has a libidinal dimension absent from the social relations that the state aims to produce.

It is often argued that the notion of citizenship treats individuals as an abstraction by defining them outside some of their concrete particularities: age, sex, class, body, and so on. What is less acknowledged is that this is not simply how the law thinks of people—this is how it constructs them. The law of state, through making us into citizens, brings forth, in a sense, that quality of us all to be abstract citizens, and in essence this abstract version of ourselves is an ontological reality, not just a way of seeing us. Insofar as we are captured by the law, this is what we become. The state evacuates us of particularity at the same time that it evacuates us of our capacity for violence. It is this abstract legal sense of the self that diminishes in the outside-the-law, negotiated, one-to-one reality that concerns us. This is something also noted by Simmel in his analysis of "dyads," one-to-one relations unmediated by a third party, similar in this regard to our relations of negotiation.[23] As Simmel argues, such relations have an intimate dimension that "derives from the individual's inclination to consider that which distinguishes him from others, that which is individual in a qualitative sense, as the core, value, and chief matter of his existence."[24] In much the same way, in existing outside the law, negotiated being stages interactions between "singular" particular, libidinal, and emotional subjects rather than abstract citizens. There are echoes here of the psychoanalytic arguments concerning the libidinality assumed by mother-child relations in the absence of the abstracting law of the father.

It is worth noting how in Jeannot's rant against queuing for one's *man'ousheh*, the law symbolized by queuing becomes articulated to both bland people and bland sandwiches. As he put it, "I can't bear the thought of standing in a line, idiotically waiting for my turn to buy a sandwich tasting as bland and sterile as the people who are queuing to buy it." It is, first, an association of the law with the bland/abstract/sterile citizen such as we have examined earlier, but second, these two are interestingly also seen as associated with a further bland experience: that of eating a tasteless sandwich. Eating, the most libidinal of all everyday experiences, is thus transformed into a formal/abstract experience by the law. It is against this that the tasty Lebanese sandwich comes to represent access to the Lebanese libidinal mother.

This opposition between bland abstract people being served and eating bland "neatly wrapped" food within the law and interesting colorful particular people being served and eating, indeed gobbling, particularly tasty food dribbling with sauce is also played out in the opposition between ordering and eating a McDonald's hamburger and ordering and eating Lebanese sandwiches. Here, the abstract person queuing to be served at McDonald's is considered to be the exact equivalent of the abstract political citizen of the law: just as everybody is equal before the law, every "eating citizen" is equal before a McDonald's counter. As Beiruti writer Maher Kassar has put it:

> A friend once told me that what she loved about McDonald's is that wherever you go in the world, you can be assured of getting the same quality and the same taste. In other words, everybody is equal in savors and flavors. This is the strength of the Big Mac. And this is precisely why it will fail here in Lebanon. Listen carefully, Ronald McDonald: we do not want to be standard. We want to be an exception. We do not want to be treated like everybody else. We want to be special. When we order a sandwich, we ask the chef to prepare it *"Alla zawaak"* (to his own taste). I want him to look at me, guess how much *taratór*, how much onion and tomato would suit my palate. I want a sandwich tailor-made for me. "This falafel sandwich, Mr Kassar, is just for you. Nobody else in the world has eaten one like this, I can assure you."[25]

We have here a clear rejection of the abstract citizen in favor of Simmel's particular libidinal self. What the writer is celebrating is that while everyone gets exactly the same sandwich at McDonald's, at Barbar (well-known chain of Lebanese sandwich shops) a person walks in and the sandwich maker, despite being busy serving tens of people surrounding him, will recognize the person he is about to serve. He will also recognize the specificity of the sandwich this customer wishes to eat: "Extra garlic for you, right?" It is in such spaces that one comes to experience the jouissance of libidinality in a "maternal" Lebanese space where one is a body existing with others' bodies, rather than an abstraction existing with other abstractions. "Americans like to say that eating hot dogs represents their democratic egalitarian ethos, because it doesn't matter who you are, you will always be served the same hot dog. That's fine every now and then, but in the long run, I like it to matter who I am," Jeannot tells me while we're discussing his attack on queuing. "You've just defined the essence of democratic desire in Lebanon," I jokingly tell him. "Everybody should be equally special before the law."

In this concluding chapter, I have tried to show that existing outside the law is not just a negative attitude vis-à-vis the law and others. It does not necessarily lead to the becoming-wolf implied by Hobbesian theory. Rather, it can become the space of a different sociality, a skill, and an affirmation of a desire to coexist with others differently, which I have called negotiated being. It is a generative and creative mode of existence that puts us more on the side of Roy Wagner's conception of invention.[26]

I have made it clear that the concept of negotiation implied in negotiated being is not the same as the dominant understanding of negotiation as "negotiation with," where two parties with specific interests try to reach a negotiated agreement. What I have defined as negotiated being is a mode of sociality where one must be constantly attuned to the other as a presence. Negotiation here is closer to its meaning in usages such as "negotiating a river" rather than the more dominant meaning of "negotiating with." In the latter, negotiation is a situation where people must formulate interests and share a common symbolic order to negotiate, and as such they are already operating under at least one common law: language. Furthermore, negotiation in its sense as "negotiating with" is an instrumental strategy, a means to achieve an end.[27] This end does not have to be an interaction with the other: one can negotiate with the other to achieve a way of living as separately from the other as possible. Or, indeed, as the history of colonialism shows, negotiation can be a means of giving oneself room to lay the foundation for a more effective extermination of the other. In the meaning of negotiation that I am highlighting, negotiation is an order of being; it is itself the end rather than a means to an end. It is a mode of being where one is constantly attuned, attentive, interactive, and responsive to the presence of the other without the existence of a "law" regulating the interaction. Partly because of this, negotiation is, as I have argued and unlike the abstract order of citizenship, a far more "concrete" mode of being with the other.

It would clearly be a misreading of my intentions to see in this analysis a desire to make light of all the negative and harmful consequences of Lebanon's perennial problems created by its inadequate confessional, patriarchal, clientelist, and mercantilist state—and which have, as I finish writing this book, erupted in what has been one of the country's most significant social uprisings. I am certainly not arguing something like "instead of social problems, we have another form of sociality." But I am proposing that the experience of my returnees highlights the fact that the partial absence of the state and of any serious centralized planning does not only foster lack and negativity. It offers a space for the flourishing of what I refer to as negotiated being. Against those who advocate an uncritical modernist solution to Lebanon's problems—more state regulations, better planning, better policing, and so on—the experience I have analyzed invites us to be aware that, regardless of the gains such modernization entails, increasing the capacity of the laws of the state to saturate and regulate society, desirable as this might be, also involves certain losses.

An awareness of the diasporic lenticularity of Lebanese modernity tells us that the last thing needed is to create a sense of ethical polarity between the sociality of the law and sociality outside the law, as if one is good and the other is bad. This would indeed be a simplistic conclusion, for the two have coexisted and will continue to coexist, and each will continue to throw light on the limitations of the other.

Indeed, we are seeing a number of situations in the West today where the order of the law is regarded as having reached its limits in its capacity to regulate social life. The state finds itself obliged to supplement law by a reopening of a space of negotiated being. This is particularly true of the evolution of some forms of traffic regulation in Europe and in Australia. In the regional city of Bendigo in Australia, the municipality has transformed the center of the city into a shared space involving "the removal of traffic lights, road markings, traffic signs, zebra crossings and splitter islands" to "increase the uncertainty of space."[28] As one of the coordinators puts it, "Precedent projects in Europe have demonstrated that when a setting seems safe, this safety is taken for granted. When things seem dangerous, however, individuals take greater care resulting in less actual risk. By encouraging unpredictability and creating uncertainty in the minds of all road users, vigilance and care are improved, resulting in safer streets." And as if to ensure that this is indeed of relevance to us, the writer adds that "this creates a traffic mode of 'passage by negotiation' rather than right of way." I think examining the plurality of modes of sociality that foster different forms of social coexistence is of utmost importance today. For it could be argued that there are many spaces in our societies where we are increasingly facing the limits of a law-regulated life and where the emergence of lenticular realities requires us to refine our capacity to engage in negotiated being.

Conclusion

In this book, I have invited the reader into Lebanon's diasporic culture. This is an immense transnational lifeworld that literally spans the entire globe. Even less so than any "classic" site of anthropological research, such as "a village," "a neighborhood," or "a tribe," it can't possibly be covered, ethnographically or otherwise, in its entirety. Nonetheless, I have strived to give the reader a sense of familiarity with this lifeworld. I've done so primarily through a strategy of diversification. We have seen this lifeworld from the perspective of various Lebanese diasporic subjects located in very different parts of the world, from rural Lebanon to rural Venezuela to New Bedford to Boston to Sydney. These subjects were also of different genders, class backgrounds, cultural and educational capital, and attachments to Lebanon and to the places where they have settled. Finally, we have entered a multiplicity of different spaces inhabited by those subjects: some public and some private, some social and some deeply personal, some easily accessible and some hidden. To claim that an access to this multiplicity gives us access to the totality of the lifeworld in which the subjects exist and which they also bring into being is to say that together, in their multiplicity and despite their differences, they share this milieu and some important features of it. It is those features constitutive of the diasporic condition or diasporic culture that have been analyzed throughout this work. It could be said that in this book, I have been more interested in the commonalities than in the differences, but my analytic ethos is probably better described if we say that I am interested in the commonalities as they emerge through the differences.

Right from the start of this book, I have aimed to define Lebanon's diasporic culture by not limiting it to Lebanese migrant culture. A migratory disposition is part and parcel of this culture, and migration has been clearly crucial in shaping it into a transnational culture, yet it is crucial not to equate migrant and diasporic culture. Lebanon's diasporic culture, I have argued, is the culture of Lebanese modernity; its defining characteristics emerge before the relatively intensive migratory movements that have made Lebanon into what it is. If nothing else, those features that initially characterize Lebanon's diasporic culture are shared by migrants and non-migrants, and as such cannot be the product of migration itself; we can also say that as this culture evolved, some effects of migration were shared by migrants and non-migrants alike. The first five chapters worked their way through these features. It's worth summarizing them and reviewing them to have a clear sense of the path we have traversed to get here.

First, internationalizing the space of viability: here I argued that Lebanese modernity introduced a state of consciousness which did not simply involve considering oneself as part of an international order. More important, it created subjects with the capacity to view the whole world as a place where they can make a living and where the viability of their lives can be played out. We can't but marvel at what it took for a person living in a small village on a Lebanese mountain to start thinking something like "I am going to make a living in Nova Scotia, Canada, or Queensland, Australia."

Second, a fragmented or multiple subjecthood: against a tradition that can only think of migrants and would-be migrants as always "torn between" one place and another, one decision and another, I highlighted the equally pervasive state of fragmentation, whereby one part of the subject can be yearning to migrate while another yearns to stay home. Here the diasporic subject is itself torn in two or more parts, rather than being unitary and torn between two or more places. It is a multiplicity occupying a multiplicity of places rather than one subject unable to fully occupy any single place.

Third, a state of permanent comparative mode of existence: here, as a corollary of the international and fragmented mode of existence, I have highlighted the inability of diasporic subjects to face any situation without viewing it from an international comparative perspective. They cannot, for example, see a landscape without comparing it to another landscape they are familiar with or that they aspire to. Likewise, any life decision and any step taken in life involve a comparative evaluation. That evaluation haunts every decision and every step taken in a "here" with the possible decision or step that could have been taken in a "there."

Fourth, an anisogamic logic: anisogamy, for Lévi-Strauss, is a marriage alliance between tribes of unequal status. I removed the concept from the domain of kinship to argue that an anisogamic dimension, anisogamic logic, and anisogamic strategies are part of any situation of interaction between two parties where claims of superiority and inferiority must be managed. I showed how Lebanese diasporic culture considers the world anisogamically as the stage on which occurs an encounter between people in need of migration and people who don't.

Fifth, lenticularity: I have argued that the kind of experience produced by this photographic technique gives us a good sense of the diasporic experience of reality. The lenticularly constructed photographic surface gives us an experience of an entangled multiplicity of photos, each coming forth depending on the angle from which one is observing the surface. What's more, this coming forth is as unstable as the angle of vision is. In a moving situation, one experiences a continuous flickering and movement between realities. I have used this concept to illustrate the fact that diasporic reality is always made of subjects engaging in a multiplicity of inhabitances and forms of situatedness and, therefore, a multiplicity of realities. Continuing with this concept, I argued against the idea that being "torn between" two realities is the most prevalent form of diasporic being. Instead, I showed that diasporic subjects are just as likely to be inhabiting a multiplicity of places and to be situated in a multiplicity of realities: for example, a subject is not torn between Montreal and Mehj but situated in both.

Having developed the defining characteristics of Lebanon's diasporic culture in the first five chapters with the help of vignettes and examples, in the remaining four chapters I examined a number of ethnographic sites and situations that, on one hand, helped us deepen our understanding of the plural nature of the Lebanese diaspora. On the other hand, these sites and situations exhibited how our understanding of the diasporic culture's dominant features can help us refine our analysis of specific diasporic dynamics: from an examination of conflicts over degrees of assimilation and attachment to Lebanon among a group of people in Sydney; to an analysis of a Lebanese diasporic family situated in Lebanon, Venezuela, the United States, and Australia; to an examination of the diasporic trajectory of a Lebanese man who blames migration for his erectile dysfunction; to finally, an examination of a group of middle-class Lebanese returnees united in enjoying and celebrating the freedoms of the streets of Beirut when comparing them to the Western cities where they have been living.

In defining my general approach to Lebanese diasporic culture in the introduction, I affirmed that along with a sociological analytics of the Lebanese diaspora that offers further insights into the nature of the phenomenon, I saw my exploration of lenticular realities as part of a more specifically anthropological quest to uncover less obvious modes of existing socially in the world: the diasporic subject's simultaneous situatedness in multiple realities that are di-ontologically interacting and speaking with each other;

the experience of such realities as a continuous process of flickering between one and the other, precisely like a lenticular photograph; the anisogamic strategies of intensification of some realities at the expense of others, all aimed at enriching our conception of not only diasporic existence but all forms of existence beyond the prevailing and taken-for-granted monorealism. Again, as I already made clear in the introduction, exploring the lenticularity and ontological multiplicity of the diasporic world is not to claim that the diasporic world is unique in offering us such forms of existence. Rather, it is to say that it is unique in making them more apparent to us. This is partly because of the minimally institutionalized nature of diasporic life. As with all anthropological uncovering of inconspicuous modes of existence, their uncovering in one context where they are more visible allows us to analytically delineate their presence in places where they are less apparent.

This is certainly the case with the conceptualization of anisogamic logic. On one hand, it could be argued that any patriarchal marriage between a man and a woman is anisogamic in that the parties involved must negotiate structures of patriarchal power and inequality that distribute claims of superiority and inferiority between the sexes. In this sense, some new insights might emerge by analyzing the interaction between men and women in a relationship through the lens of anisogamy, attempting to see the way an anisogamic logic seeps into the business of maintaining an ongoing loving relation despite the violence and inequality of patriarchal power. I have also been inclined to think that colonial relations continue to exist in the form of an anisogamic relation.

In the past, the model of decolonization has been one of freeing oneself of the other's presence: Algerians could decolonize Algeria by getting rid of the French, and Indians could decolonize India by getting rid of the English. This was considered the end result that any anticolonial struggle should aspire to. This is hardly the case today. Such fantasies of elimination have become less and less possible to fulfill. In some places, they become even unthinkable. While "driving the Jews to the sea" can be used for rhetorical purposes by some and can be exploited by the Zionists themselves as an example of what they are "really" facing, the fact is that the aim of most Palestinian struggles of decolonization today cannot be (and, one might also argue, should not be) to eliminate Zionists, even if this was remotely possible (which it isn't). Rather, the aim is to radically transform the existing colonial relations that are defined by Zionism into something better.

In much the same way, Indigenous Australians are not going to eliminate the white settlers and the immigrants who have colonized their land and exploited their resources and continue to do so. Such fantasies of elimination might be entertained by some and even voiced on Facebook by a couple of enthusiastic "symbolic warriors." But the fact is that elimination of this sort is neither possible nor desirable; nor is it realistically entertained or even wished for by the various Indigenous Australians who are in a position to voice and formulate Indigenous demands.

Accordingly in the postcolonial era, we must deal with the leftovers of colonialization but also the leftovers of decolonization that marked the colonial era: unachieved colonization here and unachieved decolonization there. Indeed, we ourselves are such leftovers, neither fully colonized nor fully decolonized, stuck with each other and with whatever else these unachieved processes of colonization and decolonization have bequeathed to us.

In his foreword to the second French edition of *De la postcolonie*, Achille Mbembe makes similar arguments presented through a critique of Frantz Fanon.[1] Mbembe asserts that for Fanon, "to kill the enemy is not only a necessity, but a politico-ethical responsibility," since he sees that life for the colonized can emerge only from the "decomposing body of the colonizer." Mbembe contends that such a way of thinking about decolonization is unsatisfactory in "our context," where it is less "about taking away the colonizer's life" and more about opposing the politics that are still driven by fratricidal tendencies and the refusal to "constitute a community."[2] Thus, Mbembe argues with the help of Derrida's *Donner la mort* that the aim is to struggle against the politics of death with a politics motivated by what Mbembe considers to be the highest ethical horizon: giving death to death.[3]

All this points to the fact that rather than getting rid of the colonizer, the colonized are increasingly facing a situation today characterized by getting stuck in a relation with the colonizer. This "stuckedness," and the imperative of relating that it imposes on the colonizer and the colonized, takes us straight into anisogamic relation. Let me be clear here. I am not arguing that anisogamic relations are better suited than the concept of colonialism to describe what remain, for all practical purposes, colonial relations. Instead, anisogamic logic can open and analyze a dimension of the relation that would remain otherwise obscured. In fact, I am increasingly of the view that there are hardly any interpersonal relations that do not have at least a minor anisogamic dimension.

What is true of the general applicability of anisogamy is also true of the concept of lenticular realities. In essence, lenticularity is an argument for ontological pluralism and the way the ontological multiplicity of the real can come to present itself. It is an argument against all forms of epistemological and ontological monorealism and either/or-ism. Let me give two examples that I have come across outside the field of diasporic studies. In them I found that a lenticular conception of social reality can offer analytical insights that would have been hard to arrive at otherwise.

In my book *Is Racism an Environmental Threat?*, I argue that the ecological crisis and racism are both grounded in what I have called "generalized domestication": a mode of dominating and exploiting nature and people. I offer a critique of generalized domestication, and I highlight the existence of other modes of relating to nature and to each other that the anthropological tradition has uncovered and described. These modes are what I have called the "mutualist" mode, where we experience our lives and the life of whatever is surrounding us as mutually reinforcing, and the "reciprocal" mode, where we experience our relation to what surrounds us as a gift. In my critique of domestication, I make a point of arguing that it's impossible to conceive of life without generalized domestication, and that my critique is not a critique of domestication as such in the form of either/or but a critique of its dominance, such that it has eclipsed other modes of relating. Were it not for the lack of space, I would have been happy to argue that in fact those three modes of relating are experienced in a lenticular fashion. Being unable to develop a new language, I used Lucien Lévy-Bruhl's concept of *"enchevêtrement de réalités,"* the entanglement of realities, which conveys some of the key ideas behind lenticularity.[4] I thus argue:

> No social space is exclusively a relation of generalized domestication, or a mutualist or a reciprocal relation. I might face the tree as a domesticator and evaluate how useful it is for me, I might even cut it down because I need fire or to build a house. Still, this does not mean that this tree did not present itself to me as a gift or that I experienced it as a gift at the same time, or that I even looked at it and felt more alive at the mere fact that it existed next to me. All social relations are an entanglement of multiplicities. It is the recovery of this multiplicity to temper the overdomination of generalized domestication that we need today to oppose the proliferation of racist and ecologically destructive modes of domination.[5]

It later struck me while reflecting on the above that a lenticular perspective can be used as an ontological way of thinking about intersectionality. This was further reinforced for me in a paper on the relation between colonialism and inequality I had prepared for a conference centered on issues of inequality. In that paper, I differentiated between two types of inequality— what I called "distributional" and "extractive" inequality. I argued that these are distinct realities: they assume not only different kinds of inequality but also different kinds of experiences as well as different dimensions of what are complex multifaceted social processes. In the Marxist tradition, distributional inequality (inequality of income) is seen as a "surface" phenomenon that can be recorded through observation, while extractive inequality (exploitation) is perceived as more structural and as such requiring an analytics of phenomena beneath the surface of the social.[6]

One of the most fundamental differences between the two is that extractive inequality assumes a direct relation between, on one side, subjects doing the extracting and, on the other, subjects from whom things are being extracted, while distributional inequality assumes no necessary relation between the unequal subjects. Extractive inequality is produced by the very relation between the two unequal parts. One part gets more at the expense of the other. It is a relation of suction, through which the growth in being of one party happens via a process of dispossession of—or the appropriation of something from, and therefore a diminishing in being of—the other. With distributional inequality, the relation is of an epistemological order. It comes into being through its being noted a posteriori via a process of observation and comparison, whether by analysts or by laypeople, whether by outsiders or by the people concerned themselves. It is in comparing that one comes to experience or notice inequality. Distributional inequality, whether material or symbolic or both, can be attributed to various differentials: skills and abilities, inheritance, valorization by the state, valorization by cultural tradition, and so on. Nonetheless, there is no necessary experience of a relation between the two unequal parties. That is, an analyst can declare two groups having an unequal possession of x or y without the groups themselves noticing that they are unequal or having anything to do with each other.

Here again, I was faced with a tradition of either/or-ism concerning which kind of inequality is more "real" and more "important." Some Marxists go as far as saying that distributional inequality is pure ideology or pure appearance. As such, it masks extractive inequality, which is the essence of capitalism. While in my paper I agreed that the order of extraction and exploitation is more of the essence of capitalism, I was not particularly sympathetic to attempts to minimize the reality of the experience of distributional inequality.

I argued that the "importance" and "reality" of those two forms of inequality were not an either/or choice. I further argued that the difficulty of engaging in, and analyzing, Indigenous politics in Australia arises precisely because Indigenous society is enmeshed in both those realities, not in one or the other. On one hand, we still have a colonial situation and an extractive order of inequality, where one people are subjugating and dispossessing another of land and resources, with the state being both party to this subjugation and dispossession and an active participant in the colonizing assemblage. On the other hand, we have a postcolonial society of citizens governed by a postcolonial and managerial state that relates to all the inhabitants of Australia as citizens, its Indigenous people included. Indigenous people struggle for more services, more income, more recognition, and in the process see themselves as citizens struggling against distributional inequality. But they also struggle as colonized people to regain whatever it is possible to regain from what has been extracted from them, particularly in the form of demands for land return and for reparations. These two orders of inequality and the struggle against each are not always, or even often, clearly separated. On the contrary, often they intersect and can only be separated analytically.

It is here that I felt that understanding the relation between the two as forming a lenticular reality is necessary. Intersecting can itself conjure an image of a very tidy encounter in the manner of a road intersection. The intersection we need to imagine, however, is anything but. It is an entanglement that is better captured by the concept of the lenticular. Furthermore, as with the experience of looking at a lenticularly produced surface, the space inhabited by the colonized subject is unceasingly fluctuating between fragments of distributional and extractive inequality as well as undefined fragments that appear as an unstable combination that can become either one of the two forms at any point. The combination can even be some new form that fuses both these forms.

The analytical task in the encounter with such lenticular realities becomes one of accounting for the varieties of experiences the existence of such an entangled, interacting, and flickering reality entails: this can be an anarchic experience, where fluctuations between one reality and another follow no necessary pattern or rhythm. But the political struggles that are part and parcel of this lenticular space, and the fact that some sociopolitical and economic forces have an interest in the salience of one reality over another, mean that there are sometimes logics and patterns behind the various durations, fluctuations, modes, degrees, and intensities with which each reality and the move from one to another reality are experienced. This is primarily a sociological work of disentanglement.

Furthermore, as is often the case with colonial politics, the two orders of inequality can be played against each other. Because of extractive inequalities' far-reaching structural consequences, the most common maneuver has been for the colonial states and the colonial white subjects to suppress the existence of the struggles to redress their effects by reducing them to distributional inequalities. In so doing, the colonial state aims at repressing one side of the lenticular formation to make it into a single stable reality. There is no "extraction," there is no "colonialism," there's only disadvantaged Indigenous Australians facing their states as citizens. To this, radical anticolonial activists respond by positing a reverse monorealism: there is no such thing as Indigenous citizens, there's only colonialism and only extraction.

It can indeed be argued that all forms of monorealism are the result of institutional strategies of stabilization of one side or another of an existing lenticular dynamic. Political and economic interests are often grounded in one of the realities that make up a lenticular entanglement. Therefore, we often see a vested interest in one reality at the expense of others, which leads to a struggle against the real's multiplicity. Monorealism is therefore a long-term, structural political labor aimed at fixing, hence de-lenticularizing, reality by restricting the field of possible realities to one, and stabilizing this reduction in the service of specific political interests. Thus, it can be said that lenticular realities are always potentially present in a repressed state wherever monorealism or claims of monorealism prevail. In such cases, an analytic bringing to the fore lenticular realities will undoubtedly have political ramifications. It constitutes an intellectual labor of re-lenticularization, which is nothing other than a reopening of the multiple potentialities of life. At its most general, this whole book can be seen as initiating precisely such a process.

ACKNOWLEDGMENTS

As noted in the preface, some of the ethnographic material in this book has been published previously, though in many cases the analytical framework that makes sense of it has changed. Parts of chapter 1 appeared in "Diaspora and Migration," in *A Companion to Critical and Cultural Theory*, ed. Imre Szeman, Sarah Blacker, and Justin Sully (Oxford: John Wiley and Sons, 2017), 191–204. Some of the arguments concerning existential mobility in chapter 2 were developed in "A Not So Multi-sited Ethnography of a Not So Imagined Community," *Anthropological Theory* 5, no. 4 (2005): 463–75. Parts of chapter 3 appeared in "Migration and Food Memories," in *Memory: Histories, Theories, Debates*, ed. Susannah Radstone and Bill Schwarz (New York: Fordham University Press, 2010), 416–27. An earlier version of chapter 6 appeared as "The Differential Intensities of Reality: Migration, Perception and Guilt," in *Being There: New Trends in Phenomenology and the Analysis of Culture*, ed. Jonas Frykman and Nils Gilje (Lund, Sweden: Nordic Academic Press, 2003), 79–94. A portion of chapter 7 appeared in "Responsibility in the Lebanese Transnational Family," in *Responsibility*, ed. Ghassan Hage and Robyn Eckersley (Melbourne: Melbourne University Press, 2012), 11–127. An earlier version of chapter 8 appeared as "Migration, Marginalised Masculinity, and Dephallicization: A Lebanese Villager's Experience," in *Arab Sexuality*, ed. John Gagnon and Samir Khalaf (London: Al-Saqi Books, 2006), 107–29. Chapter 9 is the only piece that has previously been published almost as is, as "Inside and Outside the Law: Negotiated Being and Urban Jouissance in the Streets of Beirut," *Social Analysis* 62, no. 3 (2018): 88–108, though without any reference to anisogamy and lenticularity as analytical frames.

As befits a research process lasting twenty-five years, I have many people to thank for their involvement and assistance along the way—some of whom I am sure I can't even recall. But as regards the intensive 2000–2005 period, I must particularly thank Stefan Horarik for his work in gathering the existing literature on the topic in an exceptionally thorough and efficient manner. I also want to thank Fadi Bardawil for his fieldwork assistance and for his company in the early ethnographic stages of the research. And I can't thank enough those Lebanese people, in Lebanon and elsewhere around the world, who devoted so much time to working with me.

Many others have kindly discussed and commented on this work along the way, and I want to begin these acknowledgments by extending my gratitude to my friend and colleague Michael Jackson for the many conversations we have had and for his inspiring work. Another special thanks go to my longtime friends and colleagues Greg Noble, Scott Poynting, and Paul Tabar for all the discussions and debates that began twenty-five years ago and continue to this day. Other friends and colleagues invited me to present my findings in a variety of contexts: Elie Vasta and Stephen Castles at the University of Oxford, Samir Khalaf at the American University of Beirut, Diana Allen and Michael Herzfeld at Harvard, Didier Fassin at the École normale supérieure, Jason Throop at UCLA, Henrik Vigh at the University of Copenhagen, Lorenzo Canas Bottos at the University of Trondheim, Martin Holbraad at University College London, Wayne Modest at the Research Centre for Material Culture in Amsterdam, Yoshikazu Shiobara at Keio University, Tokyo, Tatjana Thelen at the University of Vienna, Christine Jacobsen at the University of Bergen, Lorenzo Pezzani at Goldsmiths, Adrian Lahoud and Godofredo Pereira at the Royal College of the Arts in London, and Matti Eräsaari at the University of Helsinki. At home, my colleagues at the University of Melbourne have commented on many of my presentations.

My daughters, Dominique and Aliya, have virtually grown up with this work, accompanying me to Lebanon at one point in the research and to Venezuela at another. As always, my partner, Caroline Alcorso, has been intellectually and logistically supportive in every possible way.

NOTES

PREFACE

1. Pearlman, "Emigration and the Resilience of Politics in Lebanon," 209.
2. Not the actual names of the villages I studied.

INTRODUCTION

Unless otherwise indicated, translations from Arabic are my own.

1. See the pioneering Hourani and Shehadi, eds., *The Lebanese in the World*.
2. Hage, *Alter-Politics*.
3. Brettell, *Anthropology and Migration*; Malkki, *Purity and Exile*.
4. Bashkow, "A Neo-Boasian Conception of Cultural Boundaries."
5. I mean "eyes" in Nietzsche's sense as involving a total sensorial and affective sensibility. See Nietzsche, *Genealogy of Morals*, 555.
6. Hage, *Alter-Politics*.
7. For an example of a rather stark opposition between the two, see Chibber, *Postcolonial Theory and the Specter of Capital*.
8. Holbraad and Pedersen, *The Ontological Turn*, 80.
9. See Castles, "Understanding Global Migration."
10. Robbins, "Beyond the Suffering Subject."
11. Canguilhem, "The Living and Its Milieu," 8.
12. Bottomley, *After the Odyssey*.
13. Lepervanche, *Indians in a White Australia*.
14. Rouse, "Mexican Migration and the Social Space of Postmodernism."
15. Werbner, "Migration and Culture."
16. Appadurai, *Modernity at Large*.
17. Schiller, Basch, and Szanton-Blanc, "From Immigrant to Transmigrant."
18. Appadurai, "Disjuncture and Difference in the Global Cultural Economy."
19. Marcus, *Ethnography through Thick and Thin*.
20. Bourdieu, *The Field of Cultural Production*.
21. Nabti, "Emigration from a Lebanese Village."
22. Castles, "Migration and Community Formation under Conditions of Globalisation"; Grillo, "Transnational Migration and Multiculturalism in Europe."
23. Anderson, *Imagined Communities*.

CHAPTER ONE

1. Thanks to Sylvain Perdigon for pointing me to this photo and to Jeremy Arbid for the permission to use it.
2. Harris and Todaro, "Migration, Unemployment and Development"; Haug, "Migration Networks and Migration Decision-Making."
3. Biao, "The Would-Be Migrant."
4. Sayad, *The Suffering of the Immigrant.*
5. Chevallier, *La société du Mont Liban*; Labaki, *Introduction à l'histoire économique du Liban*; Khater, *Inventing Home*; Traboulsi, *A History of Modern Lebanon.*
6. There has been a long technical debate about the extent to which the Lebanese Iqta' system was indeed a version of feudalism. There is no need to enter this debate here.
7. Massey et al., "Theories of International Migration," 444; Wallerstein, *The Modern World-System.*
8. For the ramifications of this formula, see Bhaskar, *Possibility of Naturalism.*
9. Gaonkar, *Alternative Modernities.*
10. See Khater and Avery, "Complicating the Lebanese Peddler Myth."
11. See for instance Schielke, *Migrant Dreams.*
12. Khater, *Inventing Home*, 47.
13. Khater, 55.
14. Polk, *The Opening of South Lebanon 1788–1840.*
15. Khuri, "A Comparative Study of Migration Patterns in Two Lebanese Villages," 213.
16. Khalaf, "The Background and Causes of Lebanese/Syrian Immigration," 27.
17. Werbner, "Vernacular Cosmopolitanism."
18. See Alonso and Oiarzabal, *Diasporas in the New Media Age Identity, Politics and Community*; Madianou and Miller, *Migration and New Media*; Nedelcu, "Migrants' New Transnational Habitus."

CHAPTER TWO

1. Maalouf, *Origines*, 82; my translation.
2. Maalouf, 70.
3. Maalouf, 70.
4. Bayeh, *The Literature of the Lebanese Diaspora.*
5. See, for example, Arsan, *Interlopers of Empire*, 183.
6. "Rami (not his real name) struggled with gambling problems for over 25 years which dramatically impacted his relationship with family and led to losses of millions of dollars." *Good Morning Australia*, "Lebanese Migrant Loses Millions of Dollars on Gambling."
7. Yue, "Ethics and Risk in Asian-Australian Cinema," 48.
8. Ma, *Asian Diaspora and East-West Modernity*, 25.
9. Lévy-Bruhl, "Primitive Mentality and Games of Chance."
10. Berlant, *Cruel Optimism.*
11. Bourdieu, *Pascalian Meditations.*
12. Bloch, *The Principle of Hope*. See also Hage, *Against Paranoid Nationalism.*
13. Mar, "Accommodating Places."
14. Spinoza, *Ethics.*

CHAPTER THREE

1. A famous gorge below the cedar forests in the North Lebanon Governorate.

2. "10,452 square kilometers" refers to the surface area of Lebanon. It also was one of the slogans of the Christian Lebanese Forces during the country's civil war (1975–90). At the time, it signified something like "We call for sovereignty over every square kilometer of Lebanon." But people use it in a depoliticized manner today.
3. See for instance Merrington, "Town and Country in the Transition to Capitalism."
4. Lévi-Strauss, *Structural Anthropology*, 2:272.
5. Lévi-Strauss, 2:272.
6. Fabian, *Time and the Other*.
7. See Hage, "Identity Fetishism."
8. See the excellent book by Berliner, *Perdre sa culture*.

CHAPTER FOUR

1. Boccagni, *Migration and the Search for Home*.
2. See for a recent example Palmberger, "Relational Ambivalence."
3. See the excellent piece by Smelser, "The Rational and the Ambivalent in the Social Sciences."
4. In this sense, I am totally in agreement with David Berliner's invitation to "bring back ambivalent sentiments and contradictory attitudes . . . as research values." Berliner, "Anthropology and the Study of Contradictions," 5.
5. Spinoza, *Ethics* pt. 3, props. 17, 21.
6. Sayad, *The Suffering of the Immigrant*, 29–30.
7. Lerner, *The Passing of Traditional Society*.
8. Lerner, 23.
9. Derrida, *The Politics of Friendship*.
10. He is referring to Gibran Khalil Gibran, of whom many Lebanese are proud, particularly the Christian Lebanese of the northern mountains, where both Gibran and Georges came from.
11. Jackson, *The Politics of Story Telling*.
12. See especially Khater, *Inventing Home*.
13. Weiner, *Inalienable Possessions*.
14. Khater, *Inventing Home*.
15. Hitti, *The Syrians in America*, 58.

CHAPTER FIVE

1. Rodman, "Empowering Place."
2. Appadurai, "Place and Voice in Anthropological Theory," 16.
3. Rodman, "Empowering Place," 640.
4. Fernandez, "Andalusia on Our Minds," 22.
5. Berliner, "The Abuses of Memory."
6. Herzfeld, *Cultural Intimacy*, 109.
7. Naficy, *The Making of Exile Cultures*, xiii.
8. See Swarowski and Schielke, dirs., *Messages from Paradise #1, Egypt*.
9. Lems, "Ambiguous Longings."
10. Pickering and Keightley, "The Modalities of Nostalgia," 920.
11. Lefebvre, *The Production of Space*.
12. Lambek, *The Weight of the Past*, 13.
13. While capturing an important aspect of the process, these descriptions are clearly romanticized. This is because such articles aim at more than just describing: they

aim at the construction of migrant eateries as a desirable object of consumption for nonmigrants.

14. *Sydney Morning Herald*, January 26, 1993, Good Living.
15. *Sydney Morning Herald*, May 23, 1972.
16. I don't want to give the impression that these practices of traveling back home in order to engage in home-building in the present leave people entirely satisfied. There is a whole dialectic of lack. As one woman puts it, "a bitter taste" is left after each such event. It takes you back home but not quite, and you are left feeling something lacking. Despite its importance, but given that it is a generalized existential condition well analyzed in psychoanalysis, I have chosen not to concern myself with this dialectic here.
17. Appadurai, *Modernity at Large*.
18. Mar, "Accommodating Places."
19. See Goffman, *Frame Analysis*.
20. Hage, *Alter-Politics*.
21. Bourdieu, *Pascalian Meditations*, 100.
22. Uexküll, *A Foray into the Worlds of Animals and Humans with a Theory of Meaning*, 53.
23. Maurice Godelier's famous interpretation of the Marxist concept of ideology: "It is not the subject deceiving himself, it is reality that is deceiving him." See Godelier, "Structure and Contradiction in Capital," 337.

CHAPTER SIX

1. Mauss, "Essai sur les variations saisonnières des sociétés eskimo."
2. Boccagni, *Migration and the Search for Home*.
3. Hage, *Alter-Politics*, chap. 2.
4. Proust, *Sentiments filiaux d'un parricide*, 200, quoted in Bourdieu, *Distinction*, 21.
5. Bourdieu, *Distinction*, 21.
6. I have borrowed the concept of being implicated by the news from Wark, *Virtual Geography*. McKenzie Wark talks of the implicating capacity of the "media vector," the vector of informational flow. The notion captures very well what a sense of gravity and intensity means when relating to news items. For Wark, the media vector has an inherently implicating capacity. Without disagreeing with this, my aim is to develop the idea that this vector's capacity to implicate is also related to its mode of reception. Indeed, subjects often use different strategies in seeking to be implicated by the vector.
7. Anderson, *Imagined Communities*.
8. Anderson, 5.
9. Hage, "The Differential Intensities of Reality."
10. Nietzsche, *Genealogy of Morals*, 507.

CHAPTER SEVEN

1. Sahlins, *What Kinship Is and Is Not*.
2. See Baldassar, Baldock, and Wilding, *Families Caring across Borders*.
3. Goffman, *Frame Analysis*.
4. Barthes, *What Is Sport?*, 9.
5. My thanks to Robyn Eckersley for highlighting this point.
6. Refreshingly, new ethnographies of the Lebanese disapora have left such restricting tropes behind. See Abdelhady, *The Lebanese Diaspora*.

CHAPTER EIGHT

1. Somehow, what I say in response never seems to be satisfactory. This is not because I couldn't explain what I was doing but because people found it hard to believe that someone who spends a lot of time traveling and talking with people can actually be doing "something." What is it for? How much money does that make? Lateef in Venezuela continuously teases me about my work. He acts as if he finds it hard to accept that it can be called work. So when I arrive in Caracas, he often sarcastically greets me with "So, back here on work, I see, you look exhausted already." A young family member working toward a social science postgraduate degree found it extremely liberating to have me around. Most members of the family thought of him as a failure for having taken such a path in life.

2. He used *ajnabi*, which means more precisely a Western foreigner.

3. The sister of Nabil, one of my main informants, lives alone and has had three consecutive "boyfriends" in the last two years. This has generated some classic moralistic arguments about her lifestyle between enthusiastically assimilated "modernists" defending her "individual freedom" and traditionalist defenders of the Lebanese moral order condemning her "moral depravity," as well as other in-between positions.

4. I have of course obtained Adel's permission to write about this, as I will note soon.

5. The Lebanese I deal with often tell me that I've become "too Australian." So it wasn't the first time that I had been constructed as "Lebanese enough" to understand what another Lebanese was on about, yet not "Lebanese enough" in the sense of both having to have certain things spelled out to me and not being part of the Lebanese world in which they participate. This also meant that that they were confident that what they tell me privately doesn't circulate in their Lebanese communal milieu. On several occasions, my "in-between" position has led people to confide in me and tell me things that I very well knew couldn't be told to anyone else.

6. Saint Charbel is Lebanon's quintessentially indigenous Maronite Catholic saint recognized by Rome. He is so because he embodies a fusion of religious and nationalist symbolism.

7. This phrase is somewhat hard to translate. It literally means, "people who have given up their God." But this is not to indicate immoral or "bad" people. Rather, it's used to signify people who are low on social and cultural capital: uninteresting, unsophisticated, of low social status, etc.

8. I am glad to say that our discussions played an important role in helping persuade Adel to see a medical doctor about his problem, which he did in mid-2003. He said to me, "When you write this, tell people that I feel much better!"

9. Tony Frangieh was the leader of another Christian militia, the Maradah, based in the key northern Lebanese town of Zgharta and with membership coming from the many surrounding villages. His assassination by Phalangist militias led to the expulsion of all Phalangists from North Lebanon.

10. He says without blinking things like *"Ana mafrood koon rabb el'ayli"* (I am supposed to be the master of the family), which is a highly traditionalist conception of the male patriarchal role for someone his age.

11. I gently confronted Adel about this one day after a particularly difficult evening with some of my Anglo-American friends. He first became very upset with me and accused me of acting superior, like his brother-in-law. I persisted, saying that I could be wrong, but I wanted him to think about it and then tell me whether he felt I was right or wrong. He thought to settle it by telling me that it's true that he feels a bit

intimidated by Americans, but only because he's living in their country. I replied, "Well, think about why you only feel intimated by upper-class Americans, then." His response: "Well, that's because they are the Americans that really count. Who else do you want me to worry about!"

12. On the effeminization of young male Lebanese migrants in Australia, see Noble, Poynting, and Tabar, "'If Anybody Called Me Wog, They Wouldn't Be Speaking to Me Alone."

13. This is strongly present in Frantz Fanon's *Black Skin White Masks* and in Edward Said's *Orientalism*, which also shows many instances of the metaphoric effeminization of "the oriental." See also Sinha, *Colonial Masculinity*.

14. For example, Adel used a very strong castration metaphor when describing to me his reaction to the assassination of Bashir Gemayel, leader of the Lebanese Forces. Gemayel was elected president following the Israeli invasion of Lebanon, which tipped the balance of power in favor of the Christians that Gemayel represented. Thus, his election gave them a strong sense that the time had finally come when they would really control "the order of things" in their country. It was a unique and even euphoric sense of social empowerment for the many Christians who had always felt until then that the Lebanese "order of things" could never be *their* social order, as it always had to be negotiated with Muslims. In describing how he felt after the assassination—at which he had been slightly injured—Adel said that it was "like having someone cut it in the middle of your best erection ever."

15. See, for example, Silverman, *Male Subjectivity at the Margins*. Slavoj Žižek, however, tries to reclaim the real penis's centrality for Lacan: *Organs without Bodies*, 87–93.

16. Bourdieu, *Masculine Domination*, 9.

17. Bourdieu, 11–12.

18. Herzfeld, *The Poetics of Manhood*.

19. In his classic ethnography of a tribe in the eastern highland of Papua New Guinea, Gilbert Herdt describes what he called "ritualised homosexuality" involving adults sucking the penises of young boys and swallowing the semen. Herdt, *Guardians of the Flute*.

20. There is still a very strong endogamous tendency within the village.

21. One should note here that this runs against Anthony Giddens's argument that what he calls plastic sexuality (i.e., sexuality for fun) emerges when it became technologically possible to free it from reproductive sexuality. He argues, "Sexuality came into being as part of a progressive differentiation of sex from the exigencies of reproduction. With the further elaboration of reproductive technologies, that differentiation has today become complete. Now that conception can be artificially produced, rather than only artificially inhibited, sexuality is at last fully autonomous. Reproduction can occur in the absence of a sexual activity; this is the final 'liberation' for sexuality, which thence can become wholly a quality of individuals and their transactions with one another" Giddens, *The Transformation of Intimacy*, 27. Many cultures have always managed to separate sex for fun from reproductive sex through a simple social technology of domain separation.

22. Gulick, "The Material Base of a Lebanese Village," 94–95.

CHAPTER NINE

1. Hermez, *War Is Coming*.

2. This enjoyment has been curtailed but not eliminated by the massive port explosion that destroyed part of the city in August 2020 and that happened after this manuscript was written and while it was being prepared for publication.

3. Taylor, *Once upon a Time in Beirut*, 233–34.
4. Monroe, *The Insecure City*. See also Fawaz, "The State and the Production of Illegal Housing"; Fawaz, "Neo-liberal Urbanity"; Harb, *Le Hezbollah à Beyrouth (1985–2005)*; Harb, "On Religiosity and Spatiality."
5. Simone, *For the City Yet to Come*.
6. Hannerz, "The Management of Danger."
7. Scott, *The Art of Not Being Governed*, 3.
8. Mauss, *The Gift*; Lévi-Strauss, *The Elementary Structures of Kinship*.
9. Sahlins, *Stone Age Economics*, 169; Clastres, *Society against the State*.
10. See Monroe, "Being Mobile in Beirut."
11. El-Zein, *Leave to Remain*, 211.
12. El-Zein, 221.
13. El-Zein, 229.
14. It should be noted here that there is no doubt that these conversations carry the mark of the period when they were recorded. This was in 2002 and 2003, soon after the rebuilding of the middle of Beirut after the end of the civil war (1990) and the liberation of South Lebanon from Israeli occupation (2000). It was before the assassination of prime minister Rafic Hariri, which signaled a return to a downward spiral of deteriorating social antagonisms. This historical conjuncture marks a specifically happy moment for the Lebanese national and transnational bourgeoisies as Beirut starts to regain a sense of normalcy and becomes again a meeting ground for all those scattered around the world who can afford to come and visit. But as I hope to show, there is a lot more to these conversations than either their class specificity or the history of this conjuncture.
15. More recently, a ban on smoking inside restaurants and cafés has been put in place in Beirut but is not always taken seriously.
16. Vigh, "Motion Squared."
17. Herzfeld, *The Poetics of Manhood*.
18. Herzfeld, 11.
19. Hage, *Against Paranoid Nationalism*, 146.
20. Sahlins, *Stone Age Economics*, 170.
21. Lévi-Strauss, *The Elementary Structures of Kinship*, 58.
22. Derrida, "Hospitality."
23. Wolff, *The Sociology of Georg Simmel*.
24. Wolff, 126.
25. Kassar and Halwani, "My Lebanese Sandwich," 21.
26. Wagner, *The Invention of Culture*.
27. Nader, "Civilization and Its Negotiations," 331.
28. Buykx, "Walk Bendigo," 17.

CONCLUSION

1. Mbembe, *De la postcolonie*.
2. Mbembe, xiv–xvi.
3. Derrida, *Donner la mort*.
4. Lévy-Bruhl, *Les carnets de Lucien Lévy-Bruhl*, 187.
5. Hage, *Is Racism an Environmental Threat?*, 123.
6. Hage, "Between Distributive and Extractive Inequality."

BIBLIOGRAPHY

Abdelhady, Dalia. *The Lebanese Diaspora: The Arab Immigrant Experience in Montreal, New York and Paris.* New York: New York University Press, 2011.

Alonso, Andoni, and Pedro J. Oiarzabal, eds. *Diasporas in the New Media Age Identity, Politics and Community.* Reno: University of Nevada Press, 2010.

Anderson, Benedict. *Imagined Communities: Reflections on the Origin and Spread of Nationalism.* London: Verso, 1983.

Appadurai, Arjun. "Disjuncture and Difference in the Global Cultural Economy." *Theory, Culture and Society* 7, no. 2 (1990): 295–310.

Appadurai, Arjun. *Modernity at Large: Cultural Dimensions of Globalization.* Minneapolis: University of Minnesota Press, 1996.

Appadurai, Arjun. "Place and Voice in Anthropological Theory." *Cultural Anthropology* 3, no. 1 (1988): 16–20.

Arsan, Andrew. *Interlopers of Empire: The Lebanese Diaspora in Colonial French West Africa.* New York: Oxford University Press, 2014.

Baldassar, Loretta, Cora Vellekoop Baldock, and Raelene Wilding. *Families Caring across Borders: Migration, Ageing and Transnational Caregiving.* New York: Palgrave Macmillan, 2007.

Barthes, Roland. *What Is Sport?* Translated by Richard Howard. New Haven, CT: Yale University Press, 2007.

Bashkow, Ira. "A Neo-Boasian Conception of Cultural Boundaries." *American Anthropologist* 106, no. 3 (2004): 443–58.

Bayeh, Jumana. *The Literature of the Lebanese Diaspora: Representations of Place and Transnational Identity.* London: I. B. Tauris, 2015.

Berlant, Lauren. *Cruel Optimism.* Durham, NC: Duke University Press, 2011.

Berliner, David. "The Abuses of Memory: Reflections on the Memory Boom in Anthropology." *Anthropological Quarterly* 78, no. 1 (2005): 197–211.

Berliner, David. "Anthropology and the Study of Contradictions." *Hau: Journal of Ethnographic Theory* 6, no. 1 (2016): 1–6.

Berliner, David. *Perdre sa culture.* Brussels: Zones Sensibles, 2018.

Bhaskar, Roy. *Possibility of Naturalism: A Philosophical Critique of the Human Sciences.* London: Harvester Press, 1979.

Biao, Xiang. "The Would-Be Migrant: Post-socialist Primitive Accumulation, Potential Transnational Mobility, and the Displacement of the Present in Northeast China." *TRaNS: Trans-Regional and -National Studies of Southeast Asia* 2, no. 2 (2014): 183–99.

Bloch, Ernst. *The Principle of Hope*. Oxford: Basil Blackwell, 1986.

Boccagni, Paolo. *Migration and the Search for Home: Mapping Domestic Space in Migrants' Everyday Lives*. New York: Palgrave Macmillan, 2017.

Bottomley, Gillian. *After the Odyssey: A Study of Greek Australians*. Brisbane: Queensland University Press, 1979.

Bourdieu, Pierre. *Distinction: A Social Critique of the Judgement of Taste*. London: Routledge and Kegan Paul, 1984.

Bourdieu, Pierre. *The Field of Cultural Production*. Oxford: Polity, 1993.

Bourdieu, Pierre. *Masculine Domination*. Cambridge: Polity, 2001.

Bourdieu, Pierre. *Pascalian Meditations*. Oxford: Polity, 2000.

Brettell, Caroline. *Anthropology and Migration: Essays on Transnationalism, Ethnicity, and Identity*. Walnut Creek, CA: AltaMira Press, 2003.

Brettell, Caroline B., and James F. Hollifield, eds. *Migration Theory: Talking across Disciplines*. New York: Routledge, 2000.

Buykx, Tim. "Walk Bendigo: A Program to Create Pedestrian-Friendly Shared Spaces in the Bendigo CBD." *Landscape Architecture Australia* 118 (2008): 17–18.

Canguilhem, Georges. "The Living and Its Milieu." *Grey Room* 3 (2001): 7–31.

Castles, Stephen. "Migration and Community Formation under Conditions of Globalisation." *International Migration Review* 36, no. 4 (2002): 1143–68.

Castles, Stephen. "Understanding Global Migration: A Social Transformation Perspective." *Journal of Ethnic and Migration Studies* 36, no. 10 (2010): 1565–86.

Chevallier, Dominique. *La société du Mont Liban à l'époque de la révolution industrielle en Europe*. Paris: Librairie Orientaliste Paul Geuthner, 1982.

Chibber, Vivek. *Postcolonial Theory and the Specter of Capital*. London: Verso, 2013.

Clastres, Pierre. *Society against the State: Essays in Political Anthropology*. Cambridge: Zone Books, 1987.

Derrida, Jacques. *Donner la mort*. Paris: Galilée, 1999.

Derrida, Jacques. "Hospitality." *Angelaki: Journal of the Theoretical Humanities* 5, no. 3 (2000): 3–18.

Derrida, Jacques. *The Politics of Friendship*. Translated by George Collins. London: Verso, 2005.

El-Zein, Abbas. *Leave to Remain: A Memoir*. St. Lucia: University of Queensland Press, 2009.

Fabian, Johannes. *Time and the Other: How Anthropology Manufactures Its Object*. New York: Columbia University Press, 1983.

Fanon, Frantz. *Black Skin White Masks*. London: Pluto, 1986.

Fawaz, Mona. "Neo-liberal Urbanity: A View from Beirut's Periphery." *Development and Change* 40, no. 5 (2009): 827–52.

Fawaz, Mona. "The State and the Production of Illegal Housing: Public Practices in Hayy el-Sellom, Beirut-Lebanon." In *Comparing Cities: The Middle-East and South Asia*, edited by Kamran Asdar Ali and Martina Rieker, 197–325. London: Oxford University Press, 2009.

Fernandez, James W. "Andalusia on Our Minds: Two Contrasting Places in Spain as Seen in a Vernacular Poetic Duel of the Late 19th Century." *Cultural Anthropology* 3, no. 1 (1988): 21–35.

Friedman, Jonathan. "From Roots to Routes: Tropes for Trippers." *Anthropological Theory* 2, no. 1 (2002): 21–36.

Friedman, Jonathan. "Globalisation." In *A Companion to the Anthropology of Politics*, edited by David Nugent and Joan Vincent, 179–97. Oxford: Blackwell, 2004.

Gaonkar, Dilip Parameshwar, ed. *Alternative Modernities.* Durham, NC: Duke University Press, 2001.

Gibson-Graham, J. K. *The End of Capitalism (As We Knew It): A Feminist Critique of Political Economy.* Cambridge: Blackwell, 1996.

Giddens, Anthony. *The Transformation of Intimacy: Sexuality, Love and Eroticism in Modern Societies.* Cambridge: Polity, 1992.

Glick Schiller, Nina, Linda Basch, and Cristina Szanton-Blanc. "From Immigrant to Transmigrant: Theorizing Transnational Migration." *Anthropological Quarterly* 6, no. 1 (1995): 48–63.

Godelier, Maurice. "Structure and Contradiction in Capital." In *Ideology in Social Science: Readings in Critical Social Theory,* edited by Robin Blackburn, 334–68. London: Fontana/Collins, 1975.

Goffman, Erving. *Frame Analysis.* Boston: Northeastern University Press, 1986.

Good Morning Australia. "Lebanese Migrant Loses Millions of Dollars on Gambling," broadcast October 10, 2018. Updated by Fares Hassan and Sylva Mezher October 10, 2018, SBS Arabic 24, https://www.sbs.com.au/language/english/audio/lebanese-migrant-loses-millions-of-dollars-on-gambling?language=en, accessed January 13, 2021.

Grillo, Ralph. "Transnational Migration and Multiculturalism in Europe." In *Working Papers Series of Transnational Communities Program,* ed. by Ali Rogers. 2001. Published online by the Transnational Communities Program, University of Oxford, at http://www.transcomm.ox.ac.uk/working_papers.htm.

Gulick, John. "The Lebanese Village: An Introduction." *American Anthropologist* 55, no. 3 (1953): 367–72.

Gulick, John. "The Material Base of a Lebanese Village." In *Peoples and Cultures of the Middle East,* edited by Ailon Shiloh, 91–99. New York: Random House, 1969.

Hage, Ghassan. *Against Paranoid Nationalism: Searching for Hope in a Shrinking Society.* Annandale, NSW: Pluto Press, 2003.

Hage, Ghassan. *Alter-Politics: Critical Anthropology and the Radical Imagination.* Carlton: Melbourne University Press, 2015.

Hage, Ghassan. "Between Distributive and Extractive Inequality." Paper presented March 15, 2018, at the New Geographies of Global Inequalities and Social Justice Conference, School of Geography, University of Melbourne, March 14–15, 2018.

Hage, Ghassan. "The Differential Intensities of Reality: Migration, Perception and Guilt." In *Being There: New Trends in Phenomenology and the Analysis of Culture,* edited by Jonas Frykman and Nils Gilje, 79–94. Lund, Sweden: Nordic Academic Press, 2003.

Hage, Ghassan. "Identity Fetishism: Capitalism and White Self-Racialization." In *Racialization: Studies in Theory and Practice,* edited by John Solomos and Karim Murji, 185–206. Oxford: Oxford University Press, 2004.

Hage, Ghassan. *Is Racism an Environmental Threat?* London: Polity, 2017.

Hage, Ghassan. "On the Ethic of Pedestrian Crossings: Or Why 'Mutual Obligation' Does Not Belong in the Language of Neo-liberal Economics." *Meanjin* 59, no. 4 (2000): 27–37.

Hannerz, Ulf. "The Management of Danger." *Ethnos* 46, nos. 1–2 (1981): 19–46.

Harb, Mona. *Le Hezbollah à Beyrouth (1985–2005): De la banlieue à la ville* [Hezbollah in Beirut (1985–2005): From the suburbs to the city]. Paris: IFPO-Karthala, 2010.

Harb, Mona. "On Religiosity and Spatiality: Lessons from Hezbollah in Beirut." In *The Fundamentalist City? Religiosity and the Remaking of Urban Space,* edited by Nezard Al Sayyad and Mejgan Massoumi, 125–54. London: Routledge, 2010.

Harris, John R., and Michael P. Todaro. "Migration, Unemployment and Development: A Two-Sector Analysis." *American Economic Review* 60, no. 1 (1970): 126–42.

Haug, Sonja. "Migration Networks and Migration Decision-Making." *Ethnic and Migration Studies* 34, no. 4 (2008): 585–605.

Herdt, Gilbert. *Guardians of the Flute: Idioms of Masculinity.* New York: MacGraw-Hill, 1981.

Hermez, Sami. *War Is Coming: Between Past and Future Violence in Lebanon.* Philadelphia: University of Pennsylvania Press, 2017.

Herzfeld, Michael. *Cultural Intimacy: Social Poetics in the Nation-State.* New York: Routledge, 1997.

Herzfeld, Michael. *The Poetics of Manhood: Contest and Identity in a Cretan Mountain Village.* Princeton, NJ: Princeton University Press, 1985.

Hitti, Philip K. *The Syrians in America.* New York: George H. Doran, 1924.

Holbraad, Martin, and Morten Axel Pedersen. *The Ontological Turn: An Anthropological Exposition.* Cambridge: Cambridge University Press, 2017.

Hourani, Albert, and Nadim Shehadi, eds. *The Lebanese in the World: A Century of Emigration.* London: Centre for Lebanese Studies in association with I. B. Tauris, 1992.

Humphrey, Michael. *Islam, Multiculturalism and Transnationalism: From the Lebanese Diaspora.* London: Centre for Lebanese Studies in association with I. B. Tauris, 1998.

Jackson, Michael. *Lifeworlds: Essays in Existential Anthropology.* Chicago: University of Chicago Press, 2013.

Jackson, Michael. *The Politics of Story Telling: Variations on a Theme by Hannah Arendt.* Copenhagen: Museum Tusculanum Press, 2013.

Kassar, Maher, and Ziad Halwani. "My Lebanese Sandwich." In *Transit Beirut: New Writing and Images*, edited by Malu Halasa and Roseanne Saad Khalaf, 10–23. London: Saqi Books, 2004.

Khalaf, Samir. "The Background and Causes of Lebanese/Syrian Immigration." In *Crossing the Waters: Arabic-Speaking Immigrants to the United States before 1940*, edited by E. J. Hooglund, 17–35. Washington, DC: Smithsonian Institution Press, 1987.

Khater, Akram Fouad. *Inventing Home: Emigration, Gender, and the Middle Class in Lebanon, 1870–1920.* Berkeley: University of California Press, 2001.

Khater, Akram, and Zoe Avery. "Complicating the Lebanese Peddler Myth." In the *Khayrallah Center for Lebanese Diaspora Studies News*, North Carolina State University, May 10, 2017. https://lebanesestudies.news.chass.ncsu.edu/2017/05/10/complicating-the-lebanese-peddler-myth/.

Khuri, Fuad. "A Comparative Study of Migration Patterns in Two Lebanese Villages." *Human Organization* 26, no. 4 (1967): 206–13.

Labaki, Georges. *Introduction à l'histoire économique du Liban: Soie et commerce extérieur en fin de période Ottomane (1840–1914).* Beyrouth: Publications de l'Université Libanaise, 1984.

Lambek, Michael. *The Weight of the Past: Living with History in Mahajanga Madagascar.* New York: Palgrave Macmillan, 2002.

Lefebvre, Henri. *The Production of Space.* Translated by Donald Nicholson-Smith. London: Wiley Blackwell, 1991.

Lems, Anika. "Ambiguous Longings: Nostalgia as the Interplay among Self, Time and World." *Critique of Anthropology* 36, no. 4 (2016): 419–38.

Lepervanche, Marie de. *Indians in a White Australia.* Sydney: George Allen and Unwin, 1984.

Lerner, Daniel. *The Passing of Traditional Society: Modernizing the Middle East.* London: Free Press, 1958.

Lévy-Bruhl, Lucien. *Les carnets de Lucien Lévy-Bruhl.* Paris: Presses Universitaires de France, 1949

Lévy-Bruhl, Lucien. "Primitive Mentality and Games of Chance." *Hau: Journal of Ethnographic Theory* 10, no. 2 (2020): 420–24.

Lévi-Strauss, Claude. *The Elementary Structures of Kinship*. Translated by James Harle Bell and John Richard von Sturmer. Boston: Beacon Press, 1969.

Lévi-Strauss, Claude. *Structural Anthropology*. Vol. 2. Translated by Monique Layton. New York: Basic Books, 1976.

Longuenesse, Elizabeth Gilbert Beauge, and Michel Nancy. *Communautes villageoises et migrations de main-d'oeuvre au Moyen-Orient*. Beirut: Centre d'Etudes et de Recherches sur le Moyen-Orient Contemporain, 1986.

Lucht, Hans. "Darkness before Daybreak: Existential Reciprocity in the Lives and Livelihoods of Migrant West African Fishermen." PhD diss., University of Copenhagen, 2008.

Ma, Sheng-mei. *Asian Diaspora and East-West Modernity*. West Lafayette, IN: Purdue University Press, 2012.

Maalouf, Amin. *Origines*. Paris: Grasset, 2004.

Madianou, Mirca, and Daniel Miller. *Migration and New Media: Transnational Families and Polymedia*. London: Routledge, 2012.

Malkki, Liisa H. *Purity and Exile: Violence, Memory, and National Cosmology among Hutu Refugees in Tanzania*. Chicago: University of Chicago Press, 1995.

Mar, Phillip. "Accommodating Places: A Migrant Ethnography of Two Cities (Hong Kong and Sydney)." PhD diss., University of Sydney, 2002.

Marcus, George. *Ethnography through Thick and Thin*. Princeton, NJ: Princeton University Press, 1998.

Massey, Douglas S., Joaquin Arango, Graeme Hugo, Ali Kouaouci, Adela Pellegrino, and J. Edward Taylor. "Theories of International Migration: A Review and Appraisal." *Population and Development Review* 19, no. 3 (1993): 431–66.

Mauss, Marcel. "Essai sur les variations saisonnières des sociétés eskimo: Étude de morphologie sociale." *Sociologie et anthropologie* (2013): 387–475.

Mauss, Marcel. *The Gift: The Form and Reason for Exchange in Archaic Societies*. Translated by W. D. Halls. London: Routledge, 2002.

Mbembe, Achille. *De la postcolonie*. 2nd ed. Paris: Karthala, 2009.

Merrington, John. "Town and Country in the Transition to Capitalism." *New Left Review* 93 (1975): 170–95.

Monroe, Kristin V. "Being Mobile in Beirut." *City and Society* 23, no. 1 (2011): 91–111.

Monroe, Kristin V. *The Insecure City: Space, Power, and Mobility in Beirut*. New Brunswick, NJ: Rutgers University Press, 2016.

Nabti, Patricia. "Emigration from a Lebanese Village: A Case Study of Bishmizzine." In *The Lebanese in the World: A Century of Emigration*, edited by Albert Hourani and Nadim Shehadi, 41–64. London: Centre for Lebanese Studies in association with I. B. Tauris, 1992.

Nader, Laura. "Civilization and Its Negotiations." In *Law and Anthropology: A Reader*, edited by Sally Falk Moore, 330–42. Oxford: Blackwell, 2005.

Naficy, Hamid. *The Making of Exile Cultures: Iranian Television in Los Angeles*. Minneapolis: University of Minnesota Press, 1993.

Napolitano, Valentina. *Migrant Hearts and the Atlantic Return: Transnationalism and the Roman Catholic Church*. New York: Fordham University Press, 2016.

N'aymeh, Mikha'il. *Kan ma kan*. Beirut: Dar Sadir, 1966.

Nedelcu, Mihaela. "Migrants' New Transnational Habitus: Rethinking Migration through a Cosmopolitan Lens in the Digital Age." *Journal of Ethnic and Migration Studies* 38, no. 9 (2012): 1339–56.

Nietzsche, Friedrich. *Genealogy of Morals*. In *Basic Writings of Nietzsche*, translated and edited with commentaries by Walter Kaufmann. New York: Modern Library, 1992.

Noble, Greg, Scott Poynting, and Paul Tabar. "'If Anybody Called Me Wog, They Wouldn't Be Speaking to Me Alone': Protest Masculinity and Lebanese Youth in Western Sydney." *Journal of Interdisciplinary Gender Studies* 3, no. 2 (1998): 76–94.

Palmberger, Monika. "Relational Ambivalence: Exploring the Social and Discursive Dimensions of Ambivalence—the Case of Turkish Aging Labor Migrants." *International Journal of Comparative Sociology* 60, nos. 1–2 (2019): 74–90.

Parry, Jonathan. "Nehru's Dream and the Village 'Waiting Room': Long-Distance Labour Migrants to a Central Indian Steel Town." *Contributions to Indian Sociology* 37, nos. 1–2 (2003): 217–49.

Pearlman, Wendy. "Emigration and the Resilience of Politics in Lebanon." *Arab Studies Journal* 21, no. 1 (2013): 191–213.

Pickering, Michael, and Emily Keightley. "The Modalities of Nostalgia." *Current Sociology* 54, no. 6 (2006): 919–41.

Polk, William R. *The Opening of South Lebanon 1788–1840: A Study of the Impact of the West on the Middle East*. Boston: Harvard University Press, 2013.

Proust, Marcel. *Pastiches et mélanges*. Paris: Gallimard, 1970.

Robbins, Joel. "Beyond the Suffering Subject: Toward an Anthropology of the Good." *Journal of the Royal Anthropological Institute* 19, no. 3 (2013): 447–62.

Rodman, Margaret. "Empowering Place: Multilocality and Multivocality." *American Anthropologist* 94, no. 3 (1992): 640–56.

Rouse, Roger. "Mexican Migration and the Social Space of Postmodernism." *Diaspora: A Journal of Transnational Studies* 1, no. 1 (1991): 8–23.

Sahlins, Marshall. *Stone Age Economics*. Chicago: Aldine-Atherton, 1972.

Sahlins, Marshall. *What Kinship Is and Is Not*. Chicago: University of Chicago Press, 2013.

Said, Edward. *Orientalism*. New York: Random House, 1979.

Sayad, Abdelmalek. *The Suffering of the Immigrant*. Cambridge: Polity, 2004.

Schielke, Samuli. *Migrant Dreams: Egyptian Workers in the Gulf States*. Cairo: American University in Cairo Press, 2020.

Schiller, Nina Glick, Linda Basch, and Cristina Szanton-Blanc. "From Immigrant to Transmigrant: Theorizing Transnational Migration." *Anthropological Quarterly* 6, no. 1 (1995): 48–63.

Scott, James C. *The Art of Not Being Governed: An Anarchist History of Upland Southeast Asia*. New Haven, CT: Yale University Press, 2009.

Silverman, Kaja. *Male Subjectivity at the Margins*. New York: Routledge, 1992.

Simone, AbdouMaliq. *For the City Yet to Come: Changing African Life in Four Cities*. Durham, NC: Duke University Press, 2004.

Sinha, Mrinalini. *Colonial Masculinity: The "Manly Englishman" and the "Effeminate Bengali" in the Late Nineteenth Century*. Manchester: Manchester University Press, 1995.

Smelser, Neil J. "The Rational and the Ambivalent in the Social Sciences: 1997 Presidential Address." *American Sociological Review* 63, no. 1 (1998): 1–16.

Spinoza, Baruch. *Ethics*. Oxford: Oxford University Press, 2000.

Swarowski, Daniela, and Samuli Schielke, dirs. *Messages from Paradise #1, Egypt: Austria, about Permanent Longing for Elsewhere*. Documentary, 44 min., Arabic with English subtitles. 2009. Austria and The Netherlands, 2010. Viewed in 2010 at a meeting of the European Anthropological Association.

Taylor, Catherine. *Once upon a Time in Beirut: A Journey to the Heart of the Middle East*. Sydney: Bantam, 2007.

Traboulsi, Fawwaz. *A History of Modern Lebanon.* 2nd ed. London: Pluto Press, 2012.

Uexküll, Jakob von. *A Foray into the Worlds of Animals and Humans with a Theory of Meaning.* Translated by Joseph D. O'Neil. Minneapolis: University of Minnesota Press, 2010.

Vigh, Henrik. "Motion Squared: A Second Look at the Concept of Social Navigation." *Anthropological Theory* 9, no. 4 (2009): 419–38.

Wagner, Roy. *The Invention of Culture.* Englewood Cliffs, NJ: Prentice-Hall, 1975.

Wallerstein, Immanuel. *The Modern World-System.* New York: Academic Press, 1974.

Wark, McKenzie. *Virtual Geography: Living with Global Media Events.* Bloomington: Indiana University Press, 1997.

Weiner, Annette. *Inalienable Possessions: The Paradox of Keeping while Giving.* Berkeley: University of California Press, 1992.

Werbner, Pnina. "Migration and Culture." In *The Oxford Handbook of the Politics of International Migration,* edited by M. Rosenblum and D. Tichenor, 215–43. New York: Oxford University Press, 2012.

Werbner, Pnina. "Vernacular Cosmopolitanism." *Theory, Culture and Society* 23, nos. 2–3 (2006): 496–98.

Wolff, Kurt H. *The Sociology of Georg Simmel.* Glencoe, IL: Free Press, 1950.

Yue, Audrey. "Ethics and Risk in Asian-Australian Cinema: The Last Chip." In *Diasporas of Australian Cinema,* edited by Catherine Simpson, Renata Murawska, and Anthony Lambert, 41–50. Bristol: Intellect Books, 2009.

Žižek, Slavoj. *Organs without Bodies: On Deleuze and Consequences.* New York: Routledge, 2004.

INDEX